COACHING VOLLEYBALL SUCCESSFULLY

Sally Kus

Human Kinetics

Library of Congress Cataloging-in-Publication Data

Kus, Sally, 1948-
    Coaching volleyball successfully / Sally Kus.
        p. cm.
    Includes index.
    ISBN 0-7360-4037-4 (softcover)
    1. Volleyball--Coaching.   I. Title.
    GV1015.5.C63K87 2004
    796.325--dc22

                                                    2003027576

ISBN: 0-7360-4037-4

Developmental Editor: Leigh LaHood
Copyeditor: Patrick W. Connolly
Proofreader: Kathy Bennett
Indexer: Betty Frizzéll
Graphic Designer: Nancy Rasmus
Graphic Artist: Tara Welsch
Photo Manager: Dan Wendt
Cover Designer: Jack W. Davis
Photographer (cover): Paul Hokanson/University of Buffalo Athletics
Photographer (interior): Terry Wilde, unless otherwise noted
Art Manager: Kareema McLendon
Illustrator: Kareema McLendon
Printer: Versa Press

Human Kinetics books are available at special discounts for bulk purchase. Special editions or book excerpts can also be created to specification. For details, contact the Special Sales Manager at Human Kinetics.

Printed in the United States of America   10   9   8   7   6   5   4   3   2   1

Human Kinetics
Web site: www.HumanKinetics.com

United States: Human Kinetics
P.O. Box 5076
Champaign, IL 61825-5076
800-747-4457
e-mail: humank@hkusa.com

Canada: Human Kinetics
475 Devonshire Road Unit 100
Windsor, ON N8Y 2L5
800-465-7301 (in Canada only)
e-mail: orders@hkcanada.com

Europe: Human Kinetics
107 Bradford Road
Stanningley
Leeds LS28 6AT, United Kingdom
+44 (0) 113 255 5665
e-mail: hk@hkeurope.com

Australia: Human Kinetics
57A Price Avenue
Lower Mitcham, South Australia 5062
08 8277 1555
e-mail: liaw@hkaustralia.com

New Zealand: Human Kinetics
Division of Sports Distributors NZ Ltd.
P.O. Box 300 226 Albany
North Shore City
Auckland
0064 9 448 1207
e-mail: blairc@hknewz.com

CONTENTS

FOREWORD

Successful coaching in volleyball—as in most sports—is not just about having knowledge; it requires good communication, consistency, control, and courage . . . to make tough decisions. Every day coaches need to develop or alter a practice plan, teach technique, systems, and tactics, conduct conditioning drills, provide motivation, and address academic or personal issues with student-athletes. Even veteran coaches find it a constant challenge to maintain all of the qualities and responsibilities of coaching.

Sally Kus has mastered the art of the coaching process, and done so in remarkable fashion. Not only has she compiled a tremendous won-loss record through her years of coaching at the middle school, high school, and college levels, but through all those victorious seasons she's maintained her wonderful sense of humor, her respect for the sport, and the admiration of her peers. Sally is special—as a teacher, coach, mentor, and friend.

In *Coaching Volleyball Successfully*, Sally shares her proven teaching methods and on-court insights on how to develop solid technical players who understand the game and how to play it. She also provides many effective off-the-court measures that are so crucial for the support and cohesiveness of a successful volleyball program.

I have known Sally over the years, and the one thing that stands out most is her enthusiasm for her work, and that passion obviously spreads to her players. That same positive energy comes across in the pages of this book, and you would do well to soak it up.

Take advantage of this chance to learn from one of the legends in our sport. Sally Kus and *Coaching Volleyball Successfully* will help you develop a coaching philosophy, a working knowledge of the sport, and a solid grasp on all aspects of coaching young athletes.

Marv Dunphy
Pepperdine University

KEY TO DIAGRAMS

- - - - - - ➤   Path of ball

───────➤   Path of player

(B)   Blocker

(S)   Setter

(S) *   Primary setter

(T)   Target

(X)   Player

(O)   Player

(A)   Attacker

(D)   Digger

(C)   Coach

(RB)   Right back

(CB)   Center back

(LB)   Left back

(MH)   Middle hitter

(OH)   Outside hitter

(RS)   Right-side hitter

⊞   Ball cart

CHAPTER 1
DEVELOPING A VOLLEYBALL COACHING PHILOSOPHY

If you are like I was when I started coaching, you may be tempted to skip right over this chapter. Back then I would have wanted to get to the meat of the book—techniques and drills! Those were the things I needed to know to win matches. Developing a coaching and playing philosophy may not seem like the most important factor of successful coaching, but don't underestimate its importance. It provides a foundation on which you can build a strong program. And you need to communicate your philosophy to prospective players and their parents from the start so they know where you stand and what you value before they even join the team.

DEVELOPING A COACHING PHILOSOPHY

I coached 10 years before someone asked me about my coaching philosophy. I thought, *What a weird question*. It made me feel as if I were in an employment interview. That was back in the '80s when parents were very excited that their daughters had opportunities in sports. Girls' sports had become popular, and Title IX had passed. As girls specialized in a single sport and college scholarships increased, so did coaching accountability.

Coaching accountability scared me. Why did I have to state a philosophy? I knew what was important to me! Now I had to examine my values and use self-awareness to develop a philosophy. It had to be based on principles that would be the foundation of my program. I knew it was important for my philosophy to be sound because it wasn't just about me; it would have an impact on other people.

I knew I was coaching for the love of kids and sports. I knew fun, technique, and tactical application were the things that were important to me. I decided to sit down and write in one sentence what was most important to me. I wrote, "Teach volleyball in a positive, technical, and gamelike manner."

Wow, that was simple! It was something I had been doing for years. But writing it down now made me accountable. I had stated "positive," so was I allowed to yell? I had stated "technical," so did I have to constantly badger my players? I had stated "gamelike," so could I do fluffy or crazy drills that generated enthusiasm more than tactical application?

I decided I could vary from my philosophy to generate enthusiasm. If I felt the need to yell, I needed to examine why. Was the drill unchallenging? Was the player not aggressive or not self-motivated? Could I improve the practice or the mental preparation of the player? I decided it was all right to yell to change lazy behaviors as long as it was a rarity. My players take heed when I talk sternly. And I reserve talking sternly for when players have poor motivation. I do not yell. Yelling turns kids off and is ineffective if done too much.

Volleyball should be fun, but some drills are tougher and less fun than others. On the other hand, tough drills can be fun if goals are set and pride is an outcome. We have a movement drill called amoeba. It is a love–hate drill. The players know it helps our transition and defensive movement, but it is a backbreaker. We must meet a timed goal or else additional time is added to the drill. Everyone works hard to perform the drill so minutes are *not* added. It is the type of drill where the players have a sense of accomplishment when they are finished (and some relief). Accomplishment is pride. Pride is fun. Pride generates self-esteem, "team-esteem," and bonding.

Writing a coaching philosophy made me accountable for believing in it, implementing it, and acting as a role model of it.

© Human Kinetics

Your coaching and playing philosophies mold your players' qualities and abilities.

DEVELOPING A PLAYING PHILOSOPHY

To define a playing philosophy, once again, I identified what was important in the style of play I wanted my players to develop. Three words came to mind: aggressiveness, self-motivation, and attitude.

The first day of practice, I tell my players they must walk through the gym doors self-motivated, aggressive, and with a positive attitude. When this actually happens, coaching is a breeze. The players take responsibility for making this part of the philosophy work, and I can focus on my coaching philosophy!

Aggressiveness

I have always been a person who takes risks. "Test your limitations" is a motto of mine. Players will take risks and be aggressive if the coach has developed a safe, comfortable environment.

My players are accountable for being in the correct posture and position on the court. Then they can be as aggressive as they are able. This has to be carried over to match situations. It may cost the coach a few wins early in the season, but the players will learn how and when to make aggressive spikes versus well-placed tips and roll shots. Of course, well-placed tips and roll shots can be aggressive, too.

If we are going to lose a match, I prefer that our hitters go down swinging. A player will ask me, "Should I have bumped it over on the third hit? If I hadn't made that error on the last play, we would still be in the game." I always reply, "Who lost the third point in that game? If she hadn't erred, the other team would only be at 24, so we would still be in the game!" Typically, everyone remembers only the last error of the game.

Self-Motivation

It seems that younger players are more self-motivated. That is why I liked teaching in a middle school. Middle school kids run through the gym doors to play! Every day is the Olympics.

Poor motivation and burnout are due to boredom, poor skills, absence of fun, and losing. Self-motivation is a powerful tool if your players possess it. Coaches can help their players achieve this intrinsic feeling by keeping the sport fun, providing different experiences off the court, varying practices, establishing reasonable goals, being sensitive to the players' needs, and providing for success.

Attitude

How many teams have you been on or coached that didn't have at least one attitude problem? Unfortunately, most people will say very few. Poor attitudes stem from the inability to accept playing mistakes, jealousies, attention seeking, playing time issues, and social problems.

The Power of Attitude

This story depicts the power that a negative attitude can have on a team.

The setting . . . Some members of a team are sitting on the gym floor. They are angry about an incident that happened. A teammate walks into the gym laughing. She stops laughing and finds out what is wrong with her friends.

The setting . . . Some members of a team are sitting on the gym floor laughing and swapping fun stories. A teammate, who is angry over an incident, walks into the gym. The entire team stops laughing and finds out what is wrong with their friend.

One negative person possesses enough power to devastate a team. One positive person is usually powerless.

I have had very few *major* attitude problems on my teams. Once you have had one, you swear you'll never let it happen again. I had a player with a bad attitude on my high school team in the '80s. She had a jealousy problem that caused turmoil for three years. She gave dirty looks to everyone. I always wanted to carry a mirror and zap it out during one of her facial contortions. I knew if she saw her face, it would crack the mirror! If I'd had the

guts, I would have cut her. But winning was too important. I didn't want to deprive the team of her excellent playing ability. I didn't want to rob our program of the status it was acquiring.

When she was a senior, I was worried about her recruitment. I decided I would have to tell the college coaches the truth about her attitude. A Division I assistant coach flew to Buffalo to watch her play. After the match, he apologized and told me he was unable to discuss the player with me. The player's parents had requested that I not be involved in her recruiting. I was SO relieved. After this "bad egg" graduated, we had more fun the next year than I had ever remembered having. It was a relief not to be on edge during every practice and event. I decided then that I would *never* have another player with a poor attitude on our team.

I didn't realize that she still represented my program. Four years later, when this girl was a senior in college, one of my current Sweet Home seniors wrote a letter of interest to this same college. This time the head coach called me. She told me she was not going to reply to my player's letter of interest because it was a Sweet Home letter. She had had such a bad experience with my first player that she never wanted to recruit another Lady Panther. The college coach said my first player had been a cancer to her program. After I told this head coach the whole story and told her that her assistant had never inquired about my first player's attitude, she backed down. My second player, who was a bright and humorous person, went to the same college and reestablished our good name. She was even a team captain!

Ability to Handle Mistakes

Some players have trouble accepting mistakes that they or their teammates make on the court. Players mishandle poor play because of embarrassment or the inability to accept others. If a player berates herself or a teammate after an error, it takes the focus off the next play. All attention is directed at the dirty look or the tantrum. If a player berates another, or if the player who has erred stresses on it, the player will become more tense. The more tense a player is, the less she can move and concentrate. Some coaches feel that a player who says "my fault" relieves her stress or has owned up to her error. I do not suggest teams adopt this method. Usually, when a player errs, everyone knows whose fault it is. Saying "my fault" only brings negativity to the court. Can you imagine how many times a team would say "my fault" if everyone performed this ritual? Making and accepting mistakes are part of the game and part of life. To get this point across, I ask my team, "Does anyone make a mistake on purpose?" If players never made mistakes, coaches wouldn't have jobs!

Boys and girls handle mistakes completely differently. Some guys will look at each other after an error and shoot a dirty look or grunt a distasteful comment. After the next serve, if the same player has an awesome spike, the teammate will say, "Nice hit, buddy!" All is forgiven! If a girl shoots a dirty look or negative comment after an error, grudges are held for weeks . . . if not for a lifetime!

A poor attitude and the inability to accept mistakes can be a problem for coaches, too. A colleague of mine, who was an excellent technical softball coach, was known for his yelling and negative antics directed at his players during games. Many of my volleyball players also played softball and struggled with his negativity. I asked the softball coach why he yelled so much. He told me that when a girl made a mistake, it was a poor reflection on his coaching and caused him embarrassment. He had coached her to play correctly, yet she was still making mistakes. He went on to say that I didn't need to yell in volleyball because my team never made mistakes. He related winning to mistakes. We were winning so we must not be making mistakes! What he didn't realize was that the girls on his team were afraid to make mistakes because they didn't want to be yelled at and embarrassed in front of the fans. They became tenser, which caused them to make more mistakes, including errors that lost games. Softball was no longer fun for the girls. Their self-esteem was shot, and they lost their drive to play the game.

ESTABLISHING PRIORITIES

Establishing priorities is a part of defining a coaching philosophy. Prioritizing winning and player development is a tough task for many coaches. As an educator and coach, I could never make winning more important than the student-athlete. Effective player development is a coaching responsibility on and off the court. It leads to players who win on the court and have fine character traits in life. When a coach genuinely cares for her players, it comes back to her threefold. A team that plays for the love of the game, for each other, and for the coach is a sure winner. Not all wins show on the scoreboard in the gym. Feeling successful, learning teamwork, creating camaraderie, and developing leadership are wins on the scoreboard in life.

Some coaches seem to have a mystical aura in the eyes of their players. If you possess this power, do not abuse it. Kids need an adult role model to learn from and respect. Coaches cannot take the place of a parent, but they can complement the parent's role. The team should be a second family for the player.

Nothing is finer than receiving a letter from a former player saying she just got a great job because of all the values she learned through your program. Nothing is finer than having former players come back to see you and stay in communication with you. Nothing is finer than having your players come back and help coach your club or school program. Nothing is weirder than coaching against one of your former players! Nothing is finer than watching your former players teaching and coaching. Nothing is weirder than sitting in the middle when two former players are coaching against each other. Nothing is finer than having former players trust you to coach their children. Nothing is finer than being an attendant in a former player's wedding or being the godparent to her child.

Many coaches have to make winning their top priority in order to maintain their jobs. Winning at any cost is a losing venture. Athletes who play under this kind of coach

When setting priorities, remember that player development is more important than winning every competition.

become ruthless, have poor role models, and have disregard for rules. To be truly successful, coaches must learn to develop their players in a tough but respectful manner, and their athletic programs must not associate winning with job security.

IMPLEMENTING A PHILOSOPHY

Applying your stated philosophy to your program is the next phase in establishing a sound coaching foundation. This requires a coach to develop her approaches to the game. Principles and rules on discipline, dedication, and procedures need to be defined. Here are some examples:

• Be a successful student-athlete. A player has to attend classes and excel in schoolwork. We want our players to strive to be scholar-athletes. A player should be given a practice, training, and playing schedule for the season so she can manage her time and make plans to meet all her commitments.

• Commitment. A coach has to state her commitment to the team. A coach also has to state what she expects from her players. A player can make a commitment only if she knows the expectations.

• Being early is being on time; being on time is being late. This makes practices, meetings, and departures begin promptly.

• Communication is a must both on and off the court. Communication is vital between the coach and player. Communication concerning players' roles is a key for starters and nonstarters. All players are important to the success of practice, matches, and the overall program. Players' roles are continually reevaluated and always changing. Communication within the athletic system, the family, and the community is important.

• Set measurable goals. Fluffy goals sound good, but they are hard to measure. If you cannot measure a goal, you don't know if you have achieved it.

• Self-coach. When a coach asks a player to try a skill in a different way, the player has to keep trying to change, or self-coach. Being coachable promotes faster learning.

• Have fun but play hard. Play hard but play smart. This is instilled during warm-up games, drills, and matches. This is instilled through team initiative games that create team bonding.

• Your feet play the ball—efficient movement is a must. Natural athletes find this easy. Others must work to develop good feet.

• Always know the score but play like your team is behind—every point counts. Play that first point the same way you play that last point in a game.

• Play to the whistle or until the ball bounces out of the gym. Referees make mistakes.

• Let your feet prove you can't get to a ball. Don't think, react. Coaches can develop this by finishing drills as if players are in a game situation. Coaches who continually stop drills to make comments disrupt the development of decision-making skills.

• Everyone helps. No one leaves until everything is picked up. Everyone shags.

• Be thankful. Hitters thank the setter; the setter thanks the passer. Don't be obnoxious but remember that the hitters shouldn't get all the credit. Also, thank the tournament director, the support staff, the fans, and so on. This goes a long way.

• Celebrate a great play but don't dwell on it—refocus. Forget the bad play—learn from it and refocus.

• Be responsible for your actions. Don't blame others for your poor actions.

• Respect your machine. Take care of your body and feed it healthy, legal fuel. Get enough sleep. Stay fit and abide by training rules.

• Repetition develops good habits. Repetition is boring but players need to repeat skills properly so they can react in a game without thinking. Single skill repetition is a must during the learning stage. Implementing the skill in gamelike drills is the key.

• Follow the rules of the school and maintain your values. Know how to weigh the consequences. If you think you will get in trouble for the action, have the maturity to say no.

• Believe in conflict resolution. Be the initiator, be tactful, and solve problems before they fester.

EVALUATING AND MODIFYING PHILOSOPHIES AND OBJECTIVES

After every season, a coach needs to evaluate her philosophy and objectives. She needs to consider the positives and negatives from the past season and make changes that correct what went wrong during that season. Also, the coach has to modify goals and objectives to accommodate the needs of new personnel for the next season. If there are new members of the coaching staff, the head coach needs to carefully blend the philosophies of the new assistants with that of the current staff to meet the program's needs. A program's philosophy may also change in order to adjust to the addition of new players and the loss of former players to graduation and transfer.

There is a difference between being flexible and compromising your philosophy. There is also a difference between a coach's personal philosophy and her approach to the game. Her personal philosophy is her moral compass, which shouldn't waver. However, her coaching philosophy has to be flexible to adapt to change.

A change in staff and especially players for the next season means altering objectives. Many coaches change offenses and defenses according to annual personnel changes. Sometimes a team may change conferences, or other teams in the conference may become noticeably weaker due to the graduation of key seniors or decidedly stronger because of the maturing of their players. These changes in competition can be dealt with through subtle or overt adjustments in coaching objectives. It is also fine to change a philosophy to make it stronger and sounder in its interpretation and implementation.

In general terms, change is good. Because of the nature of competition, a coach needs to adopt the most current thinking into her own philosophy and, in so doing, keep up with the times. All of the information gained from clinics and workshops needs to be carefully woven into the fabric of an individual coach's philosophical mantle. However, the overall appearance of that mantle should still reflect the individual coach's personal philosophy and her ethical values. There are certain underlying personal guidelines that a person, especially a coach, must not relinquish.

CHAPTER 2 COMMUNICATING YOUR APPROACH

Good communication is a crucial ingredient for success in volleyball. Communication among players, coaching staff, parents, school administration, and the community ensures that everyone is on the same page and aiming for the same goal. It helps prevent misunderstandings, and when they do occur, it helps to solve them. Communication is necessary for teaching skills, correcting mistakes, promoting unity, and being effective in the program.

FORMS OF COMMUNICATION

Communication can be verbal, nonverbal, written, or through active listening. Each form can be positive or negative. People respond to the different forms of communication in different ways. Learning to use these forms effectively goes a long way toward avoiding miscommunication or hurt feelings.

Verbal communication is the actual words a person speaks when someone is listening. The words can be clear or confusing. The tone can be sincere, enthusiastic, sarcastic, or cruel. The message can be in a loud, soft, or normal voice.

Nonverbal communication is a reaction or demonstration a viewer understands without words. The action is usually the result of something that has happened. Sometimes it is just an action of choice. Between a coach and a player, an example is a coach not playing a player who skipped a practice before a game. Between players, an example is a setter not setting a hitter who has stolen her boyfriend. Between a coach and an official, an example is a coach throwing a clipboard in reaction to a call or an official giving the coach a red card for throwing the clipboard! Coaches have to be careful to avoid, "Do as I say, not as I do." This is an excuse for poor role modeling by a coach. Coaches are under constant scrutiny when it comes to demonstrating fair play, integrity, tactfulness, and following school rules. The old adage, "Actions speak louder than words," expresses the importance of nonverbal communication.

Nonverbal communication also includes body language. It includes facial expressions, flailing arms, shrugged shoulders, stomping feet, a head tossed around, a head buried in the hands, and many other motions. I had a player tell me once how much it hurt her when I dropped my shoulders after she served into the net. Body language can also be positive. A smiling face, clapping hands, jumping up for joy, and "raise the roof" or high five gestures are a few positive examples. As a coach, it is difficult to have perfect body language on the bench. I am sure many coaches have their players sit or stand at the other end of the bench so they cannot see the expressions shown behind a clipboard!

Most problems that arise between two people develop through misunderstandings or unclear communication. If a coach says, "Do you understand?" the players respond with a yes or no answer. It is better if a coach asks a player to rephrase what the coach has just said to ensure that the message has been properly conveyed.

Drawing Communication Activity

A creative activity that allows your team to practice communication can be done with a pencil and piece of paper. Two teammates, or a coach and player, sit back to back. One player, who is the verbal communicator, has a piece of paper with a simple picture on it (for example, a stick figure turkey). The other person is the receiver of the communication. The receiver is only allowed to draw on her blank sheet of paper. She cannot ask questions or talk. The communicator describes the picture to her partner without using words that describe what the picture actually is. An example of what the communicator could not say is, "Draw a foot." She would instead say, "Draw a straight line and put three spokes at the bottom of the line." The receiver draws the image from the explanation given. It is fun to see how well communication works when it's not two-way.

Try the exercise again with a different picture. This time allow the receiver to ask questions. Again, neither person can describe what the picture actually is, but two-way communication is allowed in the activity.

Coaches sometimes accuse players of actions before knowing the whole story. It is smart for a coach to ask a player, "What happened?" instead of "Why did you do this?" Asking a player to explain a situation gives the athlete the benefit of the doubt and allows for two-way communication. It may also give an athlete an opportunity to make up a whopper of a lie. To encourage honesty, a coach may say, "When I was young, I did some things I am not proud of" or "Please tell me the truth. I can deal with the indiscretion better than I can deal with a lie."

Active listening is an important skill a coach must possess. A coach can misunderstand a player when the coach is too busy to give the player his full attention. If a player wants to talk to a coach, the coach should direct all his attention to the player. If a coach listens while doing other work, it shows the player she is not important. This usually compounds the original problem. The coach should sit next to the player (with no desk in between them) and maintain good eye contact with the player. The coach should display positive body language while the player talks. He should listen and not interrupt. He should then rephrase what the player has told him. This ensures that he has understood the player and shows the player he has listened and cares about her. Usually, through calm conversation, the problem can be resolved.

Written communication can be a memo, a letter, e-mail, a recommendation, an evaluation, or an order form. Coaches need to be careful what they write because a written document is a tangible form of communication that a coach can be held accountable for. A coach who is angry or upset should not deal with issues on paper unless he has taken the time to calm down, decide this is the correct method of communication, and choose his words wisely. Written statements need to be proofread and edited, and order forms should be double checked for accuracy. A coach wants to set a good example by using proper English in written and verbal communication. A coach should make a copy of each written communication for future reference.

CORRECTING MISTAKES POSITIVELY

A coach has to accept the role of mentor, advisor, parent, and role model. It comes with the job! As previously stated, kids need positive role models in their lives to guide them through experiences. I have a friend, Patricia Rawson, who has been NYS Teacher of the Year twice. An administrator from her school described how her positive attitude affected the kids: "Patricia Rawson has bus duty every morning and says something positive or funny to each child as they get off the bus. Sometimes this is the only positive thing the kid hears in his day." The more positive a coach can be with her players, the more fun the kids will have. Being a positive person also makes it more fun for the coach.

It is difficult to be positive when correcting technique and game play. Players don't make mistakes on purpose, so a coach must be tactful when correcting their mistakes. Corrective criticism can be positive if the coach corrects the mistake and then finishes with a positive statement. An example of this is Coach Pollyanna saying, "Sue, if you plant your feet wider, your base will be stronger. Your platform was good and directed toward the target." This is better than Coach Gruff saying, "Sue, your base is too narrow. Your base is weak." Coach Pollyanna made her point and gave a reason why Sue should change her base. She went on to compliment what Sue had done correctly. A little sugar goes a long way. Coach Gruff made two negative statements. This coach did not comment on why, what, or how to change in order to do the skill better. The coach only told Sue what not to do. As far as Sue is concerned, her passing stinks.

A coach has to correct many mistakes throughout a practice, but the coach should try to find the root of each problem. Many times, it is not obvious where the skill has gone wrong. Coaches often focus only on the end result when assigning the blame. An example of this is the spiker whose ball hits the back wall. The coach assumes what the problem is and yells, "You dropped your elbow. Next time swing up and hit the top of the ball." In this example, what actually had happened was the player did not transition correctly off the net. The coach should have evaluated the problem more closely and then said, "You did not transition far enough off the net. Next time add two steps to your transition. It will give you more room to approach the ball. Make sure you plant your feet so the ball is in front of you. Then you can use that great power on top of the ball." Let's say that the player is still having difficulty adding two steps to her transition. The coach should check to see if the player recognizes when she can release from the net. The player may not be taking in the whole picture. If the player is watching the ball instead of how it is being played, she may not transition as soon as she could have. The point is that making corrections is an art. Effective coaches need to find where to start coaching from!

Another coaching concern is correcting mistakes that are bad habits. To help a player correct a bad habit, a coach needs to see the player make the mistake repeatedly. For this reason, it is good to use drills that require a player to contact a ball 5 to 8 times in a row. This allows a coach to assess the skill and form opinions on how to help the athlete. If a team is doing a circle drill, where a player plays a ball once in 10 contacts, it is too difficult for a coach to remember how the player contacted the ball 10 plays ago. A player may only make a certain mistake once. If this is the case, coaches should ignore the mistake.

USING CUE WORDS AND VOLLEYBALL LINGO

When teaching a skill, proper cue words are important. Cue words are descriptive and concise for the learner. Cue words can also help create a picture for the learner. Start by showing the whole skill a few times to give the players the big picture. Then identify specific

From the bench, coaches can call out cue words to remind players of technique points they learned in practice.

parts of the skill with short phrases such as "Feet under the ball" or "Face the target." Then go back and focus on the execution of each part of the skill that you identified with cue words. During a game, you can call out your cue words, and players will know immediately what segment of a skill you are talking about. Cue words are quick reference points for both the coach and the player.

Volleyball lingo includes words that are common among teams. Some words or phrases are universal in the volleyball world. Examples of these words include kill, six pack, ace, used, facial, and high five.

However, other words become distinctive volleyball lingo for a specific team. These are developed through experience and are special for a team. An example of volleyball lingo my team has acquired is a "Maribel" toss. Many of my players were at a camp together one summer. Their court coach was a wonderful woman whom they all enjoyed working with. There was one problem: she had trouble hitting free balls during drills. After the camp experience, any time someone hit a poor free ball during a drill, we would say, "Nice Maribel." It was a great, descriptive term but also reminded many of the players of a coach who had been special to them.

Another favorite expression of my players was, "We voted on it." In the early '80s, we had a formidable team. Our offense was aggressive enough to win matches without even playing defense. One day when we were playing our toughest competitor, we were challenged to play our best defense to win. Our players thoroughly enjoyed the competitive experience and the opportunity to counterattack our opponents. The other team was blasting hits on us. We had to play defense and counterattack to win the first game 15-12, and we were looking forward to the second game. During the second game, our opponents changed strategy and repeatedly passed the ball over on the first hit. At first, they scored points because we were expecting three hits. As soon as we could see it was going to be a tendency, we changed our defense and took charge. We won the second game 15-2. After the match, I commented to the opposing coach on what a great first game her team played. Then I asked her why her team changed their tactics in the second game. She replied, "Well, we didn't win the first game playing three hits with an attack, so we voted on it. We decided to send the ball over on the first hit." From that match on, any time our team would accidentally pass a ball over the net on the first hit, you could hear someone on our team bellow, "We voted on it!" A team's volleyball lingo is meaningful, adds camaraderie, and allows the team to relish past experiences.

COMMUNICATING WITHIN THE PROGRAM

Communication within a program keeps peace and harmony. It helps create a supportive, family atmosphere among the teachers, support staff, administrators, and fellow coaches.

A coach needs to make sure he follows the proper chain of command in communication. No one likes it when someone "goes to the top." A coach should work through the proper channels. If the gym is not sufficiently clean, he should speak *with*, not *to*, the custodial staff. A complaint through the athletic director will result in bitter feelings. One of the first lessons I learned when I became a physical education teacher was to make good friends with and appreciate the support staff. They make the behind-the-scenes portion of your job easier.

Many of my lessons came on the job at Sweet Home. Our athletic director at Sweet Home, Bob Barczak, used to send coffee and donuts to our bus drivers, mechanics, and grounds crew. He hosted a summer party for them at his cottage on Cuba Lake. He hosted a golf tournament for the coaches in addition to a party at the lake. He took care of the people who took care of him.

Communication with the administration is key. Administrators hate hearing things secondhand, good or bad. Administrators love to be included and share the success of a team. If a team receives public accolades, a smart coach will include the superintendent, principal, and athletic or club director. It may not seem like administrators have anything to do with a win or a success story, but they provide the opportunity for a program to thrive.

The administration needs to be informed if a coach, team, or player has a problem that affects the program. In a school setting, the athletic director should be informed; in a club setting, the club director. Administrators appreciate knowing problems ahead of time so they know the story before they receive the dreaded phone call. The director can help defend the situation if warranted. Directors hate finding out about a mishandled situation after the fact. It may be painful for a coach to admit a wrongdoing, but it is always better to be up front with the boss.

Coaches have to prioritize program needs. At budget time, directors are given coaches' laundry lists of needed equipment and supplies. Some coaches submit extra items knowing that each program's list will have to withstand cuts. If this is a fact, a coach has to know what items to push for. Coaches must be able to substantiate needs. If a coach has a poor rapport with a director, the director may find it difficult to go to bat for the coach.

A coach needs to learn what battles are worth fighting. A coach who complains about every little thing may win a small skirmish but will ultimately lose a big war. No one likes a whiner. A coach also needs to be careful not to vent his problems to the players. Players will side with the coach, and this promotes bitter relations between the athletes and the administration. In the end, it is bad for the athletic program. If everyone understands and supports the total program, everyone will benefit. A coach must have open and continual dialogue with the administration to maintain a healthy, nonthreatening environment for all.

In my office, I have a poster of Snoopy sitting on his doghouse. Snoopy is quoted, "Tact is for wienies." I keep this up on my wall as a reminder of the college recommendation my high school coach wrote for me. It was a wonderful, complimentary essay until one part: "Sometimes she lacks tact." Here was a woman I idolized stating I was tactless. I was devastated. However, it made me reflect and realize that it must be a major fault or she wouldn't have written it in a document as important as a college recommendation. Over the years, I have tried to clean up my act! I am still sarcastic and outspoken, but I try to stay tactful and positive. Staying tactful with your staff and players is important. People become tactless if they let problems fester without being addressed. Solving small issues helps prevent the development of major problems. Most problems occur due to misquoted, poorly worded, or tactless communication.

An effective coach makes time to have regular meetings with her staff, her captain, and her players individually. A coach should speak individually with her players in preseason, midseason, and postseason. Captain meetings should be scheduled at least once a week, and staff meetings should be daily. All of these regularly scheduled meetings provide a comfortable forum in which a coach can get the feedback she needs to facilitate open communication.

Staff Meetings

Staff meetings are important for keeping cohesiveness in the program. The coach has to first determine who is considered a member of his staff. The staff could include an assistant coach, a trainer, and the match crew. The match crew includes the scorer, timer, music controller, announcer, statistics recorders, linesmen, and camera operator. Once their roles are delegated, learned, and understood, the members of the match crew are usually self-sufficient.

A coach needs to talk to the trainer daily to be apprised of ongoing injuries and playing exemptions. The coach and assistant coach should meet daily to evaluate the last practice or match and to plan for the next practice and match. The two coaches may also need to evaluate scouting information and game film, prepare specific offenses and defenses to improve play against certain opponents, or discuss individual players' needs, skills, and problems. In high school and club situations, daily meetings might be impossible. Daily communication by telephone or e-mail can ensure that both coaches are on the same page. A head coach should delegate responsibilities to all staff members to define their roles and strengthen the program. To delegate effectively, the head coach must tap people's strengths.

Player Meetings

Toward the end of preseason, a coach should meet with each player to discuss goal setting, expectations, and concerns. Playing time and position are usually major issues for any athlete. Each player is excited to play and eager to start the season. The coach should define the player's role and her importance to the team. Of course, if the player's role is that of a substitute, the coach discusses what the player needs to do to earn more playing time.

The coach needs to help the player gain confidence in her ability to become a better player. If the player is a starter, the coach needs to express her sincere confidence in the player's ability to make an impact on the team. The coach wants to make sure all players leave the meetings informed and positive.

In midseason meetings, these issues should be reassessed. When players talk with a coach, relationships, attitudes, and playing time are usually the issues. Sometimes individual goals need to be altered. Midseason is a time for coaches to listen to the athlete's concerns. It is the most important time to be tactfully honest in order to maintain team cohesiveness. It is a time a coach can discover and work out problems that she had not been aware of. A coach must maintain her cool or the player will not be honest with her. This does not mean that the coach has to kowtow to the player, but the coach should reinforce team goals and affirm how the player relates to the success of the season.

At the postseason meeting, goals are assessed. The player and coach reflect on the season and discuss improvements for the next season. Goals are developed for practicing during the off-season. If it is a high school situation, the coach may encourage the athlete to play club ball. If it is a postseason club meeting, the coach may promote the high school season. Club players can sometimes bring the wrong attitude to their high school program. After many exciting experiences with their club team, some players come back to the high school team knowing that their scholastic team is not as competitive. The club coach should remind the player to be a contributing leader on her high school team and not a know-it-all show-off.

Some coaches do not have the time to hold preseason, midseason, and postseason meetings. It is important for any coach to have an open-door policy. A coach who listens to players' concerns has fewer personnel problems throughout the season.

Captain

A coach should have continual communication with her captain. A captain knows all the "skivey" and can help the coach put out fires. These problems are usually about playing time, jealousies, or personal problems. The coach can direct the captain to handle some of the problems. A coach needs to learn when to back off and let players solve problems. Becoming too involved in all of the players' problems is as deadly as ignoring a problem. This is usually truer with a girls' team. Girls' teams tend to have more sensitive issues and allow these problems to carry over onto the court. Guys tend to be able to play and forget their off-court issues.

Setter

A coach and a setter must have excellent communication and rapport. A coach has to train a setter to understand and implement his philosophy. This is usually taught off the court and developed in practice. During a match, a coach should be able to sit on the bench and know where the setter is going to set because of this training. When the team is in trouble, the setter and coach need to have simple communication from the bench to the court. Hand signals are normally used. Time-out communication and game communication are discussed in chapter 14.

COMMUNICATING WITH PARENTS

Communication with parents is essential. A preseason meeting where the coach explains his philosophy, goals, and objectives is a beneficial orientation for the parents. They want to know the background of the person influencing their child. Parents want to know the coach's approach to coaching and want to be sure that their child is being positively influenced.

Difficulties with parents begin when playing time is an issue. Many coaches have a policy of refusing to discuss playing issues with parents. Most parents want to play a role in the success of their child's team. Booster clubs can positively channel some of this energy. Booster clubs can help the coach with the normal operation of the program. If the coach

can identify a parent who has good leadership skills, that parent can be an invaluable asset to the coach. Delegating some booster club responsibilities to parents will reduce the coach's duties. These responsibilities can include fund-raising, travel plans, publicity, promotion, and setup and takedown for home matches. A coach has to coach, but parents need to support that coach, the team, and their child. A word of warning: Some parents expect more playing time for their child as payment for helping as a booster. Conversely, some coaches feel obligated to play that booster's child more.

A coach who is having a difficult time with a parent should keep his director informed. Many parents feel that if they tattle on the coach to the director, the coach will be in trouble. As stated previously, a coach who keeps his director informed can depend on him to be supportive if a parent approaches the director. A coach can also suggest to the problem parent that he discuss the issue with the director. When a coach knows his director is informed and supportive, he can stand by his director's decision.

Some parents want to inform the coach of problems with their son or daughter. Many times parents want to keep the meeting or information confidential. I prefer having both the player and parent at the meeting together. It shows all involved that the parents and the coach are working together for the benefit of the child.

COMMUNICATING WITH LOCAL COMMUNITY

Communication with the community can help boost attendance. Encouraging area residents to attend matches and tournaments will have a positive effect on the program. Displaying schedules in business windows and on bulletin boards in schools reminds people of upcoming events. According to your state laws, some businesses may support programs monetarily. In Muncie, Indiana, I saw a donation can for their club program in a McDonald's. Senior citizens are always looking for interesting activities to attend. Posting a season schedule in the community's senior citizen center may reap positive results. It will also be positive public relations for your program. Many local newspapers will print schedules, too.

Club programs need to maintain positive communication with sponsors. A club should not be a "show me the money" venture for a sponsor. Usually a business that sponsors a club expects a return for its money and efforts. A club needs to display the sponsor's name on uniforms and banners, print it in programs, and mention it in referrals. Teams may pass out token gifts before a match to promote the sponsor's product. A team should send its sponsor a team picture and updates on tournament schedules and results. Including the business' name in media coverage is positive publicity for the sponsor. A business that knows a club team is promoting its product will be more likely to continue its sponsorship in the future.

Coaches need to keep the media informed of their team's schedule, roster, results, highlights, and important upcoming events. A coach should make contact with reporters for the newspapers, television stations, and radio stations in her area and keep them well informed. After a match, the coach should have the scores, stats, and highlights ready when she contacts the reporter. If the reporter has received a roster, he will not have to ask for the spelling of players' names. Large city newspapers tend to write more on successful teams. Local newspapers will support most local schools and clubs. Many local newspapers need written stories submitted to them. Be careful to proofread the story.

A coach needs to keep the media informed about upcoming big matches that warrant a photographer or a news camera. Smaller newspapers will accept photographs. Make sure you know what type of photograph format they require. The media likes to know about an upcoming match between two rivals or undefeated teams, a match that will determine first place in the standings, a play-off match, the postseason play schedule, or a human interest story.

COMMUNICATING WITH OFFICIALS

Communication with officials has to be calm, tactful, and substantiated. When an official comes to the gym for a match, he is to be respected. The official should be introduced to the match crew, including the scorer, lines judges, and timer.

The coach and the captain need to have good communication with both officials. During a match, the captain is the only person allowed to address an official. We all know this is not always true! The captain has to know when to question a referee and how to do so effectively and politely. The captain must understand the rules and know the score.

A coach has to know how and when to ask for a substitution. A floor official is trained to be aware of the coaches during dead balls and to be aware of a player rushing up to the substitute area along the sideline. The coach needs to make sure the substitute is ready on time to avoid delaying the game or being too late to enter the game. In a noisy gym, the coach may have to stand up to draw the attention of the referee if the floor official is busy with an opponent's substitution or at the scorer table. Some coaches disrupt play by trying to ask for a substitution right before the whistle. This tactic is intended to rattle the opponent's server, but it usually causes confusion and alienates the officials. It is generally better to ask for a substitute in a timely manner.

Coaches need to know and understand the rules. Some coaches argue with officials because they do not understand a referee's call or the rule. If a coach doesn't understand the interpretation of a rule, she should ask the official for clarification before the match. If a team runs an unusual serve receive where the hitters or setters are stacked to confuse the opponents, the team's coach should inform the floor official before the match. If the floor ref is informed, an erroneous whistle may be avoided. The intention is to fool the opponents . . . not to make a fool of the official.

If a coach has a difference of opinion with a referee over a call, the coach has to remember she is on display in the gym. She is a role model and a representative of the program. In USA Junior Olympics, coaches sign a sportsmanship oath and have to take an IMPACT course to maintain proper coaching ethics. Coaches can get their point across without making a spectacle. Bantering with the floor ref, talking to the officials between games, and body language are better ways to demonstrate disappointment over a call than shouting and clipboard throwing.

After a match, a coach should shake hands with the officials and support crew. If the coach does not agree with many of the calls made during the match, it is best not to discuss them at this time. Officials usually rush out of threatening situations anyway! A phone call the next day is more effective. Coaches have to remember that officials don't play favorites but call plays the way they see them. One call rarely causes a loss. Coaches have a good basis for complaint if the official has been inconsistent in ball handling calls. If it is a serious situation, most official boards have evaluation forms that can be used to express concerns. Many times coaches are allowed to blackball one or two officials from their matches. Coaches should not make a habit of being argumentative with officials.

Bad reputations are hard to shed, and they clearly indicate a lack of sporting behavior.

COMMUNICATING WITH COLLEGE COACHES

Varsity coaches and club coaches who coach older age divisions need to develop good relations with college coaches. Coaches should help with the college recruitment process for their players who want to play volleyball after high school graduation. This includes written and verbal communication with college coaches. Scholastic coaches must be familiar with college volleyball so they understand the different levels of play and know how to recommend their players. A coach has to remember that her credibility and the school's reputation are on the line when recommending a player. If a coach says her player has a good work ethic or good attitude, it had better be true. The coach must demonstrate integrity behind each recommendation.

To me, communication is preventative. Frequently, after a conflict has been resolved, a person will say in hindsight, "Why didn't you tell me sooner?" My concept of communication is an ongoing dialogue where people feel comfortable in discussing their position. Many coaching difficulties can be prevented if players and staff have the freedom to express themselves.

CHAPTER 3 MOTIVATING PLAYERS

Motivation is the responsibility of both the coach and player. A player must come into a practice or a match self-motivated, but a coach should enhance the player's enthusiasm. The coach can do this by running a well-organized, motivating, and competitive practice. If players train hard, they know they have the ability to play well, and they know they deserve to win.

I loved teaching and coaching my "farm system." Middle school kids love to have adults care for them. To young teens, having a positive and fun-loving coach is enough motivation to keep them happy and productive. Some coaches have charisma. If you can get a young kid to have fun and to want to play hard for *you,* it's a great start.

Volleyball is a sport that is tough to teach children because it doesn't produce instant success. Forearm passing hurts, the ball hits the floor too much, spiking takes too much timing, and serving requires good contact. Heck, it's easy for little kids to dribble a ball and make a basket on a Fisher-Price hoop or kick a soccer ball into a goal. Other sports give children instant gratification!

After a little kid's first volleyball experience, her arms may have red marks that last for days. Achieving a pass, set, and hit doesn't happen. When a youth team finally achieves a pass, set, and hit, if the coach is really good, she'll go crazy with excitement. Kids love to see their coaches display positive reactions. They love to see that look of pride on their parent's and coach's faces. That's what motivation is all about with children.

My first super group of girls, whom I had developed up through the volleyball ranks, just loved to make me react by producing great plays. I made sure I pleased them by being demonstrative on the sidelines. When they were middle school and junior varsity players, they couldn't get enough of me. It was an ego booster for me and kept *me* motivated, too! By the time they became varsity players, they had developed into very good players. I no longer had to go crazy on the sidelines, but the players knew by my expressions that I took great pride in their play. They were a joy to watch.

The best compliment I ever received (which initially hurt my feelings) happened on a van trip to a tournament. The trip was with these same super kids when they were in 11th grade. In the van, we were playing the "questions" game. Everyone had to ask a question. Each teammate had to answer each question honestly. We would have great discussions based on the answers, and the game was also a great way to learn more about each other.

When it was my turn, I asked the team, "Why do you like to play volleyball?" I must have needed "stroking" because I expected answers such as, "Because we love to play for Kooz," "Because we have so much fun with Kooz," or "Because of all the extra things Kooz does for us." Instead, I heard, "It's a game of many reactions and fast decisions," "Every play is different and you really have to rely on your teammates to be successful," "It's a game of many specialties that have to blend together to produce great chemistry," and "It has taught me how important cooperation is." I was so hurt that I could barely drive the van because my eyes were blurry from tears. How dare they omit me! When I originally asked the question, my head was swollen enough to barely fit through a door frame. The answers deflated my head flat enough to slide under a door! Then I started seeing the big picture. As their answers replayed through my thoughts, I realized that I had the privilege of helping develop kids who were self-motivated, loved the complexities of the game, and developed lifelong camaraderie. I realized that their positive character traits and intense love for the game made me prouder than I had ever felt. These girls were truly self-motivated!

Believing in children is motivational. When I was a teacher at a middle school, our school taught "real" volleyball in physical education class. In the '80s, our school had an honors physical education class. That meant teaching zone defense and full-court press during the basketball unit, synchronized swimming and lifesaving during the swim unit, and spiking and blocking during the volleyball unit. It was like having a practice for our sport teams during the day! Our students were learning skills so quickly we started teaching over their heads. They were wild about the challenge of playing floor defense, playing an offensive system, and hitting combinations. Our students would run through the gym door in between classes to set and hit quicks. We soon realized that they were achieving so much because we were complimenting their ability to learn. We did not limit their potential.

These days, kids have so much pressure to do well in school, to hit the most home runs, to get a scholarship, or to be better

Wins can be great motivators, but they can also cause players to be too confident when playing an opponent they previously beat.

than the Joneses. I don't remember feeling pressure as a child. I'd come home from school, change into my play clothes, and go to the playground. It was a great life! I didn't get to play on real teams until high school field hockey and basketball. I didn't have the opportunities that young women now have in sports. But my parents believed in me. My high school coaches believed in our team. We were so excited to play on a team. No one had to motivate us. We were thrilled to have a uniform on with the school name and our own number.

REASONS FOR LACK OF MOTIVATION

Why do children today lack self-motivation? One reason is that they are provided with so much. Most decisions are made for them, too.

Mom or Dad taxis kids from practices to lessons to fast-food dinners and home in time to do homework or play on the computer.

Do kids lack self-motivation because they have so many choices? Video games, hot cars, jobs, shopping at the mall, MTV, and the Internet are a few of the reasons kids choose not to play sports. One day I was trying to convince an eighth grader to go out for volleyball. She said, "I did the sports thing from the time I was four. I got tired of trying to win a college scholarship in fifth grade. My coaches yelled, my dad lectured me, and my mom kept telling my dad to quit hounding me. I hardly knew the girls on my team. It just wasn't fun."

What can coaches do to make sports fun and help athletes be self-motivated? The first thing they should do is create a safe, nonthreatening environment for practices and matches.

WAYS TO MOTIVATE

My son played in a town basketball league. The league commissioner held a meeting for the players' families in a huge auditorium, and attendance was mandatory. He said, "Anyone who berates an official, a coach, or a player—including your own child—will be thrown out of the gym, and your child will be out of the program!" Whoa! We had all heard the old speech about getting kicked out of a gym for bad sporting behavior. But I liked the comment about not being able to yell at your own child. The comment about the child being tossed out of the program was a shocker. Everyone numbly nodded his or her head in agreement, and the meeting went on. During the first basketball game, the parents sat along the sideline in silence. At halftime, the commissioner went to center court and announced, "It is okay to cheer *for* your son and the team!" Cheering for positive plays was a novel idea in motivation, and the team was the best one my son ever played on.

Coaches should insist that their players be self-motivated. If players are not motivated, the coach has to determine the reason. Practices must be challenging and include objectives, developmental skills, gamelike and pressure situations, fun activities, and activities that allow players to experience success. If an athlete is aggressive and has a good attitude, a well-planned practice will be productive and enjoyable. If players are not producing and playing hard, the practice may be boring. Some drills are tough to make challenging all the time. But most drills can be made challenging by adding scoring, a time limit, points for positive versus negative repetitions, rewards for winning, or consequences for not winning.

A skill that can be boring to practice is serve receive. Players tend to make it their goal to get serve receive practice over with as quickly as possible! There are various ways to make this skill more motivating. If you're working only on serve receive, a score can be added to the quality of each pass. If the pass is on target to allow a setter to set a middle or perimeter hitter, it earns 3 points. If the pass is off the net and would make a setter move to the ball and only allow the setter to set a perimeter hitter, it is assigned a 2. If the pass is off the net so much that it causes a down or free ball return or the setter has to call for help, it scores a 1. If the pass is shanked and no one would be able to save the ball, it is assigned a 0. A player can pass a certain number of serves, a time can be assigned to a drill, or a set number can be assigned to the serve receiver—for example, the player must attain 50 points before she is done.

The same drill can be conducted using a setter instead of a target. The setter now gets to practice setting live passes, and the passer and setter are working together as a team. The setter can also be challenged by setting away from the pass or setting a certain direction assigned by the coach.

I have always felt that adding attacking to any drill makes the drill more fun and competitive. It fosters teamwork. A 2-, 3-, 4-, or 5-person serve receive drill can be performed with the setter either setting away from the person who passed the ball or setting the person who passed the ball. It can be a front row attack or a back row attack depending on the goal set by the coach. The coach can make this drill more competitive by dividing the team into groups who compete against each other for a score. The scoring can give points for executing set plays assigned by the coach. For younger teams, the points could be earned by successfully executing a pass to the setter and the setter setting up an attacker to return the ball over the net.

As long as the team is working on quality first contacts, the coach is happy. The players are happy because the drill is fun and game-like. If a drill is challenging but the goal is attainable, a team will feel successful. Success is motivational.

Customized Motivation

It is idealistic to think that coaches do not need to motivate players. Some coaches feel that they should treat each player the same and that the player has to adjust to the coach's style. This is true to a degree, but most coaches agree that each player learns and is motivated differently and should therefore be dealt with differently.

Some players learn from watching, some from listening, some from reading about the skill, some from performing the skill, and some from visualizing or mental imagery. During a practice or match, some players are motivated to improve or play harder when a coach yells, some when a coach explains what is wrong, some from positive cues, and some from one-on-one pep talks. When a coach learns how each player is coached most successfully, she can tap the appropriate resource at the right time. It is difficult to always use the correct approach with each player. In the heat of a match, the coach has to do her best to motivate the team and keep the players focused on the play.

Motivational Comments

A good way to motivate individual players is to have motivating comments that are special to the player. Our team had an awesome setter and middle hitter. The two of them connected on quicks at will! During a pregame talk, I was discussing strategy with our team. One of the statements I made was that if we got into trouble, we could always go to our bread-and-butter play of running a 31 quick with our setter and middle hitter. It was not meant to exclude any other player's ability to be successful. But one of our dynamic outside hitters took offense at being excluded as a bread-and-butter player. This dynamic player, Jodie, was 5 feet tall, could jump 33 inches, and was the spark plug of our team. She dug the ball better than anyone did. But I had deflated her ego. She sulked through the entire first game. I had to take her out of the match. After the match was over, we had a blowup over the situation. I didn't know what was wrong with her until she admitted it had hurt her feelings. I accused her of being a prima donna. Again I deflated her ego. The next day in practice, she apologized. All was forgotten, and I didn't use the term *bread-and-butter* again.

The next week, Jodie made the most unbelievable dig in a game. The crowd went wild. I looked at her and signaled "key dig" with my hand. I did this by turning my wrist as if I was starting a car. Then I pointed my fingers toward the floor like a digging shovel. It turned out to be a signal that was used exclusively between Jodie and me. It was special and I never overused it. But Jodie played defense tougher to make me use it with her. I had won her back and found a great way to applaud my little leader.

Another player admitted to me after she graduated that she loved to make seemingly impossible plays so I would shake my head and mutter, "Sweeeeet." I didn't even know I was using the term. I still use it for special occasions. Treating each player as a special individual, with respect, is motivational.

Prematch Pep Talks

Motivating a team before a match can be similar to a stand-up comic routine; you have to know your audience. The most difficult pregame talk is when a team has played the opponent before and had no trouble with them. Playing down to the level of a lesser opponent is a difficult barrier to overcome. Coaches try to convince their teams to use this opportunity to practice offenses. Coaches can set scoring goals, assign play sets that the team has been working on, try new combinations of players, or promise pizza for a good match.

If a team plays an opponent they have previously lost to, the previous loss is usually motivation. A revenge win is great. A coach must make sure her team doesn't have a fear of playing the team. Fear restricts movement and takes focus off play. This coach has to motivate her team to play their best against a tough team. In practices leading up to the game, this coach should have drilled what her team did poorly against this team in the first meeting. This coach also needs to point out the plays the team did well and accentuate the positive. Some coaches say, "We practice hard to play better teams. We have an opportunity to rise to the next level." If a team feels prepared, knows what to expect, and has a few tricks of their own, they will be more confident. Confidence enhances self motivation.

If a team plays an opponent they previously defeated but had a close match with, they have to be prepared for one of two things. The opponent might start strong and then lose confidence and roll over and play dead. They might not even play tough at all. Or, they may come in gunning for the other team. The latter is the team the coach has to prepare for. This opponent has nothing to lose and everything to gain. This team usually brings hundreds of obnoxious fans and noisemakers. This team will play insatiable defense and make the most unbelievable plays with long rallies. Winning long rallies is motivational and turns the emotional tide in games.

A smart coach will face an adversary with respect. She may keep her previous lineup and say, "Try to beat us." She may change her lineup figuring the opponents are changing theirs for better hitter and blocker matchups. The coach has to be ready to keep her team emotionally stable in case they start losing or the score is close. If her team has practiced and played under gamelike pressure, the team will be prepared to play tough. This coach wants to play to win; she doesn't want her team to play not to lose.

Before playing in a "big" match, the coach wants to motivate her players to play their best. Nothing is worse than players on the bus ride home regretting how they played . . . they can never get the experience back. If each player on a team has played her best, a coach and team can be proud of the outcome, win or lose.

A method of scoring I have used to motivate players in practice is called *floor score*. Every time the ball hits the floor inside a team's court lines or off the hands of a blocker and lands off the court, a team receives one floor score. It is actually a negative, minus point. The team does not want to earn these points. Assigning floor score to a drill tends to increase movement to the ball. The team with the lower floor score wins. A consequence is assigned to the losing team.

Assigning consequences is very motivational. A coach will see an instant increase in the level of defensive play. Floor score can be incorporated into competitive drills and scrimmage situations. I have used floor score in actual matches when we were winning without much effort but embarrassing ourselves by not passing balls we could have with little effort. Floor score is a way to motivate a team to pursue all balls and refocus on quality play.

Gimmicks

Gimmicks are another way to motivate a team. Our Sweet Home team was playing Horseheads High School. Horseheads was an excellent team and was our favorite rival. We usually played them in the final four of the state tournament. The morning of the match, the Horseheads setter, Sara, was quoted in the paper. A reporter had asked Sara if she thought they could beat Sweet Home this time. Sara said, "I think we can beat Sweet Home 'cause we play with more heart." Our team read that statement, and it was like throwing raw meat to a panther! Because we had a friendly relationship with Horseheads, we decided to react to the statement. We sent the Horseheads team a heart-shaped cookie. We purchased hair twistees with hearts on them to give as token gifts before the match during the ceremonial good-luck handshake. We bought a tape with the song, "You've Got to Have Heart" on it and played the tune as our warm-up song before the match. Needless to say, the Horseheads team just kept shaking their heads because of our gimmicks. It was also fun!

Make sure the gimmick is ethical and true. A friend of mine, whose team was very competitive, made up a fake news article to show his team. He created the fake article in the technology lab, and it looked like it had been copied from an actual newspaper. The pretend article quoted the opposing coach berating the team. My friend's team ended up playing inspired and won the match. After the match, the team captain went up to the opposing coach, whose name had been quoted in the article, and told him off. The opposing coach sputtered in disbelief. He didn't know what this player was talking about. In the end, the coach who manufactured the hoax was reprimanded, and apologies were made. One coach almost lost his good reputation for the sake of motivating a team. A team lost respect for a coach because of the prank he pulled to help achieve a win.

A gimmick that caused a positive reaction was using a gold medal in the pregame huddle when I was coaching in the Empire State Games. Right before our cheer, I would pull the gold medal out of my pocket and have everyone touch it. We felt the transfer of power from the medal to the players as the girls made sizzling sounds and rubbed the gold! Gimmicks can redirect team spirit, reduce anxiety, and add fun to a competition.

I used another gimmick on a team that was a split team made up of an even number of great hitters and great passers. Of course, the hitters were receiving all the media attention. We all knew that we wouldn't be playing as well without our passing machines. But the defensive specialists were the Rodney Dangerfields of our team—they got no respect. So, I went to a jewelry store and purchased two silver charms. One charm was a tiny volleyball and the other was #1. I put the two together on a necklace. After each match, the top passer was awarded the necklace. The player wore the necklace until the next match. It was a coveted award on our team. It even made our hitters work harder at passing. I gave attention and recognition to the cog that made our machine work!

Some gimmicks are promises, promises! I have made many promises in an attempt to promote better play, including pizza, stopping at Burger King, ice-cream cones, having a special practice, cutting a practice short, and buying new garb. A promise should be carried out if a coach wants to stay credible. Some promises are in the negative form of threats, such as practicing longer, not stopping for food, a conditioning practice, or other consequences. A player who loves volleyball should feel it is a punishment if the practice is cut short!

Awards and Praise

Tournaments generally give trophies, plaques, T-shirts, and medals to all-stars and winning teams. These are tokens for players to cherish as a fond memory of a successful tournament or match. Extrinsic awards are very motivational for younger players. After one club tournament, I was at the tournament desk when the mother of a 14-year-old came up to the director and asked, "Where are the awards for the third place team?" Kids love to line their shelves with awards. But an award without meaning and justification promotes false self-esteem. I don't mean to say that a player who has finished third shouldn't feel proud of her efforts, but rewarding a team for mediocre play is showing teams you can get rewards without accomplishing the goal. It also shows a team they don't have to work hard to receive awards.

As players mature, the thrill of competition and the ability to win are the reward. I love it when I hear a girl whose team has played hard but didn't win say, "We were beat by a better team. We know what we have to practice to be a winner next time." The accomplished player still likes to have the medal put over her head,

© Human Kinetics

Motivating players requires knowing which blend of encouragement, goal setting, challenge, and praise works best for each player and for the team as a whole.

but the celebration of the goal achieved is more meaningful. Intrinsic feelings of accomplishment, success, good play, and teamwork are a coach's goal.

Another motivator is displaying performance accomplishments. Players enjoy seeing their name in print. This can include media releases, bulletin boards, match booklets, and any pictures or printed material that broadcast the player's and the team's successes.

Praise is a motivational tool a coach can use during practice or a match. Developing the correct blend of encouragement, drive, goal setting, and praise is tough to do. Some players like to be verbally driven to play harder.

A friend of mine just accepted a coaching position at an NCAA Division I school. The team interviewed her. One player asked the new coach if she would please yell at her . . . even if she was playing well! I have had many players tell me they would resent being yelled at in practice or a game. As previously stated, a coach has to know what motivates a player. The tough part is blending all these different personalities and getting them to work hard, play tough, and develop team chemistry.

Exposure to Higher Levels of Play

A good way to motivate players is by exposing them to a higher level of play. This can include taking them to an area college match or a national team exhibition, or even showing them a video of an exciting match. When junior clubs were first developing in 1980, I took a team to the National AAU Junior Olympics in Chicago, Illinois. We thought we were pretty tough so we were excited to play. Our team's families thought we would come home as national champs. We did well but were awed by the level of play. It was inspiring and the team couldn't wait to practice harder to become better and return the next year. Taking advantage of teachable moments can be motivational on its own.

ENCOURAGEMENT DURING SLUMPS

The toughest part of motivation comes during a match when a team is in a slump—the team's players take turns serving into the net, serve receive passes get shanked into the bleachers, or the best pass is the one a girl got from her boyfriend last night! It drives coaches crazy. A coach hates calling time-out to break a serve and waste time saying, "Move your feet and pass the ball." What a coach really needs to do is divert the players' attention away from the mistakes and the pressure and refocus the team. This can be done by suggesting a different play or trying to lighten up the mood so the players can shake off the jitters. Some teams react to negative talk that motivates them to play better. Usually, what works best is for the coach to use her time wisely, keep it light, make suggestions, and display confidence.

When I was coaching at Sweet Home, we were playing a tough league match against Lancaster. We were doing nothing right. I had used my time-outs, and I was making substitutions as if they were unlimited. My assistant coach, Kathy Neelon, leaned over and whispered, "You just used your last substitution." It was the first time in 20 years I had ever used the limit! I leaned back in a panic and replied, "What should I do?" Kathy said, "Sit back and enjoy the game!"

BEING A GOOD EXAMPLE

A game has highs and lows, but a coach must be careful to keep her body language at an even level on the bench. If a game is close and a coach is going crazy on the sideline, the team will likely take on the same anxious behavior. A team in trouble cannot look to a coach who is ranting and raving on the sideline. They need to see a coach in full control supporting their play.

I had a coach in our club who had so many emotions that other teams would come watch our matches for entertainment. Our team emulated the personality of the coach. If he was nervous and verbally abusive, the team played panicky and helter-skelter. If things were going well, the coach was carefree and the team was light and fluffy! The best was when the team was playing poorly; he would call a time-out and sit on the end of the bench. He refused to coach them until they started playing better.

As players become mature, if a team is on an emotional high, the coach can show plea-sure but should leave most of the celebrating to the team. The coach needs to be in full control even if his insides are ready to rip out. Nothing is worse than a team celebrating too early; the match is not over until the fat lady sings.

One season, our Daemen team was playing in the conference finals. We had won the third game and were ahead in the match two games to one. You could feel victory in the air. We had played to perfection, and our opponent's setter was crying. But I could feel the celebration becoming too intense, and I didn't hear the fat lady singing. Never underestimate a setter's ability to run plays while crying. Yep, they beat us. They came back wanting to win, and we played not to lose. It was one of the toughest games I have ever coached. Nothing worked—not tricks, gimmicks, promises, pleads, praise, or threats. I felt like I was fishing and had snagged my line on a rock on the bottom of the lake. I kept trying to reel it in, and it wouldn't budge.

As I look back, I realize we did not have the court maturity to work through problems and refocus on what we had to do to win. We almost felt that we were lucky we were winning. When opponents started playing harder, we lacked confidence in ourselves. The worst part was that, after the match, many players regretted how they had played. I knew that our program had to seek higher-level competition to learn how to compete and to gain confidence. Volleyball is such an emotional roller coaster of high and low play. We needed to keep our highs high and learn to recover quickly from our lows.

The most important motivator is caring sincerely for your athletes. Taking the time to get to know each player shows that you sincerely care about her as a person and as a player. Many times this will raise a player's self-image, improve communication, and create a family atmosphere. When a person knows you believe in her, she will believe in herself.

BUILDING A VOLLEYBALL PROGRAM

Patti Perone, the Horseheads coach, once said, "When the Sweet Home volleyball team walks through the gym door, they have points in their pockets." Program building and maintenance of that program lend authority, tradition, and chutzpah to team pride.

Coaching a team and building a program stem from two different goals. Some people coach for money, control, and power. Other people coach for the love of children, for the love of a sport, as a method to pay back what others have given them, as community service, or because no one else would take the team! Some coaches truly enjoy coaching year to year without any game plan for building a program. They are content to put their time into the season and become as successful as they can between the first day of practice and the last day of the season. If a coach is working for the paycheck, the last day of the season can't come fast enough. We used to play against a team whose coach wore his bowling shirt to matches. As we walked in the gym door, he would check his wristwatch and say, "Could we make this quick? I have to be on the lanes by 8 p.m." Another coach told me he never cared if his team made the play-offs because there was no extra pay, and it meant more time working.

Building a program is like building a home. A coach has to establish a firm foundation on which to build if he is going to have a strong structure. Developing a program is also similar to nurturing a loving family. Most successful programs do not happen overnight; they develop naturally and grow from success. Success builds success.

Every team's story is different. Any particular coach's success story cannot necessarily be repeated in the same way by another coach to build his own successful program. However, a lot can be learned from the defining moments of a success story. In this chapter, I share my story of coaching and point out the important ingredients that apply to most coaches and programs: setting goals, seeking challenging competition, pride in the program, the importance of psychology, a farm system, teaching the basics, and establishing a support system.

SETTING GOALS

When I started coaching, I was coaching a team and not building a program. I had no plans or goals. I was only coaching volleyball as a favor to our athletic director. I wanted to coach basketball, softball, or field hockey. Because there were no openings in the sports I wanted to coach, our beloved athletic director begged me to accept the girls' volleyball job for a year. I had no idea what volleyball was all about. I survived the first season by asking the players what they had done the year before. I also made up some very dynamic drills!

We would start practice with bleacher bumps. This wonderful drill placed the girls in groups of three. One girl would stand up on the top of the folded bleachers with a ball (this was before lawsuits were common); another girl had her arms out ready to dig, and the third girl would run around and shag the errant balls. The girl on the bleachers would hit a ball down on the digger. The defensive player would slide on her knee pads and dig the ball up. We went through many knee pads our first season!

Our next drill was serving from behind the end line. It looked like an artillery line. Then we would toss, set, and hit from the right and left sides. If the left-side player was set, the hitter would spike with her fist. If the right-side player was set (we called her the "off-hand hitter"), she would hit with the back of her hand. We took all terms literally! To finish the two-hour practice, we would scrimmage for one hour.

That was my practice plan. We rarely passed a ball to a setter. Primarily, we double fisted the ball over the net on the first hit. We had devastating serves, and we spiked over-passes. This strategy earned us second place in our conference. The first place team won because they were ahead of us at the end of the third timed eight-minute game (the score was 11-13).

At the end of the season, I evaluated the experience. I had great athletes. They were self-motivated and loved playing sports. They knew more about volleyball than I did. This last fact bothered me. My athletic director asked me to take the volleyball team "just one more year." I told him about my season evaluation, and he suggested I attend a volleyball clinic during the off-season.

I went to my first clinic in the spring of 1975 in Rochester, New York. The clinician started off by asking us what offense we used. Hmmmm, offense? Did I go to a basketball or football clinic by mistake? She went on to ask us if we employed a 6-2, 5-1, or 4-2. What was she talking about? Was she talking in code? Only 5 coaches out of 50 raised their hands admitting they used an offense. The next six hours was the most eye-opening experience of my short coaching career. I learned about skills, drills, and tactics. By the way, I also found out that off-hand hitting didn't mean spiking with the back of the hand! By 5:00, I was driving home excited for the next season. Heck, I was ready to coach the national team!

The next year, we finished first in our league. We used a 4-2 offense and thought we were quite unique. I knew more than my players did and felt like I had actually taught skills and tactics. Most teams in our league did not know what we were doing! We lost in sectional play-offs to a team that used a player to set out of the back row. It looked cool, but it also looked illegal!

Before my third year, I attended another clinic and brushed up on the 6-2 offense. Yes, you guessed it. We used a 6-2 offense during the next season. We had great hitters, good passers, and athletic setters. We won sectionals and thought we were cool. We started playing in recreation tournaments during the off-season. This lasted a few years until some of my players decided to attend a summer camp. When they came home from camp, my players knew more about volleyball than I did . . . once again. They taught me what they learned at camp, but I realized I had to stay ahead of my players. I had to keep growing in the sport.

In the late '70s, one of my setters was being recruited by the University of Georgia. We had to send the coach, Sid Feldman, a super eight game film for recruiting purposes. Through this experience, I met one of my first mentors in volleyball. Sid invited me to coach at his camp in the Pocono Mountains. I was so excited! Two of my best players went with me as campers. There were 12 outdoor courts. I was asked to coach court number 4.

At a local pub the first night of the camp, I asked Sid why he had asked me to coach at his camp. He said, "I watched the recruiting film and noticed none of your kids prayed."

I replied, "Sid, Sweet Home isn't a Catholic school." After the roar of laughter at my expense ceased, Sid asked me a question. "I could see you were running a 6-2 offense. I couldn't figure out what defense you were using. Were you using a red or a white?" I didn't know what he was talking about, but I replied, "Neither, Sid, our colors at Sweet Home are blue and gold." After another roar of laughter, Sid took a cocktail napkin and drew a red defense, 6-up, and a white defense, 6-back. I have framed that napkin as a reminder that a coach should never be afraid of asking questions and should always be a student of the game.

I had the opportunity to meet and network with other coaches. I learned more in one week than I had in five years. During the evening, the camp coaches had the opportunity to take Level I and Level II USVBA coaching accreditation program courses from Sid and Tom Tait, the Penn State coach. I was so naive about the sport. Every evening I would listen, take notes, ask questions, and absorb all the knowledge these two learned men provided. I found myself trying to coach like Sid and Tom. In previous clinics I attended, I had fallen into this same pitfall. I didn't have a mind of my own. I just believed my teams could do everything and used other coaches' information. Every year my team learned new techniques that I had learned at a new clinic. I realized that to be successful I had to start using what would work for *our* team. From Sid I learned that it is okay to have fun, but you'd better stay intense to be successful. Sid was a great "cue word" coach who taught me how to teach skills. He also had gimmicks! From Tom I learned to be more analytical and technical in coaching. I learned there were times to be calm, listen, take in the situation, and work out the problem. I learned to figure out things for myself and to keep developing my own coaching style and philosophy.

As I look back now, I know we started changing from a team into a program at this point. I didn't do anything methodically or on purpose to develop a program. But I can point out some significant things that had happened. We were successful, we were improving, we were learning, and we were staying ahead of

Ingredients for a successful volleyball program and happy players include training, learning, camaraderie, having fun, and always seeking to improve.

our competition. If I had had a recipe for developing a successful program, my success could have happened sooner! The main ingredients of this "recipe for success" are to have fun, to share success, to keep learning, to train hard, to develop a farm system, to play during the off-season, to role model the best, to give the kids things other sports don't, to enhance the development of the whole person, to demonstrate that lifelong learning is a priority, to develop camaraderie, to network, and to believe in your kids. Success breeds success. Everyone wants to be part of that warm, tingly feeling that comes with winning. But success takes patience, perseverance, and caring.

SEEKING CHALLENGING COMPETITION

Once we had tasted winning, we liked it! We were winning in our area. We had to start challenging ourselves by scheduling the top programs in New York at various tournaments. The next step would be scheduling competitive tournaments out of state as another way to seek competition.

We won our league and section five years in a row. We did not have a state high school championship, but New York was the first state to develop all-state games during the summer. This was another avenue for some of our top players to play with and against the best. All-star teams were chosen for the Olympic events. I coached the western New York scholastic volleyball team, for which some of my own players qualified. We became exposed to players from other New York areas and how they played. We loved the opportunity to play at a higher level and to play in an organized tournament off-season. It also helped me network and develop volleyball friends. Joe Gillespie, the boys' varsity coach at Eden High School and an Empire State Games coach, became my fast buddy. We shared the same intensity and the desire to develop our players during the off-season. Joe developed the largest camp for boys and girls in the Northeast. My network was expanding and so was my knowledge through the great coaches at this camp. My new mentors were Joe Segula, Jon Wilson, Bob Bertucci, Oleg Moiseenko, and Ralph Hippolyte. I didn't know what worked best for my team, but I kept trying new things to see if they were effective. By this time, all my kids were going to camp. Going to camp for a summer was like adding a season to their development.

In 1979, Charles Michlin, a coach from Rochester, New York, took four of my players to the National AAU Junior Olympics in Lisle, Illinois. When they came home, they were very excited about their experience. They begged me to form a team and go to the tournament with our own players the next year. It sounded like fun, so we did it. I took an 18-and-under team. It was quite an eye-opener. We did well, but I was in shock at how well the other teams played. This club level competition was evolving across the country, but it had not yet affected the East. I also saw that there were 14-and-under and 16-and-under age groups. This club situation seemed to me to be an important element in player development. It was a way to combine a farm system and off-season play in a competitive situation.

In 1979, we officially formed the Cheetah Volleyball Club. We had one team in each club age level, coached by three progressive coaches from our area. We practiced on Sundays and went to any tournament we could find. The player development increased drastically. Hmmm, high school, club, camp, and state games . . . wow, these kids were fantastic. They were also playing basketball and softball for their high schools. Our club became well known, and the kids reaped the benefits by gaining volleyball scholarships to college. Things were snowballing. Several coaches wanted to coach in our club, and many area players wanted to play Cheetah.

TAKING PRIDE IN THE PROGRAM

In 1980, our state chairperson, Judy Hartmann, told me Sweet Home was only a few wins away from breaking a national high school record for the most consecutive wins in volleyball. It was good timing because our team needed a new goal. We were good before our time. Looking back now, I know it was the club experience that was making our players more seasoned than our opponents were. We were traveling out of our area to seek higher competition to make us a better team. In fact, we often traveled out of state to high school tournaments and still won!

Sweet Home broke the National Federation of High Schools record, which had been at 92 wins. It caused celebration in our area. The press gave us publicity, and college coaches took notice. It also brought pride to the program and instilled a feeling of invincibility in our players.

Sweet Home kept winning. We were using a diverse offense that included running quicks and combination plays. We had powerful hitting. We lacked defensive maturity, but we were very athletic so we counterattacked broken plays. We rarely gave up a free ball.

Most of our opponents had one or two good hitters; we had five or six.

Our setting was also superior. Our setters were receiving advanced training at the same camp where I coached, so I, too, learned as my players were trained. Ideally, a setter touches a ball more than any other player on the court. Therefore, it makes sense to give them separate quality training sessions. With our Cheetah VBC, we have a specialized practice one evening a week. We have two courts available. For the first part of the session, the young setters train together with an expert setter coach. On the other court, the middle hitters are trained by another coach. For the last part of practice, the two groups combine. The same procedure is done with our older age group setters and middle hitters. It has helped immensely and taken some burden off the team coaches in regular practice.

Our program started getting national attention. We were consistently ranked by *USA Today* (Mizuno poll) and *Volleyball Monthly*. We kept maturing in the sport and enjoying the camaraderie that success brings to a program.

Judy Hartmann contacted me again and said, "Do you know that you are getting close to breaking another record?" I couldn't figure out what record she meant. She added, "The National Federation of High Schools record for the most consecutive wins in any sport, male or female, is 218." Another volleyball program was also pursuing the record. Evergreen High School in Colorado had about the same winning record as we did. Sweet Home was playing about 30 to 40 matches a season, so we were a couple of years away from achieving 218 wins. It was just what we needed to motivate our players. However, we wanted to stay with the philosophy of seeking quality competition because without formidable foes, the record wouldn't be credible.

During the next season, Evergreen lost to Coronado High School, coached by a friend of mine, Joannie Powell (who always reminds me that we owe her!). So, with Evergreen out of the running, Sweet Home had to focus on our goal and maintain excellence. We had a very diverse and strong team, so I knew we

could achieve the record as long as we didn't become too mental! We had to play to win and avoid playing not to lose.

As the record grew closer, we started to realize the magnitude of the event. I normally play one match at a time, but I couldn't resist looking at our schedule to see who our opponent would be for the 218th win and 219th win. I am superstitious, so I felt like I was "putting the bats away before the ninth inning." But, in the end, I was glad I did check out the schedule. The 218th match was a home match, but the 219th match was an away match at West Seneca. Our athletic director called them, and they agreed to flip-flop our home and away schedule. I always felt very indebted to them for agreeing to that change. If and when we broke the record, it would be so much more memorable on our home court.

On the night that we tied the record at 218 wins, the Buffalo television stations covered the event. It was fun and exciting. We played in front of a crowd of a few hundred. I could just feel the intensity inspired by the record. The media started publishing information about our past accomplishments and set the stage for the possible record-breaking match versus West Seneca. When we were only two days away, the press was clamoring! We were getting calls from national media such as *Sports Illustrated* and the Associated Press.

On the morning of the fateful record-breaking match, our school phone was ringing off the hook. Our principal said, "We are calling in a substitute teacher for you today. We can't keep up with the phone calls." All I could do was giggle and shake my head. Many people told me that the city of Buffalo latched onto the record because of the urban ownership and pride. Many said it was because our area needed a winner. Both the Buffalo Bills and Buffalo Sabers had recently experienced tough seasons. A TV broadcaster was quoted, "It is taking a girls' team to draw national notoriety and bring a winning atmosphere back to Buffalo."

My athletic director called and asked me if I thought we needed to pull out all the bleachers. The gym was large and legally held 1800. Normally for a home match we pulled out the bleachers on only one side of the gym. I told him I thought it would be better to pull out both sides—better safe than sorry! By afternoon, my athletic director called back and said he had hired parking attendants and off-duty police. The athletic office had fielded a multitude of phone calls. The whoopla was inevitable!

All three local television stations had hauled in huge equipment to "go live" on the 6:00 news. The whole atmosphere was exhilarating. After the live interviews, we secluded ourselves in the locker room away from the junior varsity match. We changed into the new uniforms our athletic director had purchased for this event that we hoped would be historic. Our opponents were warming up in our auxiliary gym. Neither team had any idea of what we would soon be entering.

When we were given the signal, we ran out of the locker room and were met by over 2500 screaming fans who wanted to witness a national record. There were cheerleaders, the pep band, over 50 photographers from newspapers and magazines, and portable live-cams blinking shots of us warming up. All I could do was smile and drink in the scenery . . . 'til I felt drunk. My junior varsity coach, Ken Fournier, and I could barely see the court over the media members who were all crouched down around the court during the match.

In the end, we broke the record . . . on a controversial "touch" call. Maria "Looper" Guererri made the last kill to register the record in the books! She later went on to become an NCAA Division I All-American at the University of New Mexico.

The media surrounded us. Our superintendent and athletic director presented us with plaques. The players from both teams were interviewed. Our district threw a huge party for us, and we relished the record that was now at 219 consecutive wins.

USING SPORT PSYCHOLOGY

The next hurdle, aside from promoting our program and playing with a winning style, was to prepare for the big loss. It was inevitable that our team would lose and the win streak would be broken at some point. It was not a subject on which I wanted to dwell; however, I also felt that I had to properly prepare my players. So, I would tell each team that if the fateful day arrived, we would be stoic in defeat and laud our victors. We would go off privately and share our tearful emotions as a team. That seemed to satisfy the team each year.

One of our favorite teams to play was Horseheads. In the finals of our own Invitational, they had driven us to a three-game match. We had to play them again in the Eden tournament in two weeks. I could feel the fear mounting in our players. Instead of feeling excitement about challenging our skills again, our players were scared. All around school, people were asking them, "You almost lost for the first time?" "Are you nervous?" and "Do you think you'll lose?" I kept saying, "We beat them in a well-played three-game match," "We can't wait to play them again," and "If we play our best, we will win." I have always been a person who sees the glass half full . . . not half empty, but I could see that my players were drinking from a glass half empty. I felt powerless.

On that fateful day, we played well enough to reach the finals against Horseheads. We lost the first game. In the second game, Horseheads had a huge lead on us. Somehow we struggled back and stole that game. My hopes were lifted by the fortitude we had shown in the second game. The third game was close, but I could just feel it slip away in the end. Playing not to lose instead of playing to win is not a pretty picture.

As we had previously prepared, we were stoic in defeat. We were so stoic that two officials became emotional. A national win streak was halted at 292 wins. We congratulated our worthy opponents, thanked our officials, and went into the locker room. The seniors sobbed, the juniors cried, the sophomores shed a tear, and the freshmen hung their heads. I felt like someone had died. I promised the kids that the sun would rise the next day and told them I was proud of our record.

At our camp, we try to satisfy five goals:

1. We teach the basics 'til they're basic. This goal makes the players' high school coach happy.

2. We try to achieve each player's personal objectives. At the beginning of camp, we ask each player what her three immediate goals are. These goals usually include becoming better skilled at her primary position, such as setting or hitting.

3. We try to have fun and stay competitive.

4. We try to give them tough workouts. Players feel like they have accomplished more if they are pooped. This produces a sense of accomplishment!

5. Lastly, we teach them something over their heads. Then each player can go home and brag that she learned something incredible. We also challenge them to continue to work on this higher level of skill.

The following experiences can all help raise a player's skill level and knowledge of the game during the off-season: attending camps, playing club ball, playing in competitive off-season leagues, attending open gym, participating in player clinics, playing in state all-star games, playing in beach competitions, and playing in grass tournaments. A high school coach should recommend and then route his players into positive off-season experiences to enhance their development. A high school coach should also include himself in as many of these experiences as possible. These situations will help the coach network with other coaches and players, acquire new learning experiences, and show his players how much he is interested in them *and* in their improvement.

Providing special experiences for players also gives my athletes what some other programs don't offer. A special tournament out of town is always fun. Offering such an experience to any player enhances the player–coach rapport and encourages lifelong learning. Attending a camp with the entire team provides a key off-season experience and promotes a family type of bonding that demonstrates caring between a team and the coach.

ESTABLISHING A SUPPORT SYSTEM

Programs need support and leadership. The support system includes the administration, the faculty, the athletic department, the coach's relatives, and the players' families. Schoolwork and family are the top priority in a student's life. Fortunately, the families of our volleyball players schedule many functions around the volleyball season. This can be accomplished by meeting with parents before the season to invite their help, communicate, and make them feel like an integral part of the program. Many parents want to help, and a coach should use them to help with noncoaching tasks. A friend of mine, who coaches at a rival program, had a parent who was known for his antics and negative outbursts during matches. The coach invited this man to become his announcer. Now he had a job of prominence and responsibility; he also had a microphone in front of him. He became the perfect announcer and fan!

Along with support staff, a team always has the coach to support them on- and off-court. But the team also needs a peer leader to role model, encourage, and be a level-headed decision maker. A leader is expected to maintain an atmosphere of calmness on the court and to focus her teammates during long rallies and close scores. I have been blessed with my share of great leaders. I didn't know what it was like to have a team without a leader until I experienced one. It was the toughest year I have ever coached. After that season, I sought leadership in my middle school recruits and during my high school tryouts. I also tried to develop it in players. Some players are natural leaders, and most athletes have leadership abilities; however, not all athletes have the wisdom and confidence to use it. Having a leader on a team is like having a coach on the court.

SETTING RULES AND EXPECTATIONS

A team that establishes "family rules" becomes closer and learns to depend upon each other. These family expectations can include keeping and solving problems between team members, being supportive and confiding in each other during good and bad times, representing their school program with pride, developing lifelong character traits and proper behavior, tutoring each other, and doing off-court activities together. Members of a family are expected to take care of each other. Within such an atmosphere, cliques are much less likely to develop. Some members may have certain favorite members, but acknowledging, respecting, and accepting each other's differences are vital.

Overall, a program has to demonstrate class! It is always a fantastic feeling when I receive a report on how polite one of my players has been to an official, to a tournament director, or to a teacher, or when I receive positive feedback about any situation that represents our program. As a program becomes established, each player's behavior reflects that program all year long. Sometimes during softball season, for example, I will receive a call from the principal asking me for help in handling a situation involving a softball/volleyball player who has broken a school rule. The principal will typically say, "Well, she is a volleyball player, and we know you will support us in behavioral or attitude adjustment." Above all other successes are the compliments I receive when players represent themselves and our program in a positive manner outside of volleyball. These truly are acquired behaviors, which players develop through the help of positive sports experiences.

Attitude is everything. We can't always make up for a lack of natural talent, but most coaches would rather coach a player with great attitude and average ability than a player with a poor attitude and great ability. Attitude, positive or negative, will carry over from the volleyball court into everything else a player does throughout life.

In 1998, I had the opportunity to take a coaching position for a small NAIA team that had just organized in 1997. We were a young team with no tradition, few goals, and no off-season volleyball involvement. We were dysfunctional. It was my privilege to help create new traditions with these young women. It was also fun to be calculated in the development of this program, as I drew from the experiences I had brought with me from my scholastic years. I once again had the opportunity to help expand a team into a program and to be a long-term part of young women's lives.

CHAPTER 5
PLANNING FOR THE SEASON

Most people think of the volleyball in-season as the competitive stage. A volleyball program entails a preseason, competitive season, postseason, and off-season. Most colleges have a spring season during the off-season, too. A master plan has to be configured to include all segments of a program's year. Good planning will maximize players' potential during each phase.

OFF-SEASON

For most high school programs, the off-season is the time between the end of the competitive or play-off season and the start of the next preseason. For colleges, it is the time after the play-offs but before the spring season. For club players, it is usually the high school season.

The off-season between the competitive season and the start of spring season is usually sacred. Many college coaches allow this period to be downtime for their players. It is usually the time during semester break. Some college coaches encourage their players to maintain a certain fitness level. This makes it easier to retain muscular strength and endurance for the spring season. Unfortunately, there are other coaches who say, "Hey, just don't eat too many holiday cookies."

High school players, who usually play a fall season, either play another sport or play junior club ball after the volleyball season is finished. Most high school coaches do not have the luxury of working with their players during the off-season. In many states, it is illegal for high school coaches to conduct off-season practices. Some states allow open gyms or let coaches conduct all-state games, summer team camps, clinics, and other forms of legal play. Junior club ball is legal in all states; however, not all states allow high school coaches to coach their own athletes. Some states limit the number of players from the same high school on any club team.

If a high school coach does not coach his own athletes during the off-season, it is important for that coach to confer with his players after the school season is complete. The coach can make recommendations on how an athlete can increase her movement, skills, and conditioning. He can suggest options such as playing other sports, playing on a junior club team, attending summer camps, playing in recreational leagues, and following a fitness routine. Most serious high school volleyball players play on a junior club team during the off-season.

Conversely, a junior club's off-season is usually the high school season. Many times the club player returns to her high school team primed and ready for action. If the high school team does not have many skilled players, this can be a letdown for that returning club player. It is important for the club coach to talk with his players about attitude, effort, and expectations. The club player is often called upon to play a different position on her high school team. The club coach should encourage this because versatility is good for any player. A player's acceptance and willingness to play a new position enhance team continuity. Occasionally, some club players return to their high school team with more knowledge than the coach or, at least, more than is needed to compete in that high school league. Humility, leadership, helpfulness, and knowing when to keep your mouth shut are important qualities to instill in club players.

College coaches give their players extensive workout programs to follow during the off-season between May and mid-August. These include any combination of the following: weight training, aerobic or endurance activities, plyometric or jump training activities, swimming pool workouts, bounding, agility, and movement training. Some coaches require the players to mail or e-mail weekly, bimonthly, or monthly results, and many coaches test the players the first day of preseason.

Strength and fitness trainers within a college's athletic program develop workouts that focus on the objectives of coaches. These workouts should be well rounded to include all phases of fitness and should have particular emphasis on an athlete's specific sport. Such a workout is usually scheduled for an every-other-day rotation, which allows for recuperation. Some workouts vary the activities or give the athletes choices to help maintain their interest. Any workout has to become part of a player's daily routine, so if an athlete is from out of town, she may have to join a local fitness center to execute the workouts. Also, it is beneficial for each player to have a workout partner. Motivation and pride are the keys to following a workout regimen. Coaches should send feedback and inspirational quotes to their players after receiving workout results.

Coaches differ in their philosophies on cross-training during the off-season. Some coaches think that playing other sports is good because it keeps an athlete from burning out in one sport and helps an athlete remain active and happy. Some coaches feel that it is too risky to allow their athletes to play other sports. Their feeling is *Why take the chance?* Each coach has to weigh the consequences. Nonetheless, most coaches do limit other activities for their players during their own competitive season.

High school coaches often have to rely on players to come into preseason in good physical condition. Some high school coaches give players summer workout schedules, rely on captain practices, or encourage their players to cross-train or play in summer leagues. Summer camps are a great way to get ready for the season. Many high school players are able to attend a camp on a particular college campus where they are interested in attending as a student-athlete. This gives the athlete the opportunity to live on campus and be instructed by that college's coach. Many high school community education programs conduct summer day camps that are more affordable. Some town recreation programs and YMCAs have summer programs that help promote fitness or provide wholesome activities for teenagers. Team camps, where an entire team trains together before preseason, are very popular. Some team camps are instructional, but most involve team play in a tournament format.

PRESEASON

Preseason is the time designated to ready a team for competition. It is the time allotted before the first competition. Some coaches include preseason scrimmages and non-league matches in this definition, but other coaches consider nonleague matches part of the season because the wins and losses are reflected in a team's overall record.

The major goals of preseason are player assessment, physical conditioning, skill development, and team development.

Player Assessment

Player assessment in the preseason includes the "dreaded" tryouts. In chapter 15, actual assessment methods and considerations will be discussed. Coaches must develop a meaningful yet efficient evaluation procedure. A coach can usually watch a group scrimmage on the first day of preseason and subjectively identify the best players based on performance, attitude, and hustle. Ideally, a coach needs to develop an objective method to choose a team, based on skills, performance, and athletic ability. The activities the coach uses to test these traits need to be measurable and meaningful. If called upon, the coach must be able to explain and verify the results. Even the intangibles—such as effort, attitude, aggressiveness, and potential—need to be evaluated in a somewhat objective format. The coach needs objective methods to prove his subjective feelings!

Physical Conditioning

In many instances, high school coaches have to initiate their players' conditioning on day one of the preseason. High school preseasons usually begin two to three weeks before the first match. Therefore, many coaches find it beneficial to conduct double sessions during the first week or two.

Some coaches conduct one long practice each day during preseason. However, when coaches add clock time to each practice session, their goal should be to teach and drill volleyball techniques, not to wear down the players with exercise workouts. Conditioning is important, but an exercise crash course will be counterproductive to the skill-learning process. Physical conditioning has to be a continual process throughout the season but it should be encouraged especially during the off-season.

The learning and conditioning processes are greatly enhanced if players start the preseason already in good condition. Most players dread preseason because of the conditioning. It is not fun, and their muscles become sore. Sometimes it is not easy to differentiate between an injury and sore muscles. When players are sore, it is difficult for them to move; therefore, it is difficult to teach them movement and skills. So, as much as the average coach would like to come in the first week and crack the whip, he must also remember that crippling his players will be counterproductive. Coaches usually include some conditioning in agility station work, during drills, as a consequence activity, or at the end of practice. Endurance conditioning should be done at the end of practice or at a separate session so that it doesn't reduce players' stamina during practice. If a player has no vitality in practice, her movement, learning, and performance will diminish.

The players should come into practice hydrated and ready to warm up (see chapter 6 for more on warming up). Coaches should provide drink breaks regularly in practice. Punishing players by refusing drink breaks is a deadly tactic. Most players do not realize how important it is to hydrate before, during, and after practice. Once a player is thirsty, it is actually too late.

As previously mentioned, endurance training is best performed after the practice is finished. The players should hydrate before and after the endurance exercise. After the endurance training is complete, the players must cool down and stretch. This is a good time for coaches, captains, and players to reflect on that practice, give motivating comments, and make announcements.

Basic Skills

Development of basic skills is the main objective in preseason. Varsity, junior varsity, and grassroots programs usually start at the beginning teaching levels. There are usually new team members each year, and the coach needs to make sure each player understands the footwork, technical jargon, and progression for each skill. This is also true of junior club programs. Each coach has her own teaching style, emphasis, and expectations. Many veteran players find this review silly and tedious, but without it, players do not have the basic knowledge to proceed to tactical application.

It is wise to throw in some work on aggressive skills with the "ho-hum" skills. It is also smart to instill pride in basics. This can be done by varying the scoring in drills and making them competitive. Movement needs to be incorporated into the basics as soon as possible. This will help with anticipation skill work and a smooth progression into tactical application.

Team Development

Preseason is also the time for coaches to set standards, verbalize their expectations, and engage in team-building activities. It is important for a coach to present a consistent outline of standards and expectations. As the season progresses, these standards must be maintained in order to achieve the team's goals. Team building is an ongoing process. Teammates don't have to be best friends; however, team members who enjoy each other's company but respect each other's differences usually bond successfully and consequently play harder for each other. Teams need to develop chemistry and camaraderie through different team-building experiences . . . planned or unplanned.

Different methods of team building include cooperative games, group initiatives, outdoor education courses (e.g., ropes course activities), camping excursions, captain's practices, and any other positive team-bonding activities. I have taken my team to our summer cottage on Cuba Lake. It sleeps 15 people "if no one breathes." There is one bathroom and a small kitchen. We practice in the morning and evening at Cuba Rushford High School. During the afternoon, we ski and tube on the lake. The players are responsible for planning and preparing the meals. Each grade is responsible for an evening activity. These trips to the lake always bring us closer together because they provide the opportunity to share experiences.

IN-SEASON

The early season is a time to reinforce basics, develop team play, and stress serving and serve receive. Teams who can serve and side out will win the early season games. Players love to work on attacking. Spiking takes time to develop and must be worked on every day to achieve timing and consistency. Coaches work on defining players' roles and establishing lineups early in the season. Conditioning is an ongoing process.

During the early season, players need repetitious drills to become consistent in a skill. The player should repeat the skill until she can do it on "automatic pilot." Opposing team members used to say, "Your team passes like machines . . . it can't be fun." Little did they know that was a compliment. When a team can pass like a machine, they can play at the next level. My teams always felt pride in their basics; it was part of their work ethic. Repetition drills can be fun if designed properly. The goals and scoring in a repetition drill are centered on one skill, but these drills can also include other skills. When the drill includes two or three skills, it is more gamelike and leads teams into tactical application more effectively.

Once each movement and skill has been instructed and drilled, it is time to scrimmage and prepare for nonleague matches. Combination drills that incorporate basics into game play, or *tactical application*, are worked on at this time of the season. Many players are great at passing, setting, or spiking in repetition during a controlled drill. But to be successful, players must be able to read and anticipate the opponent's play so they can move into the correct position and posture. This will allow players a quality first contact to initiate offensive play. Coaches must also drill players on how and where to move after completing the offensive play so they are ready before the opponent's next play. A player who thinks "the next ball is coming to me" is always focused and ready. These drills are easy to design because they are like a segment of the game. The players enjoy combination drills because they are gamelike and can be scored competitively. A coach can also let a combination drill continue until its gamelike conclusion. The action after the combination portion may not be included in the score, but the anticipation skills that are derived from allowing a drill to finish normally are beneficial to learning. A coach can always wait to make his comments until the ball hits the floor. Another option is making the score for the combination portion of the drill a higher amount but still awarding a point for winning the rally. This will give the teams a competitive surge to win a rally and be awarded for it. It teaches and drills perseverance. Winning rallies also gives an emotional edge over opponents in match play.

Once the conference season begins, most practice time is spent reviewing the basics, running combination plays, fixing mistakes made in past match play, getting ready for the next opponent, and working on new ideas. Team play supersedes basic skill work. Basics are usually covered in warm-ups. Work on serve receive and conditioning is always an ongoing process. Tactics become more important as the players understand team play better throughout the conference experience. By midseason, players' roles are understood. A coach has solidified lineups and now works on improving defensive and offensive schemes. Coaches develop practice plans from errors in match play. Drills are developed to improve consistency and to work on weak areas.

Coaches can also experiment with different lineups during practice at this time of the season. Is it better to have the setter follow the middle hitter or for the middle hitter to follow the setter? Should the outside hitters switch positions? There are so many questions and possibilities concerning playing personnel to work on at this time. It is important to plan it on paper and try it on the court. Perception on paper is very different from performance during play. Coaches must also explore all their creative avenues of play so that they will have no regrets.

Volleyball *programs* normally develop teams that are ready at the start of the season. This is due to off-season development and the serious commitment by its players and coaches. These are the programs that are known for their volleyball. Other teams develop throughout the season. Volleyball is important during their season, but program development is not a priority during the off-season.

Programs often start off the season well and then struggle to maintain excellence. This usually occurs in the second half of the competitive season. Here are some reasons why:

• The team might get bored playing the same way. They do not see improvement when their only improvement is playing more consistently. I had a player who went on to play for an excellent Division I team. During her junior year of college, I asked her how things were going. She said, "Oh, it's okay. We don't learn anything new." This same girl went from hitting .202 her freshman year to hitting .387 her junior year. Improvement and consistency are learning. It's all in the presentation and delivery!

The program team is skilled enough to have different lineups, offenses, and defenses. This helps keep the season exciting. Working on new plays is important for program teams. They will eventually need them during play-offs. These new lineups and plays can be used in scrimmages, nonleague action, and tournament play. Teams need playing experience and confidence with new lineups and plays, but they usually save them until they're needed in play-off time against unwary opponents.

Some coaches would rather say, "Here we are, just try to stop us." This is great in theory. A coach still needs to be able to change a lineup that doesn't work. A team has to be comfortable with the change from past experience with the lineup.

• Some opponents can't play at a high enough level to create a challenge for the program team. The program coach should seek tough competition. It is great to notch wins, but meaningful wins are the memories. An early season loss can refocus a team to work harder in practice. An early loss can also keep the stigma of losing off their backs during play-off time. Sometimes the pressure of being undefeated can play havoc in the minds of a team during play-offs. During play-off time, fortitude and confidence in play are most important.

• A team might need some time off or some cross-training. It might also be a time to do some team bonding. A team that is playing well can be rewarded with a surprise day off from practice, a team outing, or a special practice filled with "carnival" drills or spent doing a unity activity. A coach may see this as a wasted day, but it usually turns out to be an emotionally rejuvenating experience!

Peakers

After a team has played a program team twice, they will usually approach a third meeting with one of two mind-sets. The team will either roll over and say, "Don't hurt me too much" or they'll say, "We have nothing to lose . . . let's play hard." The program team will inevitably come in saying, "We've played them twice and they were nothin'." The coach will properly say, "Don't come in cocky," and "It's hard to beat a team three times in a season."

These are the teams the program team has to watch out for. They're the *peakers*. The peakers are the teams who start poorly and progress throughout the season. Peakers are usually multisport athletes who play insatiable defense and always come out shining! Peakers are teams that peak at the right time—play-off time. Beware! These are the teams you have to be emotionally prepared for and ready to play with tenacity. Peakers play with wild abandon. The program team needs to be aggressive, consistent, and unriled. They have to be playmakers and win the rallies.

Peakers always have the most unruly fans. Their fans are obnoxious and full of tricks. The match can even be played on your home court, and it seems like you are playing away! Peaker fans will outnumber home fans and work on weakening confidence. They find pride in cheering harder for their opponent's mistakes than their own team's accomplishments. Peaker fans wear you down. There is only one way to silence peaker fans: play out of your mind! Peaker fans do not know how to react when their opponents play great. They have to sit in the bleachers and grumble. So, that has to be the plan . . . silence the peaker fans!

POSTSEASON PLAY

The overall program does not change in the postseason. The changes needed are subtle. For example, a younger player may be brought up to the active squad as a reward or incentive, or to enhance practices. An assistant coach from a lower-level team may become available because his season has ended. Scheduling court time may become a problem because the season is extended.

Postseason practice includes team play and tactics. Review of basics is routine. Coaches are developing strategies to defeat opponents that they have played several times. They are also preparing for new opponents from other conferences. Teams now practice the new plays they've been working on for the play-offs. Review of film, networking, and scouting are critical tools for identifying an opponent's strengths and weaknesses. This is a time when most teams are highly focused. Coaches need to blend motivational activities with meaningful practice that prepares the team for the play-offs. It is a time to maintain excellence and make sure the team is emotionally ready to play their next opponent. An undaunted attitude toward the opponent and confidence in play are the feelings the coach should establish in practice. Essentially, the season continues as is. The overall program and preparations should remain the same because that's what got the team to the play-offs.

PLANNING THE DETAILS

Planning for a season includes gobs of paperwork. Most of the paperwork is related to the organization of a season, the safety of the players, and the liability issues that are inherent in working with children. It includes athletic rules, physical examination forms, first aid procedures, travel arrangements, permission slips, match management, and various organizational charts. Budgeting is usually planned with the athletic director during the postseason.

Athletic Rules

Athletic rules will define and establish a program's parameters. They help develop the lifelong character traits that make a player a better person. The regulations are intended to instill self-restraint, moral values, and the ability to weigh the consequences, make good choices, and set priorities.

Along with rules comes communication. A preseason meeting must be held to explain the regulations and consequences. This meeting should be mandatory for the athlete and parent. Most schools and organizations insist that players sign a pledge to abide by the athletic rules before the player is allowed to try out for the sport.

Rules must also include the consequences for negative action. A coach has to be able to work within the rules and deal with any infringements, or else lose credibility. It is best if the regulations identify the consequences for violating a rule. This takes the burden off the coach and gives consistency to an athletic program.

Some rules include progressive consequences for multiple offenses. An example is being late for practice. The first offense may be a warning, and the second offense may have a physical consequence. Our basketball coach has the team run one lap for every minute the late player has missed. The late player must stand in the middle of the court and watch the team run the laps. Peer pressure has been highly effective, and tardiness usually occurs once a season!

Other rules need stricter consequences. An example is skipping a practice. Sweet Home High School allows one illegal skip. After the second skip, the player is off the team. Along with this rule, a concise list of "legal" excuses must be written. A legal excuse could be illness, field trip, college visit, death in the family, family emergency, family vacation, religious obligation, special examination, overlapping seasons, or after school academic help. It is smart for a coach to insist on prior notification of the absence. A player should be held responsible for informing the coach of the reason for the absence *before* the missed practice. This teaches responsibility, respect for the rules, and commitment to the team. Also, it is helpful for a coach to know how many players will be in attendance when planning a practice. Coaches must keep good attendance records.

Other rules involve breaking laws and school regulations. These include skipping class or school, stealing, and illegal use of drugs or alcohol. Sometimes the school administration will decide the consequences. Some schools have nonnegotiable rules or no-tolerance punishments. Some athletic rules include dismissal from the team and suspension from the next sport season, too. Some schools include an alternative to expelling a player from a team. This might include attendance in a rehabilitation program and a suspension period. After the suspension, the player is allowed back on the team and allowed to play. Some rules may allow the player to practice but not dress for the match or not play. Many schools believe children need education in drug abuse to solve the problem instead of throwing them off a team. The philosophy is that a player who is ejected from a team will act out and repeat the rule infraction if she isn't counseled. A school has to define its role and philosophy regarding serious rule infringements.

Other rules that most schools and organizations include are sporting behavior, vandalism, fighting, and academic eligibility. Rules on sporting behavior include conduct in regard to taunting, vulgar language, disrespectful attitude, fighting, and being ejected from a contest. Most of the consequences for violating a regulation on sporting behavior include suspension from the event and possibly from future contests.

Academic eligibility is another athletic rule that takes the support of the school administration to enforce. The devil's advocate would argue for punishing the athlete tougher than the student who is not an athlete. Educators agree that students are in school for the education. Sports are an important part of a student-athlete's education. Many agree that sports keep some kids in school who would normally quit. So if you put a tough eligibility standard on the student-athlete, it will exclude her from the reason she stays in school. Perhaps the player is more of an athlete than a student, but she will gain a diploma by staying in school.

Many organizations find it helpful to use laws as a guideline. The first year I coached at the college level, no one on the team was 21 years old, so it was illegal for any of them to consume alcohol. I would be a fool to believe college students don't drink because it is against the law. But it did give me a legal guideline to use. College programs have to decide on and hold strongly to their rules, too. Most colleges have a no-tolerance rule during the season. It is important for colleges to spell out the rules and consequences because most of the players are of legal smoking age and some of the players are legally able to buy and consume alcohol. Scholarship programs have more to barter with when applying consequences. The bottom line for any level of player is that she should follow the rules because of understanding and appreciation of the rules and pride in the program.

Some coaches use the athletic rules as a basis and develop stricter policies for their own sport. An example is a coach adopting a no-cut policy for practices and matches, meaning a player is not allowed any unexcused absences, even though the athletic rules may allow one absence. The coach might feel that the list of legal excuses is sufficient to give players any needed time off. If the athlete is committed, practices and matches are a priority. This coach may also believe that having a one-cut system is telling the student-athlete it is okay to miss one practice. The devil's advocate would say that everyone is entitled to a mistake. Regardless, if a coach strengthens a rule, communication is important. Players and parents need to read, understand, and sign the rules of the sport.

Junior club teams need to have similar rules. They are not governed under the auspices of a school but generally respect many of the same philosophies. A club's board of directors, or a committee comprised of the club director and the coaches, must develop rules that reflect the philosophy of the club. Junior clubs usually do not punish players for school incidents.

Forms

Other athletic participation forms include parental consent, permission for emergency medical treatment, and transportation approval. Most of these forms are for liability and safety issues to protect the player, coach, and organization.

Emergency Medical Treatment Form

A statement that there is an element of risk that cannot be eliminated even when all precautions are taken is an important legal issue to include on an emergency medical treatment form. Parents must be informed of the element of risk inherent in the sport of volleyball. Common injuries are floor burns, hip pointers, and ankle, shoulder, and finger injuries.

Most schools do not carry medical insurance because of the cost of the policies. When this applies, parents must sign a statement agreeing to be responsible for all medical and hospital expenses that are not covered by their own insurance. Permission for emergency medical treatment, in case the parent cannot be contacted, is important for the safety of the player and liability of the designated personnel. Along with this information, coaches or trainers should carry each player's emergency treatment card with them to all practices and contests. Included on this card are parent home and work phone numbers, emergency contact in case a parent cannot be reached, medical insurance carrier and policy numbers, and important emergency care information (including any allergies to medicine or treatment). A coach or trainer can carry these cards inside the first aid bag.

Travel Consent Form

A form frequently used by a coach to organize trips more efficiently and protect the program legally is a travel consent form. This must be in accordance with school rules. Some schools make it mandatory for the team to travel to and from a contest on the team bus. Many schools allow a player to go home with her parents or a teammate's parents if she has a written note. Very few schools allow a player to drive to and from a contest or ride with another student or non-family-member. Whatever the rules are, a coach can develop a travel form to conform to the school rules.

This kind of form, if legal for your school, will save time and aggravation after a match. Many coaches feel that bus trips to and from matches are part of the bonding experience. Some coaches feel it is more important for a team to get home quickly so the student-athlete can finish her homework and get adequate rest on a school night.

In junior clubs, either the coach or travel coordinator coordinates the travel. All travel arrangements should be made before the season starts. Liability issues are always a stickler and must be handled according to the policy of the governing agent.

Sometimes players need to be housed overnight. Some teams do a team exchange and stay in the homes of opponents who are hosting the tournament. This is a great way for the kids to meet new people. Coaches may have to instruct proper behavior and courtesy! If a team is going to stay overnight in a motel, proper supervision must be planned. Of course, permission slips are a must and sometimes have to be notarized.

Physical Form

Most schools have regulated that the only professional approval that is acceptable for participation in athletics is that of the school physician. This keeps the examinations consistent and protects the school legally. All athletes must have the physical prior to the first day of practice. If a problem, such as a heart murmur, is found in the physical examination, the school doctor may insist that the athlete get further permission from her own family physician.

Health History Form

Most school officials allow parents to fill out the player's health history form. Some districts insist that personnel at the family doctor's office fill out the form and sign it to ensure correct information.

This information is vital knowledge for the coach, trainer, school nurse, and school doctor. It is also important for hospital staff if emergency treatment is necessary.

Safety

Safety is the prime concern for every athletic administrator and coach. No one wants athletes to get hurt, and no one wants a liability lawsuit.

Before and throughout the season, a coach should check all the equipment and facilities he will be using. This includes standards, safety padding, net cable, lighting, and the gym floor. Coaches must also make sure they have strict rules governing the use of water near the play area and the wipe up of spills. The area around the court should be clear of obstructions or paraphernalia that could be considered a safety issue if an athlete pursued a ball off the court.

An administrator needs to keep records on equipment and the environment that athletes play in. Administrators also need to supply first aid equipment and medical personnel in case of injury.

The administrator must make sure every coach knows the emergency action plan and make sure it is posted by each phone in a gymnasium. Coaches must go over the action plan with their players in case a coach needs assistance during an emergency. For outdoor sports, most first aid kits include a cell phone or walkie-talkie for communication during an emergency. Many schools provide cell phones for teams when they are competing away at an opponent's facility.

Many schools are hiring part- or full-time athletic trainers. Some school districts are providing a training room for evaluation and rehabilitation of injured athletes. This helps prevent coaches from guessing about the seriousness of an injury. It also increases the chances of getting the athlete safely back to the court as soon as possible. Athletic trainers can assess an injury and recommend a course of action. Medical doctors still have to handle the diagnosis, X ray, and rehabilitation of serious injury.

Since volleyball is not a contact sport (except with the floor and sometimes under the net), trainers usually spend most of their practice time with teams in higher risk sports. Most colleges have a staff of trainers. Some universities have their own trainer travel with each team and attend every practice. Smaller colleges usually have a trainer on staff to cover practices and all home events. Tournaments always have home trainers on duty. Visiting teams are welcome to use the services of the training staff but should provide their own medical kit, including athletic wrap and tape.

Budgeting

Every year athletic directors have many decisions to make when distributing money into sport budgets. Safety is the main concern. Sports that generate revenue are a second priority, and sports that attract publicity are third. Successful sport programs are sometimes given preference. Spreading the budget across the rest of the sports is done according to need.

In interscholastic sports, the main budget items include equipment, uniforms, officials, and travel. Coaches should prioritize their equipment and uniform needs through accurate inventory. Official costs are governed by contract. Support staff costs might be included in this budget for paid scorers, announcers, and linespeople. Travel costs within a conference are easy to estimate from past seasons. Tournament entry fees, transportation, lodging, and meals are either included in the budget or paid for through fund-raising efforts by the team or booster club. Most postseason play is supported within the school's or conference's athletic budget. Other considerations in budgeting could include scouting mileage, clinic costs, coaching apparel, and costs for hosting tournaments.

In junior club sports, budgeting includes coaches' expenses, tournament fees, equipment, facility rental, membership costs, added insurance or liability costs, administrative costs, and uniforms. Some clubs include the cost of travel, and some rely on individuals to "pay as they play and go." Most established clubs include salaries for coaches, directors, treasurers, tournament directors and planners, and secretaries. Certification conferences and clinic attendance also are usually included in the budget.

No matter what level a person coaches, he has to prioritize items and sell his needs and wants to the athletic director or board of directors. Many tournaments are located on or near college campuses, historic sites, and fun sites. Volleyball is about more than just the game on the court. When I took my club team to the California Festival, we toured San Francisco for two days. These players are all adults now. When they reminisce, they talk about Alcatraz, cable cars, Fisherman's Wharf, the Golden Gate, and the Pacific Ocean. It doesn't mean they didn't enjoy the tournament . . . we came in fourth; it was a great showing for us. But the experiences we shared will never be forgotten.

Scheduling

Many schools' schedules are set by conference play. Junior clubs can make their own schedule according to their budget, their level of play, and their goals. If a junior club team has aspirations of qualifying for nationals, then they must follow the correct tournament schedule to qualify.

The head coach usually chooses nonconference opponents and tournaments. The coach must schedule a good mix of play for her team. Early in my season, I like to schedule a beatable team so we can work on our offense and gain some confidence. Then I like to schedule a team who plays insatiable defense and shows us that offense doesn't win games. It also shows us our team's weaknesses, and we know it's time to buckle down and work harder in practice.

During the season, I like to schedule some matches where I know I can play my substitutes or work on different lineups and systems. Tournament play should be against equal or better teams. Rolling over teams leaves players lackadaisical and flat. Winning a tournament is always nice as long as it is a reputable tournament with competition of your caliber.

Equipment and Uniforms

An inventory should be recorded at the end of every season. This will give the coach an accounting of what needs to be ordered in the next budget. The inventory should include all team levels of the program. Some athletic programs incorporate the "hand-me-down" system—for example, the varsity passing down uniforms to the junior varsity. Other programs are more fortunate and receive new uniforms at every level. Sometimes fund-raising is necessary to obtain new uniforms. In any case, several factors need to be considered before ordering uniforms, including safety, freedom of movement, style, and durability of material.

Safety is the most important consideration when ordering equipment. Proper padding, ease in setup and takedown of net systems, and how the equipment will enhance practice should be considered. Constructing or ordering hitting platforms that are safe to use in practice (instead of hitting off chairs) is a must for every program. Most schools provide first aid equipment to every team. Chapter 6 contains more information on equipment—that which is necessary and other "fluffy" equipment that is helpful but not essential.

Facilities

The use of practice and game facilities needs to be scheduled before the season. Usually, an athletic director or club coordinator is responsible. Facilities need to be safe and clean. The room should be cool and arid. An emergency action plan should be in place with a working telephone nearby. First aid equipment has to be at every practice and event. Overhead projections, such as basketball baskets, need to be raised. Any equipment along the perimeter of the courts needs to be moved or padded.

The floor should be clean and dry. Court towels should be handy to wipe up spills or sweat marks. It is always better if a team can practice on two courts instead of one. This is usually difficult unless teams are willing to alternate evening and morning practices, but the benefits outweigh the inconvenience!

DESIGNATING STAFF RESPONSIBILITIES

A great support staff is essential to helping the coaching staff with the organization, communication, procedures, and responsibilities of a sport program. A support staff includes many different personnel.

Most high school volleyball programs do not have the luxury of an assistant varsity coach. Junior varsity, modified, and middle school coaches are all considered assistant coaches to the varsity coach. College programs have a variety of staff depending on conference rules and the program's budget. A college bench can include an assistant coach, a graduate assistant coach, stats keepers, and a trainer. Many junior clubs provide a head coach and an assistant coach for each team. Teams usually function more effectively with at least two coaches. The only potential glitch in this theory is that the coaches must be able to work together collaboratively for the benefit of the program.

An outlined job description is important for each coach. This will define responsibilities for each staff member and define his role on the team. Communication with the staff is important to reduce overlap of responsibility. Players need to know each coach's role so there is less confusion and the chain of command is clear.

The head coach is usually responsible for the following:

- Hiring the immediate coaching staff. Some coaches inherit assistant coaches, and some schools rely on the athletic director for hiring. It is important that the head coach has a say in choosing his assistant coach.

- Meeting with the administration.
- Meeting with parents—preseason meetings and perhaps any social opportunities.
- Meeting with players.
- Organizing preseason, in-season, and off-season, including any team-bonding or other types of team experiences.
- Scheduling. Many league and conference schedules are predetermined. Nonleague or nonconference and tournament play is usually a choice of the head coach.
- Securing contract agreements.
- Arranging transportation to all events, meals on the road, and lodging if needed.
- Obtaining tax-exempt forms.
- Faxing rosters to tournament directors and arranging overnight accommodations during tournaments.
- Arranging any "bonus" side trips while traveling.
- Defining, communicating, and enforcing team rules.
- Distributing and collecting all pertinent paperwork: health forms, emergency forms, team rule forms, class schedules, travel forms, and roster information.
- Developing guidelines for players to follow when missing a class for a volleyball match or tournament.
- Developing and distributing information for the faculty, including the roster, schedule, and policy on missed classes.
- Facilitating media guide publication and team pictures.
- Defining the practice schedule and securing the practice facility.
- Reviewing film and scouting.
- Arranging for statistics to be kept.
- Ensuring safety during practices and matches. The coach must make sure the first aid kit is brought to each practice and match.
- Working closely with training staff or parents concerning injured athletes.
- Budgeting.
- Securing money or a school credit card for travel, and reporting expense account and reimbursement information.
- Ordering equipment and uniforms.
- Organizing tryouts and determining final team selection.
- Recruiting.
- Establishing practice procedures.
- Establishing bench procedures.
- Establishing time-out procedures.
- Making decisions on the offense and defense.
- Making decisions on substituting during a match.
- Completing public relations duties.
- Facilitating pep rally participation by the team.
- Planning off-season physical conditioning programs with the training staff.
- Providing nutritional education.
- Helping players get academic tutoring.
- Using sport psychology.
- Deciding how awards will be earned.
- Planning the awards banquet, party, or assembly. Ordering awards and thanking all people who have made the program a reality.
- Maintaining community involvement.
- Recommending camps and clubs for the off-season.
- Helping recruitable players with college choices.
- Assisting the farm system.
- Providing opportunities for staff education and clinics.
- Helping with fund-raisers.
- Ensuring the chain of command by staff members.
- Arranging special events to promote the program.
- Sending thank-yous to tournament directors.

These all fall under the auspices of the head coach. Great head coaches delegate responsibilities to staff members. Smart head coaches think before they delegate. It would not be a good idea to delegate recruiting to a coach who is shy. It would be good to delegate stats to someone good in math.

When a head coach delegates a responsibility, it is important to communicate to the staff member what is expected. But the head coach must also allow input and development from the staff member to whom the job is being delegated.

Some high schools and many colleges have staff already hired to accept many of these responsibilities. A sports information director fields questions and sends information to opponents, the media, the public, and conference stat reporters. This includes faxing rosters, sending and receiving scouting tapes, sending conference paperwork, collecting and formulating information for media guides and home programs, arranging team photos, providing directions to events, and so on. Athletic trainers normally handle injury care, practice and match safety, emergency action plans, emergency care information, and nutrition guidance. They also help in developing off-season conditioning programs. Athletic secretaries may make travel arrangements, organize rosters, keep forms on hand, help with budget and uniform/equipment forms, arrange for copy work and mailings, type recruiting letters and organize information from recruits, handle home and away contracts, type schedules, and so on. Many colleges have sport psychologists, publications directors, and assistant athletic directors.

The head coach needs to be the person in charge but also needs to create an atmosphere of give-and-take with his staff. A head coach who makes his staff feel subservient will not benefit from the talent of his assistants. Head coaches should ask for and use suggestions offered by the staff. If a coach is democratic, his staff will feel it is safe to let their creativity loose. Even though a head coach is responsible for all the important decisions, he should include his staff in the decision making. Each has been hired for a particular strength. The head coach should use that strength and share any success with the assistants. Effective communication and strong organizational skills are key when working with assistants. Role modeling these character traits will promote dialogue in meetings.

Provide cool coaching apparel for the entire staff to wear during practices, matches, camps, clinics, and public appearances. Other small tokens of appreciation mean a lot to the people who do the behind-the-scenes work for your program. These can be given on special occasions or on any day throughout the year to show special appreciation. Staff members also appreciate understanding when personal emergencies arise. One of our secretary's daughters was cut from an athletic team. Listening to her problem, helping her with the reasoning, and leaving her a chocolate bar went a long way!

One of the most important traits to be leery of when choosing an assistant coach is disloyalty. Many head coaches have found out too late that some assistants have trouble accepting the role. A few tend to be power hungry. Some of these coaches work their way through the players planting seeds of discontent.

Assistant Loyalty

One of my good friends, who coached at a Division I university, found out that while she was driving one of the team vans, her assistant was causing dissension in the other van. Through investigation, she found out that the assistant coach had been back stabbing her for most of the season. The assistant had been setting the head coach up for failure by blaming her falsely for many things. My friend felt that part of it had been her own fault for not giving the assistant enough responsibility and credit for successes in the program. After dismissing the assistant coach, my friend reorganized her staffing philosophy. Not only did she delegate more responsibility and offer more praise to her new staff member, but she also found that this made her own job more enjoyable, too.

There are so many separate facets to a volleyball program within a calendar year. Each one must be handled as its own entity, in spite of the fact that each one contributes to the total volleyball program. So, because each facet is so distinct, the planning has to be unique for each as well. In essence, planning for the season really means planning for the whole year.

6 PLANNING FOR PRACTICES

Planning a practice involves many essential considerations. The coach's philosophy is always the basis for all of his plans. Secondary to the coaching philosophy are several logistical concerns: the time allotted for each practice, the amount of gym space, the number of participants, the available support personnel, and the equipment on hand. Various points during the course of the season dictate the contents of each practice according to the coach's master plan. The basic outline of each practice includes announcements, warm-up, review, focus on current objectives, conditioning, cool-down, and closure. In addition, a coach has to repeatedly set the stage for success by continuing to teach and redefine his expectations of each player.

PRACTICE LOGISTICS

Nailing down the logistics of practices is something that's best done early. Logistics such as length of practice, number of courts, and the maximum number of players to plan for at any practice are important to get settled. These things can be influenced by the age of your players, the facility's time restraints, the equipment available, and the number of coaches. Identifying these factors before your season helps you to plan accordingly.

Length of Practice

The factors that dictate the length of a practice are the age level of the team, the physical condition of the players, the time of the season, and the availability of the gymnasium.

The younger age groups (10 to 13) need shorter practices because they have shorter attention spans. Modified, middle school, and grassroots programs normally practice between one and two hours. Teaching segments and practice drills are changed frequently. Related games can be interspersed to add variety. It takes a coach who is both creative and technical to plan and implement an effective practice for younger players. These coaches must be positive and need to be able to change activities when the players get restless. They almost need to possess a magic wand!

Older age teams (14 to 18) can practice longer, but this doesn't mean that long practices are the key to success. The quality of each practice and the objectives achieved are the most important aspects. Most varsity, junior varsity, and club teams practice between two and two and a half hours. College teams usually practice two to three hours. The added time allotted for older teams is used for multiple skill drills and tactical instruction.

Number of Courts Available

Two courts is the ideal number for a team of 12 to 16 players to practice adequately. Some college teams have the luxury of three or four courts because they usually have adequate space and support personnel to implement individualized position training and game situations. Most high schools have one court per team, and some varsity and junior varsity teams have to share courts. This is where creativity is a necessity, for example using off-court space for announcements, warm-up, stretching, conditioning, and cool-down. It may become necessary to use off-court space to teach certain aspects of the game, such as conducting a chalk talk. It is essential to use the actual on-court time for technical development, skill instruction, situation training, and gamelike drills.

Some coaches use flexible scheduling and multiteam teaching to make practices more effective. If the junior varsity and varsity teams each usually have a court, a combination practice session can gain court time. For example, one court could be used for setter training, and another court could be used for serve receive or defensive drills. Another option is to conduct a junior varsity team practice for the first time segment, then have a combination varsity and junior varsity setter training session, and finish with a varsity practice. Another option is to practice before classes or in the evening when more court space is available. Of course, a coach can beg the school administration for more court time, but usually a coach has to work wonders with what she has been given.

Additionally, a coach must be ready for the surprises that may greet her as she walks into the gym—the gym is being decorated early for the homecoming dance, the gym is filled with confetti from an earlier pep assembly, or the gym is filled with desks to prepare for standardized testing the next day . . . "Sorry, we forgot to tell you!"

Number of Participants

When planning any practice, the coach must know the number of players expected to attend. Most teams have 9 to 18 players. Some modified and grassroots teams have huge numbers because of policies against cutting players. Flexible scheduling and creativity in drills are essential when planning a large group practice.

A coach must have a policy governing absences from practice. It is smart to put the responsibility on the player. If a player is going to be absent for any reason, that player must notify the coach before the absence. Consequently, the coach must supply the players with his phone number and e-mail address at the beginning of the season. The coach should also put the burden on the player to find out what happened at the missed practice and to be informed of any announcements that were made to the team. If the coach mistakenly assumes this responsibility, he will be on the phone more than he'll be at practice! A team Web site is a great communication tool, if you have the option available, to use for additional updates and schedules.

When formulating drills, a coach needs to know how many athletes will be attending practice; however, a coach has to be ready for the unexpected. It is not uncommon for a coach to walk into practice and find out that Suzy went home ill from eighth period class, Jennifer had to stay after school for extra help, or the bus from the field trip is returning late. At the middle school level, where participation in many diverse activities is encouraged, kids are pulled in many directions, so priorities must be established. It is important not to pit kids and activities against each other. The supervising adults need to work out agreements with each other ahead of time. If two activities, such as volleyball and orchestra, are practicing simultaneously, the coaches/supervisors must split the time. It often is necessary to share practice time unless individual position training becomes a priority.

SUPPORT PERSONNEL

Support personnel are very important to a program. They provide logistical assistance and help take some of the tasks off the coach's plate. Assistant coaches, volunteers, and parents all play a role as support personnel.

Assistant Coaches

Support staff (i.e., assistant coaches and managers) play an important role in making practice effective, so the coach should specify the role each support staff person is expected to perform. A coach should use the strengths of each support staff person to help develop player skills.

Support staff may be used to run drills, coach players in a specific position, demonstrate proper skills, score drills, or keep statistics during practice. Colleges have the luxury of one or two assistants on staff, but most high schools have only one coach per team. Some varsity coaches take advantage of the individual strengths of their feeder program coaches by assigning them to help occasionally with other squads in the program.

Volunteer Coaches

Volunteer coaches are another consideration for a program. Volunteers usually have to be approved by the board of education or be certified because of liability reasons. All volunteers must be adequately trained, must uphold the program's philosophy, and must understand their roles. Good volunteers to consider are former players, student teachers, physical education teachers, or academic teachers who are interested in becoming staff coaches in that program in the future.

Parents As Assistants

Generally speaking, parents don't make good volunteer coaches. It gives them too much inside information and control over a team. However, parents can make great volunteers for other duties within the program. These duties include assisting in fundraising; becoming a scorer, linesperson, or announcer; making travel arrangements; organizing refreshment stands; developing game programs; and helping with court setup and takedown. Our Junior Olympic club utilizes parents to do all fund-raising and travel arrangements. They also have a "father's club" that sets up and takes down all of the equipment for practices and tournaments. Parents usually want to participate in their children's endeavors, so they can be used effectively to help a volleyball program.

EQUIPMENT

The equipment and instructional aids available will determine the kinds of drills a coach can organize for a practice. There are two categories of equipment: equipment that is necessary to develop players' skills, and equipment that supports and enhances drills and the rules of the game.

Volleyballs

Every volleyball association, league, or conference adopts a ball for use in their competition. In practice, teams should use balls that are the same size and weight as those used in competition. Many grassroots programs use a smaller or lighter ball. Junior Olympic club programs use a light ball for ages 12 and under and a regular size and weight ball for all other ages. Middle schools and high schools use a standard size and weight ball. Programs should purchase and maintain leather balls for practice. It is better to have a small number of good quality balls than to have a large number of plastic or synthetic balls. Most synthetic volleyballs do not respond the same as leather balls and sometimes hurt the players' arms.

Ideally, a team should have about two dozen volleyballs per court for any practice. If that is not possible, one volleyball per player is adequate. Some teams have only one to three balls per squad and also have to share them with the physical education classes. Trying to secure more volleyballs should be every coach's constant effort. The more quality ball contacts each player has in every practice, the more a team can develop.

Volleyballs should be maintained at the recommended inflation level. The balls should be stored in an environmentally secure place. Storing volleyballs in either a very dry or humid storeroom will deteriorate a ball faster than overuse.

Antennas

A net should always have antennas in place. Players need to familiarize themselves with court markings to keep the ball in bounds. Additional antennas can be used to divide the court in half for mini-court drills or for use as a target marker along the net.

Poles, Nets, Referee Stands, Padding

Most schools have drop-in volleyball pole systems to satisfy insurance liability issues. Schools that use older standards with wide support bases are inviting injury. Most volleyball net systems have referee stands that will attach to a pole. The important issues when purchasing a volleyball system are the anticipated ease of setup and takedown, the tautness of the net itself, and the ease of storage. If properly cared for, a quality net system will last many years. Be sure to investigate systems from a variety of manufacturers because each system has its pros and cons.

To protect players, padding of all equipment near the court is essential, including poles, referee stand, and any exposed metal wire supporting the net. Sometimes towels are taped to this metal wire as temporary protection.

Supporting Aids

Supporting aids are various devices that help a coach conduct a drill in a gamelike fashion. They are not essential, but they do enhance the flow of drills.

• Coaching boxes. Some coaches stand on specialized hitting boxes for defense drills. It is best to pad the sides of these boxes with something such as carpet remnants.

• Flip score. Many drills are scored using some kind of flip card device that shows the score for each team. If that device has a game indicator, coaches can use it to indicate a "wash" or for other drills that require winning a best of three or five series.

• Ball carts. Ideally, each court should have four carts, since four activities can be initiated on any court. Carts help drills stay organized, but more important, they keep the court safer. Balls underfoot are an accident waiting to happen. The ball carts need to be kept away from the player movement in any drill. If carts are too expensive, you can substitute plastic garbage cans.

• Cones, rubber floor markers, and floor tape. These resources are useful for indicating floor areas, changing court lines, and developing targets. Cones are frequently used for the players to run around, but for safety reasons it is very important to keep cones off the playing area during play.

• Elastic cord. Some coaches stretch an elastic cord from antenna to antenna in serving, hitting, and blocking drills. This cord can also be used for agility drills.

• TV, VCR, camcorder. Taping individual players, specific drills, or entire practices can be helpful. Taping a practice can help a coach evaluate his own effectiveness as well as the team's performance. Sometimes during drills, it is difficult to watch the whole process, so replaying a tape provides an opportunity for the coach and players to watch, review, and evaluate performances. Taping individuals is most helpful if a coach is on the court at that time to appraise and correct performances.

• Whistles. A whistle commands attention, starts and finishes drills or races, and is a quick way to keep a practice organized. The sound of a whistle is part of the game, so players need to become accustomed to it during practices. But a whistle can easily be overused, especially in situations where players should be alert to the sound of the coach's voice to anticipate instructions, such as during a rally. So, although a whistle is an absolute necessity, it is not a replacement for verbal communication.

• Stopwatch. A stopwatch is helpful for timing drills, consequences, or contests.

Additionally, a wristwatch with a timing mode can be set to remind the coach how much time is left in a drill. This enables the coach to efficiently manage practice time.

• Towels, water bottles, and cups. Towels must be kept handy to wipe up spills and to wipe sweat marks from the floor. Try to keep water, cups, or water bottles on hand for players during drink breaks. You can also have each player bring a filled water bottle to practice (but store them off the court). Having an area in the gym where the players can congregate during a break provides a pleasant oasis, and it keeps the kids in the gym. Setting up this area is a good job for a manager or parent volunteer. If time is an issue, a coach can talk to the team during the water break to evaluate the last drill or introduce the next drill.

• Dry erase board or chalkboard. Some gyms have a large writing surface mounted on a side wall, and others have a portable board. Many times chalk talks are conducted during off-court time because teams should use all court time for ball handling. Boards can be used to list the agenda, to post the theme or quote of the day, to write cue words and plays, to indicate players divided into groups, or to show particular drills (although court demonstrations are usually more effective).

• Gadgets. Every coach develops or purchases volleyball gadgets to be used as teaching and coaching aids. The following are some of the more popular gadgets:

1. Blocking aids for practicing coverage behind an attacked ball. Some coaches use a baseball pitch back, a folded chair, or a board. The surface should be padded in case player contact occurs. Admittedly, it is difficult to replicate the actual rebound effect of a blocked ball during a simulated exercise.

2. Attack aids, which include a volleyball hanging from a basketball basket via a bungee cord, a ball hanging from the ceiling of the gym by an adjustable pulley system, or a ball attached between two foam pieces that are mounted on a pole. These aids are used for practicing spike approaches on a stationary ball or for teaching full arm extension over a ball. The coach can just hold a ball with his fingers directed downward and his arm extended as a player then attempts to hit the ball out of the coach's fingers. But a device allows the coach to watch and evaluate the player better.

3. Vertical jump testing devices, most of which are mounted on a pole or suspended from a wall bracket. These devices have targets that players hit to mark the highest measurement from their jump. Some coaches use the vertex device as a maximum target during blocking drills to motivate hitters to explode during their jump. Some coaches label measurement markings on a wall. This is not a suggested practice because the jumper could crash her body into the wall during flight!

MASTER PLAN

When you have become comfortable with your coaching philosophy, have assessed all the logistical factors, and have gotten to know your team, you will be able to establish a structured master plan for practices. You may deviate from the plan a bit, but an organized outline is essential for keeping your practices moving. You will find your own specifics, but as an example, my practices usually include an introduction and team meeting, warm-up and stretching, ball handling, drills for reviewing skills, new instruction, combination drills, scrimmages, conditioning, cool-down, and a closing team meeting.

Introduction and Team Meeting

The first part of the practice is the time when the coach redirects his players' thoughts toward volleyball. Most high school practices come at the end of a long day for both the coach and players. The coach has to set the stage for the day's practice. This meeting should not last longer than five minutes. Players are usually anxious to be active, and they enjoy a motivating and aggressive practice. Topics included in the initial team meeting could be review from the previous day's practice or match, themes and objectives of the day's practice, or some groundwork preparation for the next opponent. Team meetings that entail more time should be scheduled during off-court time. If a team meeting is needed at the end of practice, a coach should schedule the time so it does not detract from the goals of the practice.

Warm-Up

The goal of a warm-up is to stimulate blood flow in the body. This will increase the body's temperature to permit adequate stretching and range of motion, which, in turn, will optimize muscle and joint flexibility. Stretching should always be performed *after* warm-up when the muscles are flexible and ready for adequate movement. The warm-up period should last between 10 and 15 minutes depending on time restraints—just long enough for players to break a sweat and warm up the major muscle groups.

Warm-up activities can include limited ball handling drills, specific volleyball movements (e.g., spike approaches or footwork for blocking along the net), or any aerobic activities that cause a player to break a sweat, such as jogging, jumping rope, or agility routines using bungee cords. Movements can be designed to work on position skills or proper posture if a coach wants to combine volleyball footwork with warm-up. Movements can also be continuous basic motor movements.

Warm-up games can be elementary games such as tag variations, active group initiatives, or cross-training. For example, one of my team's favorite games is hand soccer, because it's fun and physically exhilarating. Games such as this are a great way to start a practice, and they can promote competi-

tion, develop teamwork, and provide consequences. These games should motivate players and set an aggressive atmosphere for the rest of the practice. See the following warm-up drills for ideas.

If actual court time is limited, warm-ups should be performed in an unobstructed hallway or in a limited space off the court. Court time is precious and should be used for quality ball contacts in drills and activities. If court usage is not an issue, warm-up activities can be volleyball related, including activities related to a current lesson's goals. Warm-ups can be routine, can vary, or can include stations.

After warm-ups, players must stretch to prepare the joints and muscles for activity. If the players' muscles are sore, stretching (and holding the stretch) will help relieve some of the soreness.

Warm-up and stretching should not include physical conditioning. Anaerobic conditioning can be done in conjunction with drills or between drills, but aerobic conditioning should be done at the end of practice.

WARM-UP DRILLS

Hand Soccer

Purpose: Fun game for practicing low posture

Equipment: Half a volleyball court, two sets of floor goals (e.g., four shoes, four travel bags, or four cones), one volleyball

Procedure: Two goals (about six to seven feet wide) are set up on each sideline. The team divides into two teams of five to seven players (see figure 6.1). In the middle of the court, the game is started by a ball dropped between two players. Each team tries to score by passing and propelling the ball on the floor. A player cannot pick up the ball and must roll it, push it, or punch it along the floor. Each team may have a goalie. The game is won by achieving a set number of goals.

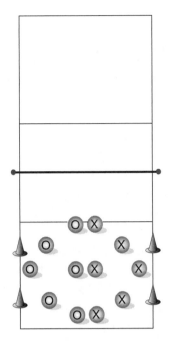

Figure 6.1 Hand soccer.

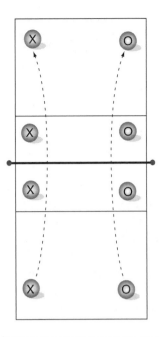

Figure 6.2 Control drill.

Key points: Players will have to stay in a low posture and dive along the floor to block shots, steal passes, and propel the ball to pass and score.

Variations

- Two volleyballs can be used.
- For larger teams, divide the team into four teams and use both sides of the court.

Control Drill

Purpose: To work on basic ball control and communication; to warm up early in practice using the basic skills

Equipment: Two (if possible) regulation courts and net setups, one volleyball for each group of four

Procedure: A group of four players sets up in a row, two on each side of the net. On each side, one player plays back row and one plays at the net. The drill is initiated by a back row player sending the ball over the net to the other back row player (see figure 6.2). The players attempt to rally in a controlled manner. They must contact the ball according to different goals set by the coach:

- Every contact a forearm pass
- Every contact an overhead pass
- First contact a forearm pass, second contact an overhead pass, third contact an overhead pass
- First contact an overhead or forearm pass, second contact an overhead pass, third contact a roll shot
- First contact a forearm pass, second contact an overhead pass, third contact a full approach and tip
- First contact a forearm pass, second contact an overhead pass, third contact a full approach and controlled attack

Key points: To maintain continual play, players must send the ball over the net in the area of the backcourt player. Players must ready themselves by adjusting their posture and position to receive the next ball.

Variations: There are endless variations a coach can challenge a team to achieve. Number of repetitions over the net in a row can be used as a score to challenge groups.

Pepper

Purpose: To warm up and work on technical skills and posture

Equipment: Floor space, volleyballs

Procedure: Players can initiate and perform this drill on their own (without the coach). The drill can be performed with two, three, or four players. The drill is always started with a toss. The players' goal is to perform a pass, set, attack, and dig in order. When only two players are participating, the drill continues with a dig, set, attack, dig, and so on.

With three players, one player acts as the setter, and the other two players are diggers and attackers (see figure 6.3). The setter starts on the right side of player A. The setter tosses the ball to player A, who passes the ball back to the setter. The setter sets player A up to attack the ball on player B. The setter runs between the players after she sets so she can be on the right side of player B. Player B digs the ball to the setter, who sets the ball back to player B to attack the ball back to player A. Once again, the setter runs between the players so she can receive the dig from player A on her right side.

With four players, two players act as setters (one for player A and one for player B) so no setter has to run through the drill.

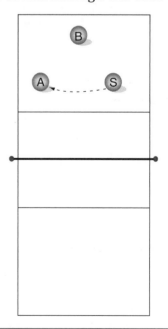

Figure 6.3 Pepper.

Key points

- Two-person pepper is the least advantageous form of pepper because it teaches players to dig back to the attacker.
- Four-person pepper is good for beginners because it is more controlled and teaches diggers to pass right.
- Players should plan ahead and get into the correct posture early.
- Players should work on their footwork for passing, setting, and attack approach.
- Setters should set the ball up well in front of the hitter's shoulder so the attacker can work on her approach.
- Players should be aggressive and not overuse the tip because of laziness.

Variations

- Pepper can be played with a full spike approach and jump.
- Pepper can be played over the net with three or four players.

Shuttles

Purpose: To warm up and work on controlling passing

Equipment: Regulation court setup (optional), volleyballs

Procedure: Use one side of the court. Player B is lined up behind player A near the end line, and player D is lined up behind player C near the net (see figure 6.4). The groups are facing each other. Player A tosses a ball to player C to pass. Once player A tosses the ball, she runs to the right and gets behind player D. Player C passes the ball to player B. After player C passes the ball, she runs to her right and gets behind player B. The drill continues and is scored by time or number of contacts.

Key points: The players must hustle to get behind the line so they are facing the incoming ball and use the proper footwork for an effective pass. Players must say "mine" on every contact.

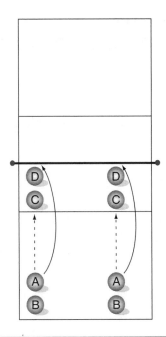

Figure 6.4 Shuttles.

Variations

- Either forearm or overhead passing (or a combination of both) can be used.
- Three players can perform this drill (to begin, the ball is tossed from the side that starts with two players).
- More than four players can perform this drill, but there are fewer contacts and more waiting.
- Different areas of the court can be used to create tempo passing (short passing or deep court passing).

Touch and Run

Purpose: To warm up and work on control while passing, setting, and down ball attacking

Equipment: Regulation court setup, bucket of balls

Procedure: Three players (team A) are on one side of the court, and three players (team B) are on the other side of the court. The drill is initiated with a toss or serve. Using all three players, a team must pass, set, and attack the

ball with a standing down ball overhead swing (see figure 6.5). After a player executes her skill, she drop steps and runs and touches the back line and then returns to focus on playing the ball on its return. If a team has to send a ball over on the first or second contact, the players who did not contact the ball do not run and touch the back line.

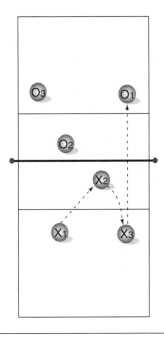

Figure 6.5 Touch and run.

Key points: The players should maintain eye contact with the ball while running to touch the back line. Proper posture and technique can be coached. The players should prepare early and stay focused.

Variations: The drill can be scored by the number of successful three contacts achieved in a certain time limit, or versus teams on an adjacent court performing the same drill. A team can be penalized for not achieving three contacts.

Backcourt Football

Purpose: To warm up and work on backcourt defensive movement and meshing, and react to the trajectory of the ball's flight

Equipment: Two regulation courts, four junior footballs

Procedure: On each court, three back-court defensive players line up at 1, 6, and 5. Players 1 and 5 are spread across the midcourt (wings), and player 6 stays deep toward the end line like center back defensive system. This is a Neucomb throwing and catching game using a football. Out of bounds and net rules are in effect. The player at position 1 stands behind the end line and throws the ball over the net to the opponent's side. She tries to throw it to an area that is not well covered or between two players (in a seam). A player on the opponent's side must catch the ball and throw it immediately back over the net trying to score by hitting her opponent's floor. Fast play continues until one team scores. The players rotate when they side out. Rally scoring is used. The game is played to an assigned number of points.

Key points

- Players must balance the court when a player has to rush forward to catch a ball.
- The wings should be ready to run forward to protect against short throws. This is similar to tips.
- The wings should protect the corners by catching balls over their heads. This is similar to overhead passing. The 6 player should play sideline to sideline running through balls.

Variations

- The coach can allow the person who catches and throws the ball a two-step approach.
- If a team only has one court, a challenge court scoring method can be used, with teams waiting behind the end line to come on and challenge the winners.
- If this is not challenging enough for higher level teams, teams can be made up of two players.

Noodle Polo

Purpose: To warm up

Equipment: Floor space, two goals (cones), two beach balls, swim noodles cut in half (each player needs a half noodle)

Procedure: A goal is set up on each end of the gym. The team is divided in half with one team in pinnies. Each player has a half swim noodle. Each goalie starts with a ball and hits it (passes) using her half noodle to a teammate. The object is to try to score a set number of goals.

Key points: The goals should be big enough to encourage frequent scoring. Teams do not have to use a goalie. Kicking is not allowed.

Variations: If a team is bigger, more balls can be used, or the players can be divided into four groups (sending two out at a time).

Stretching

After the warm-up, the players should stretch together as a team, led by coaches, trainers, captains, or instructed players. Early season instruction should be given to emphasize the importance of stretching after warm-ups. Each body area should be stretched properly for increased range of motion, flexibility, and optimum joint and muscle use during physical activity. Most teams enjoy a set routine of stretches. It helps them physically feel ready and psychologically feel safe to practice.

Static muscle stretches should be used at this time, stretching one large muscle group at a time. The next step is to work range of motion and hold the stretch. An athlete should feel the stretch, but it should not be painful. Bouncing stretches can tear muscles and extend joints and muscles too far.

Ball Handling

Ball handling work usually starts with movement drills that include two to four players. Players should start with passing and setting drills, followed by hitting and blocking, or digging drills. When players have achieved some rhythm in movement and skill work, combination drills can be added. See chapters 8 through 10 for specific skill drills.

Ball handling drills usually build on the particular basic skills that the coach wants to practice every day. This repetition will reinforce these skills and refine fundamental movement. Basic skills include passing, serving, and serve receive. Fundamental movement includes spike, block, defensive, and transition footwork. The time of the season and skill level of the team will dictate the depth of any such ball handling drill.

Early in the season, drills should include more repetitions to acquire skills. Midseason drills should maintain skill levels. Late in the season, ball handling work should emphasize gamelike conditions.

Let's use serve receive as an example. Early in the season, serve receive drills usually include repetition of passing to a target. By midseason, a team may progress to repetition drills of serve receive pass, set, and hit (emphasizing the initial pass). Toward the end of the season, serve receive drills may include a back row triples game using both sides of the court, again emphasizing serve receive passing. This doesn't mean a team would never play triples earlier in the season, but it illustrates a progression throughout the season!

The most popular ball handling drill is pepper (see page 56). Pepper is not an opportunity for a coach to take a coffee break or work on practice plans. Pure coaching takes place during pepper. Constant anticipation, correct posture, fluid movement, and proper skills need to be reinforced. This is not a drill of playing it safe and keeping the ball in control. If a coach does not supervise a pepper drill and encourage aggressive play, the players will turn it into a toss-pass-set-tip-to-a-teammate drill. Players will start talking about boyfriends and having chatty conversation about their school day. Pepper should be aggressive and require pursuit.

Pepper drills can also be for control. This is best done over the net and is a good way to work on basics. A toss, pass, set, hit, and dig in a controlled manner can still develop movement and basic skills. This drill is usually timed or a number of continuous rallies is counted. The coach can vary the drill by using tips, roll shots, or two-handed placements over the net to replicate a third hit.

Grassroots teams can play pepper in this manner and practice one skill at a time. An example would be toss, pass, pass, pass over the net. This encourages movement and three hits on a side. It provides practice with gamelike angles and promotes anticipation skills. This is a form of cooperative volleyball, where the players are working for number of continuous three-hit contacts instead of trying to simply beat the team on the other side of the net with a first-contact return. Cooperative volleyball can be competitive if each group tries to score the highest number of continuous contacts.

Review of Skills

The review is a time to demand communication and movement. It is a time to prepare a team for the main objective of practice. It is a time to set a tone. The team should review the main theme of the previous practice. This helps to "instill the skill" and provides an opportunity for the coach to assess the team's progress (and their retention of key concepts) and to build from one skill to the next. Keep drills active and apply each skill in a gamelike manner. If practice time is shortened, a team can review skills as part of the ball handling warm-up. Simple combination drills can also be used.

If the level is grassroots, the coach should remind the players of the movements and cue words introduced at the previous practice. The drills at this level should be more limited than a gamelike drill, and they should be varied from the previous practice. A grassroots drill can be made somewhat gamelike by initiating the drill from the appropriate court area or by finishing the drill at an expected target area. This will help the young player see the big picture. An example of this involves the teaching of passing technique. In this instance, the coach has taught and drilled toss passing and partner passing. The next step is a drill where the ball is tossed over the net and then passed to a target. The players may not be perfect at the drill, but they are perceiving and executing the skills required in a gamelike fashion. Of course, if a player is not even getting to a ball, it may be time to regress or punt.

The review time of practice can also include working on a skill that has been a struggle for the team to master. This can be something the team struggled with in a past practice or during a match.

New Instruction

In this part of the practice a coach's long-term goals are taught, drilled, and achieved. Depending on the time of the season and level of play, instruction could include an individual skill, team skills, or positional training.

Individual skills include the six basic skills as described in part III. Team skills include serve receive play and *out-of-system* play. Serve receive play has to be performed and practiced from all positions on the court. Out-of-system play refers to how a team performs when the first pass does not go to the setter. This includes "help" plays, pursuit plays from all the areas on and around the court, and some emergency techniques.

Team skills also include counterattack plays. Counterattack plays involve a transition from defense to attacking the ball on offense. These counterattack plays may be from a dig off a block, from a tip, from a roll shot, from a free ball, from a spike, or from an attack coverage position. Counterattack could also evolve from emergency techniques or from an out-of-system play. In any case, all of these plays require a team to be able to defend all positions along the net and receive the ball at any position on the court.

Coach Bill Neville aptly stated, "A team should attempt tactically only what the players can execute technically." Everyone wants to play a diverse, multiple offense, but a coach must know what skill level his players can attain. This is not to say that a coach shouldn't have faith in his team or even sometimes teach over their heads. However, if a higher skill level is used as a challenge to motivate players to develop better basic skills, it should be tried in doses.

Quick Fix

I had an eighth grade team that struggled with serve receive. They were free ball passing machines! We also had excellent setting and hitting. So I taught the team how to run quicks. The kids would run into the gym between classes to set and hit quicks. They could achieve this attack off a free ball most of the time. In practice, they wanted to keep practicing this new play. In order to practice quicks, they had to achieve a preset number of serve receives to target. In other practices, I only let them run quicks off serve receive passes. It was amazing how quickly their serve receive passing improved.

Combination Play

Early in the season, the coach will combine skills into combination drills. A combination drill is a phase of the game, such as a pass, set, hit segment. The combination drill can include new instruction if the coach is teaching a new element of the game or a new play. A combination drill can be used for the grassroots team who is learning to combine skills in game play. These drills can be used for higher level teams as warm-up during the season. The benefit of combination drills is that they prompt players to react to gamelike situations. As the team and season progress, coaches plan less time for individual drills and more time for combination drills.

6-on-6 Play

During 6-on-6 play, players get the chance to take all of the skills and tactics they have been working on throughout practice and use them in a gamelike situation. Any 6-on-6 drill that allows normal point or side-out conclusion can work. In other words, these are scrimmage situations. The problem with scrimmages is they are usually boring because they are slow. Coaches can devise ways to keep the play moving faster. If a team is scrimmaging, after the rally is concluded, the coach can begin the next rally by tossing a ball to the winning or losing side, or by returning a ball to the person who made the last mistake.

The coach can change the scoring methods according to what she wants to emphasize. If the theme of the practice was right-side attack, the scrimmage scoring could award more points for a right-side attack. If a coach wanted to force the issue, she could add points for the right-side attack and subtract points for any other attack! If a team is being wimpy and giving up too many free balls, a coach could award points to the other team every time a free ball is returned. The coach must force any 6-on-6 scrimmage situation to be aggressive and make it achieve the appropriate goals. The following are some gamelike scrimmage drills that can be used in practice.

GAMELIKE SCRIMMAGE DRILLS

Yo-Yo Scoring

Purpose: To create gamelike, pressure scoring situations and to train a team to stop the opposition from scoring several points in a row

Equipment: Regulation court, two buckets of balls

Procedure: A team of six players is on each side of the court. A coach or manager is positioned off the sideline on each side of the court; both have a bucket of balls. There is only one game score for both teams. The game score starts at 5 points. Team A has to reduce the game score to 0 points before team B increases the game score to 10 points. A coach/manager initiates a free ball over the net to team A. Play continues until someone

wins the rally. If team A wins the rally, the new score is 4. If team B wins the rally, the new score is 6. So, any time team A wins a rally, the game score is reduced by 1. When team B wins a rally, a point is added to the game score. The team who wins the rally earns a free ball to start the next rally.

Key point: The setter must run her best attackers over her opponent's weakest blockers or defensive weaknesses.

Variations: The drill can be initiated by a down ball or by a serve.

Randy Dagostino Drill

Purpose: 6-on-6 drill that puts pressure on the offensive team

Equipment: Regulation court setup, bucket of balls

Procedure: Team A must score 4 points before team B scores 3 points. To initiate play, team A receives a free or down ball from a coach across the net. The coach initiates another ball to team A after the first rally is completed no matter who won the rally. The coach keeps initiating balls to team A until one team accomplishes their goal score (i.e., team A reaches 4 points or team B reaches 3).

Key point: This drill forces the offense to score on a rally or they are under pressure to score on a counterattack from the opponent.

Variations: The score can vary to meet the coach's needs. The drill can also be initiated with a serve instead of a down or free ball.

Tom Tait Repeat the Skill Drill

Purpose: 6-on-6 scrimmage drill that allows players to work on correcting mistakes (the consequence for erring is to receive a ball from the coach in the same manner as the error)

Equipment: Regulation court, one or two buckets of balls

Procedure: The drill can be run by one coach but is better run by two coaches. A team of six players is on each side of the court. The teams scrimmage, and play continues to a normal rally conclusion. The coach then initiates the ball to whatever player erred to cause the rally to stop. The coach tries to initiate the ball to the player in a way that forces her to repeat the skill she erred at originally. In this manner, the player attempts to fix her error and practices the skill until she corrects her mistake. This may take several attempts, but the coach keeps initiating the ball to the same player until she is successful. For example, if a player shanks a dig, the coach keeps hitting balls at the same player until she digs a ball that her team can continue play with.

Key points: The coach should try to create the same ball flight at the player to re-create the play on which she erred. The coach can verbally coach through the skill (for example, as the coach is hitting on the player, the coach can remind her to stay low). The team must be ready to play the next ball. The team should cheer the teammate on if she has to play multiple balls to become successful.

Variation: The drill can be scored by the number of extra balls the coach has to initiate to a team.

Maxwell Tip Drill

Purpose: To practice gamelike situations, communication, blocking, and run-through defense

Equipment: Regulation court setup, volleyballs

Procedure: Two teams of six players play a normal scrimmage except a team cannot spike a set unless they have created a one-on-one situation (one hitter versus one blocker). If a hitter has two or three blockers on her, she MUST tip or roll.

Key points: The hitter should see how many blockers are up and make the correct deci-sion. The hitter's teammates should communicate how many blockers are up against the hitter. The defense has a chance to work on double blocking the total net and to work on back row run-throughs.

Variation: Any scoring can be used, including rally, yo-yo, wash, and points burden.

Five Versus the Team

Purpose: To work on defensive movement, defensive positioning, and quality first contact

Equipment: Regulation court setup, bucket of balls

Procedure: Team A has five players lined up at positions 1, 2, 4, 5, and 6. (Team A has a 3 position, but she is not part of the defensive scheme.) Team B has a back row passer, a front row setter, an outside hitter, and a right-side hitter. A coach pops a ball over the net to team B's back row passer. Once the ball is passed to team B's setter, she can set the outside or right-side hitter to attack onto team A. The setter can also dump the ball onto team A. Team A sets up to defend the attack. Team A must dig the ball to the 3 player, who passes an easy ball over the net to team B's back row passer to continue the drill. The coach can challenge the players to achieve a set number of balls to the 3 player.

Key points: The defense should work on movement from base one to base two, communication, protecting the perimeter, and digging into the center of the court.

Variations

- Team A can have six defensive players by having the 3 position player be a middle blocker. This player should still be responsible for sending the ball over the net.
- Team B can have a middle hitter with a back row setter.
- Team B can have a middle hitter with the setter in the right front position.
- The coach can challenge the team to achieve a set number of digs in a row.

• The coach can require the team to achieve a total number of digs before rotating.

Feeney Drill

Purpose: To work on rotations in practice before a match

Equipment: Regulation court setup, bucket of balls (behind the end line of team B)

Procedure: This is a three-part scoring drill for each rotation to work on serve receive, counterattack, and free ball reception. Team A is the starting lineup set up in serve receive order. Team B is the reserves set up on the court as strong as possible.

1. Team A receives a serve. Team A must score on the serve receive. If they do not, they start over and receive another serve until they side out.

2. Once team A has scored on the serve receive, the coach tosses a ball to the setter on team B to initiate an attack. Team A must counterattack and score. If team A does not score, the coach keeps tossing balls to team B's setter until team A scores.

3. Once team A scores on the counterattack, the coach pops a ball over the net to team A to run a free ball play. Team A must score on a free ball play or they keep receiving balls from the coach until they do so.

Once a team achieves all three scores, the teams rotate.

Variations: Higher level teams can require a team to achieve all three scores *in a row* in order to rotate. The coach can assign a certain play to be run for each step of the drill.

Softball

Purpose: 6-on-6 drill for working on serve receive rotations and free ball plays

Equipment: Regulation court setup, bucket of balls behind the end line of the team up to bat (serving), bucket of balls on the outside of the court on the opposite side of the team up to bat

Procedure: Team A serves the ball to begin the top of the first inning. If team A wins the rally, they record a run, and a coach pops a free ball into their court from over the net. If team A wins the free ball rally, they score another run and keep receiving free balls until they lose a rally. If team A fails to win the rally on its serve, an out is recorded. Team A would serve again. If team A fails to win a rally on a free ball, an out is recorded, and they serve again. Once team A accumulates three outs, the top of the inning is over, and team B starts the bottom of the inning in the same manner. A team rotates its players when it is their turn to be at bat (serve). After six innings, every rotation has been used by both teams, and the race for the pennant is over. The seventh inning is the World Series. Each team may put out their best front row and their best back row for the last inning. The last inning is scored the same way as the first six innings.

Key points: All aspects of the game are practiced in this drill so the coach can set any goal he chooses. After six innings, allow the teams to make their own final lineup.

Variations: After six innings, if the score is lopsided, the coach can award two runs for each rally winner by the team that is behind. After six innings, the team that is behind can make a player trade to strengthen its lineup.

Erin's Chutes and Ladders

Purpose: To practice gamelike 6-on-6 situations; to work on pressure serving

Equipment: Regulation court setup, bucket of balls

Procedure: The team is divided into two teams for a gamelike scrimmage. The game is played to 15 points. Regular rally scoring is used, but the coach assigns reward points for running certain plays. If a team serves a ball out of bounds, it loses all its points and starts over at 0.

Key point: The coach can assign bonus points to any method of execution that the team needs to work on to improve play.

Variations

- A team must win their final point with a jump serve.
- The coach calls serving areas.
- A coach can assign bonus points for winning a rally by executing specific skills such as the following: serve receive, transitional counterattack, running a quick tempo attack, a block, a right-side attack, a combination play, a setter dump, or for younger teams: an attack, a three-contact play, a tip.

Conditioning

It is best to schedule conditioning before cooldown. If a team has limited court time, and a coach does not want to use this time to condition his players, he needs to find other gym space, hall space, or an outdoor area. Some coaches conduct conditioning at a time other than practice; any conditioning program that is separate from a practice session should include a warm-up and a cool-down.

There are different ways to achieve fitness goals. Because many drills are active and aerobic, they naturally include conditioning elements. At Sweet Home, my players were usually great jumpers. We never did specific jump training, yet everyone thought I had some magical jumping development technique that I was keeping secret. One day a friend of mine was observing our practice, and she couldn't believe how many times the players jumped during various drills. My theory is that my players jumped well because they jumped so frequently in practice. Nevertheless, additional jump training would certainly be beneficial for most teams!

Another conditioning plan is to intersperse it between drills. Also, a coach can have his

players do an upper and a lower body conditioning exercise before each drink break. This way they have a chance to recuperate during the break.

Consequences for being a member of the losing team during a drill are another way to add conditioning exercises. A coach has to strategize so that the same side doesn't always lose. This will ensure that all of the players ultimately receive the conditioning benefit of the consequences.

Each coach has his own philosophy concerning cardiovascular endurance training. Volleyball is primarily a stop-and-go activity—anaerobic rather than aerobic. Many conditioning activities used by volleyball teams are agility exercises that include various fundamental movements; however, endurance training is needed to prepare for playing in a five-game match or a daylong tournament. Training schedules must reflect a season's schedule. If a team plays in several tournaments or just a season of five-game matches, the players must be in sufficient condition to stay alert and aggressive. If a team is preparing for play-offs, endurance training is especially beneficial.

Energy That Lasts

One of my best setters, Alicia Bergmann, attended a Division I program that demanded a four-mile time under 32 minutes. At first we both thought it was a lofty goal. But she trained hard to achieve it and then to maintain it throughout the season. During her freshman season, Alicia was the starting setter in a 5-1 offensive system, yet she declared that she had never felt tired at the end of any tough, five-game match. This opened my eyes to the importance of endurance training. How many times had I admitted that my team had run out of gas in the finals of a competitive tournament? Too many! I didn't copy the demand for a four-mile time under 32 minutes, but I did increase our endurance training.

Cool-Down

If a team has just finished a strenuous drill, cool-down could include light jogging or walking to allow the athletes' heart rates to return to normal. Once this is achieved, move on to stretching. This is an important part of practice to protect your athletes from becoming sore. It also helps players attain better flexibility because of the stretching.

Final Team Meeting

A final meeting to bring the practice to an end may be held after the cool-down. To save time, the final "words of wisdom" and announcements can occur during the cool-down. This is a good time to pass out any written material. Also, the coach can present a quick evaluation of the practice and an overview of tomorrow's practice. If the team has a match the next day, appropriate announcements should be made, and pressing issues should be discussed and settled. Individual problems should be discussed one-on-one after practice. A team practice should end with a cheer as a final reminder of team spirit.

TIME MANAGEMENT

When planning a practice, the time for each portion should be estimated. If a coach has 2 1/2 hours for practice, he needs to divvy up 150 minutes. The time allotted for introduction and team meeting, warm-up, stretching, cool-down, and final announcements should remain fairly constant from one practice to the next.

Introduction and team meeting usually total 5 minutes. Warm-up usually takes 15 to 20 minutes. For cool-down and final announcements, 10 minutes is usually a sufficient amount of time.

If a coach has to conduct a team meeting to discuss personnel, scouting, evaluation of a tape, or travel planning, it is best to schedule this during off-court time.

Therefore, if the normal prepractice and postpractice activities take 1/2 hour, a coach has about 2 hours of ball handling, instruction, skills, combinations, and scrimmage drills to plan for the remaining practice time.

Admittedly, it is tough to remain realistic regarding efficient use of practice time. Coaches tend to overplan and run drills longer than anticipated. Drink breaks and impromptu instruction also eat away at scheduled time; therefore, it is best to schedule drink breaks. Impromptu instruction or discussions during a drill can be the best learning experience a team receives, so they should not be eliminated. Through trial and error, a coach can become more efficient with the use of time. Ideally, a coach should try his best to stay on schedule to meet his practice objectives, but he should also be flexible enough to meet the team's long-term goals.

The time of the season and the level of play will also dictate the amount of time a coach spends on the principal phases of practice. If it is early in the season, a coach will spend more time on ball handling and individual skills, gradually advancing toward team skills and scrimmage drills. Midseason practice includes continued ball handling for maintenance of skill level, drills to improve team play based on current match performances, and additional tactics and scrimmage situations. Toward the end of the season, plans should include skill-specific team play, higher level tactics, intensified scrimmage situations, and, if warranted, postseason planning.

Grassroots programs typically spend more time on skill development in early and midseason. Ball handling drills for acquisition, maintenance of skill level, and combination drills continue later in the season. Modified teams need to progress toward team play as individual skill levels increase. A youth coach who can blend these elements can then work on tactics as combination drills become successful. Grassroots players need to see the big picture early in their development so they know what they are working toward and how to play the game correctly to reach that level of play. One of the most helpful practices we conducted at Sweet Home was when we would bring the varsity team or the JV team to a modified practice for a "big sis/little sis" practice. The veteran players were wonderful role models, and the one-on-one attention was great help for each of the younger girls. The modified players, in turn, supported the varsity and JV teams by attending their matches, where they also experienced all the facets of the game played at a higher skill level.

PRACTICE BEFORE A MATCH

Most high school teams play two to three matches per week. This is in addition to weekend tournaments. It is not uncommon to have only one practice to prepare for each opponent, so any scouting information on a given opponent is very valuable when planning a practice before that match.

Sometimes a team may have to play on a Tuesday and a Friday. Possibly the Friday match is the tough match, and the Tuesday match is less competitive. Nonetheless, it is important to play one match at a time. To get ready for Tuesday's opponent, the team may need a practice filled with defensive work to prepare for a roll shot or tip shot team, because this kind of opponent can eat away at a defense that is not properly prepared. It may also be a match in which the coach feels comfortable using more of her bench players. To make sure the substitutes are ready to play a bigger role in that match, they should be included in combination drills with probable teammates. The coach needs to put these substitutes into starting lineups to scrimmage at the end of practice. The coach can also work on some drills for Friday's match without labeling them as such. Her players may need more time to work on specific tactical situations so the coach can feel secure that her preparation is adequate. However, at no time before Tuesday's match should she even mention Friday's match. That is like the kiss of death; in other words, don't put your bats away before the last out . . . just don't do it!

Because the schools within a league usually play on the same dates, most high school coaches do not have the opportunity to scout other teams. Frequently, a coach does not know anything about an opponent until she sees the roster and watches the warm-ups. If a team has played that opponent during the previous season, a coach will know some of the veteran players. To prepare for opponents like this, it is best to consider their tendencies from past history and their veteran players' habits, and, most important, to make sure your own team is ready to use its strengths.

Using scouting reports and films is a good way to help prepare a team for an opponent. If a coach has good networking, she may know the coach of another team that has already played a given opponent, and she may be able to get a secondhand scouting report. Coaches even may be willing to swap videotapes, which is a common practice among colleges.

To make sure that a team is ready in every rotation, a coach must use drills that practice serve receive options for all six rotations. Most teams have one bad rotation, which usually is one of the last rotations. It is beneficial to practice that rotation first because often this rotation is shortchanged at the end of practice. Next, the team needs to be ready for all counterattack plays from different zones on the net. Lastly, the team needs to practice against free balls and down balls from different zones on the net. If players are properly prepared and feel comfortable with various situations, they are more likely to play better under pressure because they have to rely on what they have drilled.

Players must also practice common help situations and KISS ("Keep it simple, stupid!") situations. An example of a common help situation is a bad pass that goes to the number 4 area. According to the coach's philosophy, she might have the outside hitter set a simple two ball to the middle hitter every time. An example of a KISS situation is when a setter has to turn backward to set a errant pass off the court. According to the coach's philosophy, she might have the setter always set that ball to either the right front player or right back player. A coach can prepare her players for both of these situations so their reactions become almost automatic as they "better the ball."

A good friend of mine, who coached at the University of Pennsylvania, had a good drill to ready a team before competition. I named it the "Feeney drill" after her because I stole it from her. This drill is described on page 63. As previously mentioned, it is smart to start with a team's weakest rotation, and that applies to this drill as well. A coach can also put nonstarters into the starters' positions to test other players' abilities in certain rotations.

A team must feel ready before a match. Obviously, a team will be more nervous before a highly competitive match. A coach has to make sure she doesn't project her own tension, which could add to the players' stress. If a coach can physically and emotionally prepare a team in practice, the players should feel relaxed, comfortable, and ready to play aggressively.

Unfortunately, the reverse is true before an easier match. If the practice before an easy match is filled with goofing around, a team is likely to take the opponent for granted when the two teams meet in competition. To avoid this lack of intensity before playing an easy opponent, possible objectives of a practice can include working on new offensive plays, setting individual goals to achieve in the upcoming match, or playing more substitutes in drills that reflect the opponent's style of play.

PRACTICE AFTER A MATCH

The practice after a match can easily reflect a coach's mood, according to the outcome of that match. Most high school teams do not have the luxury of several practices to review a previous match because they have to prepare for another match the next day! If a coach has more than one day to prepare for the next match, he should use his stats and notes from one or more previous matches to prepare for this practice.

The coach can develop drills to strengthen weak skills or to review combinations that the team failed to perform properly or that were ineffective in a previous match. The coach may also decide that a certain serve receive or particular offensive or defensive formations were not effective, so adjustments need to be made.

After a win, a coach will want to review what was effective and should be repeated against future opponents. He should also at least mention what was not good. Celebrating too much after a win can leave a team with a feeling of infallibility. If a team is coming off an easy win, a coach still needs to review what could have been done better. In defeating an easier opponent, a team usually plays offense well but is flat-footed on defense. Tips and roll shots used by an easier opponent continually find the middle of the court because a team feels in control of the match and can side out easily to regain the serve. With rally score becoming a reality in most levels of volleyball, better defense will be required against teams that play well on defense but just keep the ball in play as their offensive strategy. This style of offense seems unorthodox, but it is usually effective until an opponent adjusts its defense to cover those frequent roll shots and so forth. A practice after a win should immediately focus on the next match because the mood of the team is lighter, and there are fewer mistakes to review.

After a loss, a coach will want to review what was not effective. He has to decide whether or not to discuss the psychological and emotional problems that occurred in the match, and how much time to spend on those topics. If it is a team problem, a coach can use practice time or schedule a separate meeting. If it is a problem among a few players, the coach may want to talk separately with these players. After a loss, frustrations and finger-pointing are predictable because players tend to remember only what happened on the last play of the match, thinking that play only determined the outcome. A coach needs to keep the discussion positive and objective.

The Third Point Disclaimer

After our Sweet Home team lost the *big match*—the one that ended the national win streak record—we did not blame the person who shanked the ball for the final point. I have always used the "third point" disclaimer. My point is that the player who made the mistake on the third point is as much at fault as the player who made the mistake on the final point. If she could have played the ball better to avoid the third point against us, the opponent would not have scored at that time, so the game could have had a different outcome. In essence, the third point disclaimer says, "Play the game as aggressively at the beginning of a match as at the end of a match." It is a way of saying that a loss is a team's loss . . . not a loss that was caused by an individual's one mistake.

After a loss, some coaches and teams are very frustrated. The usual reasons why a team has played poorly are lack of aggressiveness, poor footwork, poor communication, or poor positioning on the court. Some poor movement is caused by the stress of playing a tough team or the emotion during a closely scored match. This causes a team to develop "roots in their shoes!" The only cure for this is to develop more drills that contain stress and competitive situations in practice. Also, a coach can play a more competitive schedule so the team experiences a greater number of competitive situations.

The coach has to determine whether a team lost the match because of emotional reasons or from lack of preparation. If all of the players have played their very best, a competitive loss can actually be more rewarding than an "ugly" win. Unfortunately, it is not recorded that way on the win–loss record! If a team has played its best but was beaten by a better team, a coach has to openly acknowledge this and show pride in their play. Regardless, there are probably mistakes to review and some goals the team must accomplish to reach a higher level of play.

Many losses are the result of unforced errors. These mistakes are frustrating for a coach and usually result in tougher practices. Although many coaches run their players hard after such a frustrating loss, they need to note whether the problems were movement related or ball related! Razzle-dazzle drills and pursuit drills can be developed to work a team hard but still be directed toward a goal. If a team has been flat-footed in a match, instead of just running sprints (which does relieve a coach's frustrations!), a coach may want to conduct footwork drills for a longer or faster pace.

Also, it is important for a coach to point out the good things that happened in a loss. Leaving a team feeling totally rejected by their coach is as detrimental to their psyches as the loss itself is. Players need to know why they didn't win *and* how they can win the next time they play a similar opponent.

GETTING THE MOST OUT OF YOUR PLAYERS

Wouldn't it be wonderful if every player reacted the same? It would allow a coach to treat each player the same, so she could concentrate solely on skills, drills, and tactics. Some coaches say, "I will treat each player exactly the same; players must adjust to my style." At some levels, this could work, especially if a player is on scholarship. It is commonly accepted that different methods work for various players. If a coach knows her players well and knows what makes them tick, she will know how to motivate each one more effectively. This does not mean that coaches should play favorites or be inconsistent in their relationships. It just means that some methods will be more effective than others when communicating, teaching, and motivating each player for maximum performance. Some players feel threatened or embarrassed if corrected in front of teammates. If a coach can correct the player in a secluded, non-threatening space, the coach's comments will be accepted better. Of course, any coach needs to work with all of her players so they learn to accept constructive criticism on the court; if players are not receptive to such comments during a practice, they cannot be coached during competition.

Another method of getting the most out of your players in practice is to make sure they know their role and understand their importance to the rest of the team.

Praise from peers is usually motivating, so a coach should encourage teammates to support each other during drills. If a player or group of players does an excellent job during a drill, the coach's praise will be well received by those who deserve it.

If learning is presented as fun, players will respond better and acquire skills faster. Most players love to compete, but some need to learn to thrive on pressure situations. Well-trained athletes love pressure and consider it a personal challenge—not a threat. If players learn to face pressure situations in practice, this mental conditioning should carry over to match play. Many players do not play as well in a match as they do in practice because of the pressure. However, there is always a *gamer* on every team, the one who competes harder in real competition. These gamers are usually not challenged in practice, so they are lazy in drills unless they feel motivated. Nonetheless, these players can become better if they are pushed to practice at a higher level.

GETTING READY FOR A TOURNAMENT

Volleyball is widely accepted as a tournament sport. Many teams host tournaments, travel to tournaments, or qualify for postseason tournament play. Tournament play entails several matches played in one day, so these multiple matches can become "aerobic volleyball" or survival of the fittest.

Tournament play requires a higher level of fitness for a team and better use of substitutes by the coach. A team with a thin bench will have to be in great aerobic shape. If a team has a well-skilled bench, the coach should utilize his substitutes' strengths throughout the course of that tournament. Accordingly, a coach has to train his players in practice to withstand prolonged competition and still have enough gas to finish well in finals. Training for tournaments includes aerobic conditioning and developing drills that include repetitive combinations and promote long rallies. Preseason usually includes endurance training, but this typically slacks off during midseason to concentrate on the needs of match play. A coach who keeps his team in good condition throughout the season will not be putting his team's aerobic fitness on a roller coaster. It is easier to maintain aerobic fitness than to try to regain it.

Aerobic conditioning can be developed from razzle-dazzle drills, movement drills, pursuit drills, repetitive drills, consequence drills, or wash drills. A scrimmage situation during which a team continues to perform because a coach repeatedly tosses balls into play is a good way to develop and maintain stamina.

Practices before postseason play should be a blend of skill maintenance and strategy-specific preparation. A coach needs to help his players maintain their confidence yet instill in them a sincere respect for the opponent. When a team concludes postseason play, no player should regret how she played. It is helpful to remind players that it is more fun to play in finals than to watch from the bleachers!

CHAPTER 7
TECHNICAL DEVELOPMENT OF PLAYERS

Coaching is finite teaching. Developing skill requires finite teaching in a simple manner for the learner. It's where players and coaches connect. It is filled with frustration. It's challenging and always changing. It is unique to each player, and it sometimes generates a warm and tingling feeling when that connection occurs and success evolves.

This chapter provides general coaching keys and advice on skills and drills, and the following chapters discuss specific skills. But coaching is an art. It is preparing for and presenting each practice and game. It is the ability to see where a player is erring, not just watching the outcome of the skill or play. It is seeing that maybe the player is off balance on takeoff, or her feet are too wide, or her knees aren't bent enough. It is knowing where to coach *from* to improve her play. It is knowing which drills to use when, and how to make them interesting and relevant to players. Sometimes it is even waking up in the middle of the night and putting a play on "mental replay," then suddenly realizing where the problem is!

Coaching is also about making sure the kids feel safe and comfortable on the court. But coaches want their players to be aggressive. If a coach trains posture and movement but praises aggressiveness, no matter the out-

come, the player will feel free to take risks and test her limitations. Players must be trained to "swing fast" not "just keep it in" during match play. As soon as you change your aggressive philosophy to a safe one, it changes the timing and tempo you have trained in practice.

USING CUE WORDS TO COACH SKILLS

When teaching skills, using descriptive and concise cue words can be very helpful. Cue words can help create a picture for the learner. Once the player correlates certain words with certain actions, you have a great way to communicate during games, too.

When teaching a new skill, the coach should show the whole skill to give players the big picture. If possible, players should also see the skill performed in a drill or gamelike situation to see the function of the skill. Many learners are visual learners and will learn from an example. A coach should first have one player demonstrate the skill. An example is player A demonstrating overhead passing for the rest of the team. Player B is tossing balls over the net to player A, who is demonstrating overhead passing by passing to player C, the target. The coach allows the team to view the complete skill a few times. Then the coach starts using his cue words. When player A is in ready position and starts moving to the ball, the coach says, "Feet under the ball." As the player is moving closer to the ball, the coach says, "Face the target." As the ball starts dropping downward toward player A's forehead, the coach says, "Ball-shaped hands." As player A sets the ball, the coach says, "Extend to the ceiling." The team has seen the skill performed, and the coach has pointed out each cue word in the total skill as part of the demonstration.

In this teaching method, the coach next teaches each part in succession. The coach has the team focus on the cue, "Feet under the ball." The coach starts a drill where a player is tossed a ball. The player runs under the ball and catches the ball above the forehead. Next, the coach demonstrates "Feet under the ball and face the target." Again, the team performs a drill where the player combines the first two cues. The player catches the ball. The coach then demonstrates the third cue, "Ball-shaped hands." The team does the coach's third drill, "Feet under the ball, face the target, and ball-shaped hands." After the players have accomplished this cue, the coach moves on to the final cue, "Extend to the ceiling." The players should now be doing the total skill. At any time in the process, if a player is not performing a part correctly, she should continue working on it until she is ready to move on. If a player is performing the whole skill and is having a problem, the coach should recognize the part of the skill that is incorrect and coach from that point. The coach may find that he has to define a cue with more descriptive words for certain players. But he should be careful not to lecture the whole team on how to correct an error if only one or two players need extra help.

In a game, if a setter sets a high outside ball that is 10 feet off the net because her feet were planted incorrectly, the coach can say, "Face your target." The setter will usually nod her head and understand that she had not squared to the target. Cue words are quick reference points for both the coach and the player.

Stinging Words

Using cue words during matches reminds me of a story that happened at NYS Empire State Games in 1984. Our team was running a new play set called a *31*. We called it a *B quick*. The B quick is an inside shoot set positioned between the opponent's middle blocker and right-side blocker. Our opponents had never seen this play set. They kept jumping in the middle, ready to block an A quick. Our team was running a B quick over and over again for points. The opposing coach finally called a time-out. During the time-out, I told my setter, Kathy, "Keep running a B quick until the other team learns to block it!"

When our team returned to the court, Kathy ran a high outside set. I yelled, "Kathy, a 'B' . . . a 'B'!" Kathy called back to me, "It was a bad pass!" As the next ball was served, I repeated, "Kathy, a 'B' . . . a 'B'!" and I ran out on the court chasing Kathy. She looked at me in astonishment as I whacked a bee—a bumblebee—off her shoulder! I have always been a nonviolent coach, but all of the fans saw me hit my setter like a mad woman. In actuality, the bee did ultimately sting Kathy, and she had to leave the court! So much for cue words between a coach and her setter!

LEARNING BEHAVIORS

People learn in a variety of ways. One method may not work for all your players. Some players need more demonstrations, some need more repetitions, some need more descriptive words, while some need tactile help (e.g., the coach helps a setter place her hands in a proper ball-shaped position).

What is important to remember is that if you don't start right, you can't finish right! Sid Feldman used to say that if a player knows how to start right and finish right, she has a great chance to succeed in skill acquisition.

Another way learning takes place is by teaching. People remember 90 percent of what they teach and 30 percent of what they hear. *Pair share* is a proven learning method that takes advantage of this fact. Pair share involves learners working in groups of two. In this learning method, one learner performs the skill, and the second learner critiques the skill. The second learner views and assesses each part of the first learner's performance of the skill.

Coaches should also stress that players need to coach themselves. Sometimes this shocks kids because they think it means the coach is leaving the gym. What it actually means is that when a coach asks a player to try something new or change how she is doing part of a skill, the player tries to change it immediately. The coach can keep giving feedback, but the player must be open to change. Some players get discouraged because they feel a coach is picking on them. Sometimes this means a coach is too verbose, but it usually means a coach is working hard at fixing the player's error. It's the silent coach who the learner should be more concerned about; this is a coach who has given up!

Players tend to learn skills better if they are drilled in doses. A drill that is performed too long is boring and causes learning to cease. If a coach wants to work on passing for 45 minutes in a practice, it is best to divide this into short drills interspersed throughout practice (four or five drills for younger players; two or three drills for more skilled players).

Practicing gamelike drills will help carry over skills into games. A player rarely plays as well as she practices because of the pressure involved in match play and the unfamiliarity of the opponent. If a coach can add pressure to a drill, it will also help in some motor transfer. Drills that allow players to break rules will not help develop proper skills. Allowing players to touch the net during drills will not help a blocker learn to control her body off the net. Playing two-person pepper that allows a digger to return the ball to the attacker will not reinforce a digger containing the ball in her own court.

COACHING KEY DRILLS

A coach needs a core set of drills to use throughout a season to help teach and prac-

Practicing gamelike drills will help players carry over skills into games.

tice skills and to instill familiarity with tactics and decision making. For each drill, he can vary the demands put on the players in order to make the drill different and challenging. One of John Kessel's favorite stories is about a coach who asked him a question at a drills clinic. It was a popular clinic because everyone wants new and better drills. After showing passing drills for over an hour, John was ready to move on to the next skill. John called for questions before he proceeded. One coach raised his hand and asked John for one more passing drill. John, a little exasperated, questioned the coach on why he needed one more drill. The coach proceeded to say, "If I have one more drill, I will have a different passing drill for every day of my season!" This coach wanted to prevent his team from getting bored doing the same old drills. But, what the coach did not realize was that he was teaching drill instead of skill. Teaching a new drill takes up valuable court time. It takes some time for a team to learn to be successful within a drill. If a coach has a core set of drills, he can vary from them but keep the organization of the drill efficient. Practice will have a better flow, and the players will stay more focused.

Here are some different ways to adapt a core drill:

- Make the initiation points gamelike—start from different areas on or off the court, introduce the ball with different methods (toss, hit, overhead, bounce), or vary whether the coach or a player starts play.
- Vary the ball trajectory, height, speed, and methods of initiation (e.g., down ball, toss, free ball, serve, hit, and so on).
- Change the movement demands placed on the players to gamelike, vary the footwork, and test the limitations by making players, still in motion, play a ball in motion.
- Change the number of players, the group of players working together, or the positions working together.
- Change the contact or rebound angle demands put on the players.
- Change the reaction time, decision making, and available options to succeed.
- Dictate different methods or skills to be used in the drill.
- Vary the scoring.
- Add a more complex skill to challenge players to pursue a higher level of play.
- Change the defensive system, offensive system, or attack pattern.

TYPES OF DRILLS

Drills can be categorized into several types. To achieve her goals, a coach can organize a drill so that it includes any number of players. The fewer number of participants, the greater number of contacts. But, for contacts to be quality contacts, they should be gamelike (creating angles that occur in games).

Instructional or Teaching Drills

Instructional drills include one, two, or three players. The drill is meant to teach and improve

the consistency of one technique. Focus is on early identification of ball trajectory, communication, movement to the ball, and key teaching cues to improve each phase of a skill. The drill is performed at a slow pace with no time restraints. Instructional drills start with a demonstration of the whole skill (by a skilled player or using instructional video). The coach then emphasizes important phases of the skill one at a time. Once a player shows some proficiency in the phase, the coach demonstrates the next key in the progression, drills it, and so on. When the ball is tossed to the performing player, it is usually kept within close range of the player. This will make less demand on movement patterns to the ball. But once the player learns to get into position to play the ball, the coach should start tossing the ball so that it places more movement demands on the player. Otherwise, the player feels she only has to play balls within her reach. If the skill has a different initiation point when used in a game, the coach should take the next step in gamelike development. The drill should be started from the new starting point (see the following examples).

- Underhand/digging/overhead passing—Instead of tossing balls from the same side of the net, start tossing balls from over the net.
- Setting—Instead of passing back to the initiation point in a straight path, the setter can start receiving the ball from an acute angle over the left shoulder and finishing to another point. The angle can increase as the setter's skill level increases.
- Serving—Instead of serving from midcourt, increase the distance until the player can serve from behind the baseline.
- Blocking and hitting—Instead of blocking or hitting on a box or from a lowered net height, the player can work from the floor or on a regulation height net.

Skill Refinement or Consistency Drills

These drills are performed once a player has learned all the phases of a skill and has progressed to a gamelike pace playing several quality repetitions within a time restraint. Movement back to base or starting posture should be stressed. Once the player is achieving better competence in the skill, the coach can advance another step in skill consistency by placing more movement demands on the player, changing the goal for drill success, and adding another skill to the drill. This drill should always include at least three players and all the gamelike angles demanded in play. These drills include good communication and should be performed throughout the season to maintain consistency of basics. Coaches can keep the drills challenging by changing the time restraint, goal score, initiation points, initiation angles, initiation velocity, or secondary skills. A coach can still coach one skill if other skills are involved in a drill. Early and midseason, this drill can finish at a point declared by the coach. The drill can also be played out to a gamelike conclusion. This is a progression to a combination drill, but a single skill is stressed and refined by the staff.

Razzle-Dazzle, Frenzy, or Pursuit Drills

These drills really motivate players because they are performed at a faster than gamelike tempo. The players play balls at a faster pace and are tested to perform repetitions by time restraint, scoring methods, or a required number of repetitions in a row. These drills are usually best controlled by the coach so he can create the tempo that will result in his objectives. Frequently used pursuit drills are defensive in nature. Frenzy drills can be produced to create out-of-system plays or plays from a position that is not gamelike. It could also include rapid hitting, digging, or other skills performed until exhaustion. A razzle-dazzle drill can be a drill that includes more than one ball.

These drills have several benefits. The first is that when the player returns to gamelike tempo play, the tempo seems slow, and it seems easier to move and perform. Another benefit is that they lighten practice, add com-

petitiveness, and develop team unity. These drills will automatically produce teammate support, better communication, positive encouragement, and pride in success. A coach must know when to use this type of drill in a practice. Some coaches use them after a slower-paced drill has been performed or after the coach has taken too much time to explain something and the kids have been put to sleep. The drill is dynamic and produces fatigue. After the drill, teams need a drink break. Another suggestion is to have a pressure serving drill after the pursuit drill but before the drink break. Another way to use this type of drill is as a consequence after a poorly played match or practice drill.

Combination, Flow, or Team Tempo Drills

These drills involve at least two skills and are most successful if gamelike in tempo and conclusion. The tempo of the drill will be determined by player reactions, decision making, communication, and skill level. The combination drills must have at least three players, and the team tempo drills should have six players on one or both sides of the court. The skills performed are dictated by the goals of the drill but usually include all skills performed in a game. Sometimes, to make the drill spicier, the coach will take away a skill or positions, or change the scoring. Team drills were once thought of as scrimmaging. Now, coaches use *continuous* team tempo drills in which they initiate a new ball immediately after the first ball is dead by serving, tossing, hitting, bouncing, or throwing a ball into the net for recovery. A coach can also return a second ball to the player who erred using a method similar to the player's original contact.

Practices involve all types of drills, and the coach needs to blend the drills to keep players motivated and achieve desired goals.

The coach, a player, or a machine can initialize play in a drill. After play has been initialized, the players may be allowed to play it out. Another option is for the coach to initiate the drill and then continue play, after the first ball has hit the floor, by tossing or hitting balls to create situations he desires. Once the drill begins, the player or coach can control the success of the drill.

Drill format can be organized by number of players, formations, play it once and rotate, repetitions, shuttles, waves, repeat the skill, or expulsion from the drill for success or failure. A drill must be designed to include spatial awareness, to be gamelike, to include specific feedback relative to cue words, to stay within the skill abilities of the players but remain demanding, and to be challenging in varied scoring methods.

Drills should have names. If I have not developed the drill, I name the drill after the person I have stolen it from! When I tell my team we are playing patriot games, they run to their positions and wait for my instruction on drill variation and measurement. Sometimes, I really want my players to be in different starting positions, but I usually allow the drill to start in the positions they sprinted to!

SCORING DRILLS

Consistency-based and combination drills need to be scored to promote competition and provide gamelike pressure. No matter what the level of play, drills can be scored using a variety of methods. The scoring for consistency-based drills usually involves keeping track of repetitions (for example, number of times in a row) and trying to achieve specific goals. Here are some examples of how a consistency-based drill may be scored:

- Timed or the coach's watch. The coach times the drill without any scoring or continues the drill until he sees what he wants to achieve. Coaches' watches tend to run slow.
- The number of successful contacts.
- Players must beat the number of successful repetitions from the past drill.
- A number in a certain time period.
- A ratio of successful repetitions versus total number of attempts.
- A set number that must be accomplished before the drill is complete.

- A set number to achieve before the other players or groups achieve it.
- Plus or minus points assigned. A successful contact would be a positive point, and a botched attempt detracts a point from the score. The coach would assign a goal score to achieve success in the drill.

Most team drills are minigames; that is, they are short segments of a game. A coach can create what he needs to work on to prepare for a match and create gamelike pressure in scoring.

Wash Scoring

Wash scoring is a method of scoring that requires one team to win two rallies in a row to win a point. If each team wins a rally, it is a wash and no one wins a point. This scoring method was created by Bill Neville, who coached three different men's national teams in 1968, 1976, and 1984. Coach Neville used big point/little point scoring. It takes two successive rally points (or little points) to win a big point. The coach sets how many big points wins the drill, creates a rotation, creates a consequence, or flip-flops the front row with the back row. This scoring system is a great method because it puts pressure on the teams to win the first rally and motivates them to win two rallies in a row. It puts pressure on the team that loses the first rally to score on the second rally in order to create a wash and stop the point. When teams can produce many washes in a rally, the coach knows his team is working hard to side out. Rallies, in match play, are the emotional ups and downs that coaches try to inhibit. With rally scoring in effect, coaches find this drill crucial for teaching teams to side-out for a point or to generate two successful rallies for control.

10 to 0 Plus–Minus Scoring

This is a fun method of scoring where both teams share one score starting at 5. It is a great method for coaches who are mentally deficient when it comes to keeping track of the score! Team A is trying to score plus points to

10 to win, and team B is trying to score minus points to 0 to win. Every time a team scores, the combined score goes up or down to reflect who won the rally. For example, team A scores a successful rally point, and the score goes to 6; team A wins the next rally again, and the combined score moves to 7; team B wins the next rally, and the combined score moves back to 6.

Number of Balls to Complete Scoring

This scoring gives a team a set number of balls to finish before the drill is completed. An example is a bucket of 50 balls and 40 must go to target. Other scoring methods or a time limit can be combined with this scoring method.

Time Bomb Scoring

The coach assigns a certain goal that each team must successfully perform before the team can freelance and start scoring points to win. The coach also sets the number of points needed to win the drill. This can also include a defensive goal by assigning a team three digs before they are allowed to attack a ball. An offensive example is a team who must run three successful right-side attacks before they can freelance their offensive attack. The other side must also strive to achieve the goal before they can freelance. The game is played to seven.

Skill-Based Plus–Minus Scoring

A coach assigns different values for specific skills performed successfully. For example, attacking a high outside set earns one point, a quick attack scores three points, a free ball return is no points, and an error is minus one point. The coach should make sure he doesn't assign too many points per skill or he will need a manager to keep score (which isn't a bad idea). Focused players will always know the score. Every team has a player who tries to cheat!

Cooperative Scoring

Cooperative scoring encourages teams on opposite sides of the net to work together. There is a second group organized in a similar manner on another court or sharing the same court. A coach can make two minicourts by placing an antenna in the middle of one net, producing two long narrow courts. For youth teams, a coach can make a shorter baseline, too. Cooperative scoring is used with youth teams to keep it fun for the kids but still practice ball control and certain contact demands. An example is 3 players on each side of one minicourt and 3 players on each side of the other minicourt. This accommodates 12 players on one court. Every time one side has three contacts and sends the ball over the net, it counts as one point. Every time the ball hits the floor or a team has only one or two contacts, the drill continues but no points are scored. The goal can be changed by counting successful three-contact plays in a row or by varying the quality or types of contacts demanded.

This same kind of scoring can be used to warm up or practice skill-based ball control for older teams. My favorite cooperative drill is over-the-net quads. Each team of 4 (2 on each side of a minicourt) has to perform certain three contacts to win a point. The drill can start with pass, set, and pass over the net. The third contact changes to tip, roll, down ball, and any contact the coach chooses. The final phase is back row attack, and the drill takes on the appearance of over-the-net control pepper. After the control cooperative phase is complete, I always finish with this over-the-net pepper phase (with the 2 players competing against each other) to keep a more gamelike ruthlessness in my players! I have also conducted over-the-net quads or triples pepper on diagonal minicourts.

Repeat the Skill

I first saw this scoring method used by Tom Tait who coached at Penn State. This scoring works well with a combination or team drill. Every time a team fails at performing a skill, the other team gains a point. The coach initiates the next ball to the player who erred, and the player must perform the failed skill. If she errs again, the other side gains another point, and the coach continues to initiate the ball into the drill at the same player in the same fashion. An example is one player fails to dig a ball that has been attacked. The other team scores a point, and the coach initiates the next ball by overhead hitting the ball on the player who erred. This drill is best done with a coach on each side of the court. One nice thing about this drill is that it requires a player to actually correct what she did wrong! A variation of this drill is where the player who erred goes to an open court and practices the skill correctly 10 times. The side that erred either plays with one less player or has a substitute player run onto the court to fill the vacant position. Another coach could be on the extra court helping the player who erred, and the first coach would initiate the ball into the drill on the winner's side. This is a common practice for a junior varsity team scrimmaging a varsity.

Handicap Scoring

Handicap scoring is devised to equal out two unequal teams or combinations. One team starts with more points than the other side. The teams might be unequal because of skill level, number of players, or because one side never receives an initiated ball or one side receives an initiated ball in a more difficult manner. One example is the starters scrimmaging the second string. In a game to 25 the score starts at 13-17 with the nonstarters in the lead. If a team has been having problems finishing a game, the score could start at 21-23 with the nonstarters in the lead. Another variation is the offense (receiving the initiated ball all the time) must win five rally points before the defense scores three. I call this the Dagostino drill because I first saw Randy Dagostino from Tampa Bay perform this drill.

Winning Points Burden

This scoring requires the player or team to win the final points in a designated fashion.

If they fail to accomplish the final goal, the drill continues. An example is a pursuit drill where the last two digs must go to target to finish. An example of a team drill is when a team must score its last two points running a quick attack to win. This scoring was developed to help a team finish strongly and not get stuck on 23!

Success Advantage Scoring

This scoring system awards a point and the next initiated ball to the team who won the last rally. The winning team continues to receive the next initiated ball as long as they continue to win the next rally. This is a scoring method to try to encourage one side to use a free or down ball and convert it to another point. It also encourages the defense to dig and counterattack to squelch their opponents from continuing rallies. A variation is to require the defensive team to perform a consequence if they don't limit the rallies to two or three in a row. This is just an added pressure incentive to motivate the defensive side to work harder. Another variation is to give the defense every initiated ball to make the other side work on counterattack to score successive points.

As a coach learns his team's level of play and assesses what they need to do to be successful, the coach can develop his own methods of scoring to make drills exciting and challenging.

PRACTICE SKILLS

Coaches, managers, and players need to know how to perform practice skills to make a drill more efficient and to create situations that will enhance the success of the drill. These skills must be demonstrated and taught to players in order to keep drills organized and maintain the gamelike quality of drills.

Practice skills include communication, ball retrieving (shagging), handing the ball to the coach, initiating practice play, balancing the drill, tempo, and the effort expected by the coach in a drill.

Communication is a skill that must be practiced so it is second nature in a game. Communication is verbal focus. Practices should be noisy. If every player is verbally assessing the play, every player is focused. Words used to communicate in drills include the following: mine, in, out, short, ball, long, help, tip, roll, go-go-go, here, and so on. As the level of play advances, examples of communication used may include the number of the set a hitter wants from the setter, helping a hitter with where to hit according to the number of blockers up (e.g., "Go line!"), the number of blockers up (e.g., "You have two!"), indicating that a second hitter is coming in on a combination play (e.g., "Second!"), and other words a team may use to relate what they see to help their systems run effectively. If teams are resisting communication skills, consequences should be incorporated within the drill.

Shagging exudes enthusiasm and keeps a drill efficient. Shagging is part of conditioning. If a player is not directly in a drill, she is responsible for keeping the drill safe by removing volleyballs from the playing area, replenishing the ball container, collecting the ball at the target area, or handing a ball to the coach or drill initiator.

Coaches like players to hand them a ball in a certain fashion during a drill. Some coaches like it placed on their dominant side hip, placed in a waiting hand, or placed in a waiting hand behind their back. Few coaches like a ball thrown to them because if the coach is running the drill, his eyes are focused on the player performing the drill to give her feedback. Some drills need a ball bounced to the initiator by a target player or shagger.

Teaching young players how to toss a ball in a drill is sometimes harder than acquiring the volleyball skill taught in the drill! Balls should be tossed to simulate a pass or set from the same side of the net, from over the net, and from off the court. If a toss is performed with two hands, it usually has less spin. As the level of play increases, the variety of tosses must increase to include a simulated down ball, free ball, set, attack, and serve.

Balancing a drill requires players to even out lines in a continuous drill where the players move from one line to another line. If a drill starts off with at least two or three players in each line of the drill, some lines dwindle for various reasons. Players who are focused will see this misalignment and fix the drill by evening off the lines.

Proper tempo in a drill requires the coach to use gamelike timing when initiating the ball into the drill. For example, if a coach is going to tip a ball into a drill from the same side of the net, the tip should be executed from a level higher than the net. Another example is a transition drill. If a coach is initiating a ball from the opposite side of the net, and the team receiving the ball is in base defense, the coach needs to give the players a few seconds to recognize the free or down ball. If the coach does not give the players gamelike time to recognize and react to the ball, it really simulates a setter dump. If the goal is working on transition attack, the team needs the time to go from base one to transitional positioning. A coach's voice inflection and body language can also accelerate the tempo in a drill!

The effort expected from players in a drill has to be stated and overstated by the coach until it is common practice. Consequences may be used to help encourage this as routine. It is the same effort expected in game play.

EFFECTIVE FEEDBACK

Questioning players during learning and encouraging self-discovery are methods that create critical thinkers. A coach should ask questions instead of giving all the answers. This will also encourage players to trust themselves and react correctly in out-of-system play and bizarre experiences as they happen on the court. Coaches should assess players at the end of practice in what they have learned. It is also true that coaches should first review in practice what was done in the previous practice. Too often coaches feel that once they have taught a lesson, the players have acquired it without further review or practice.

If a coach wants to work on skill consistency, repetition is key. A coach needs to conduct a drill where the same players perform a skill repeatedly instead of running around in a continuous drill. A coach cannot assess a player when he only sees her pass once in every 12 contacts. Continuous drills are more beneficial as warm-up drills to get the blood flowing and still have the players touch a ball. Conducting a continuous drill does not allow the coach to see if a player is habitually erring or it was just a one-time error. A coach needs to assess a player over several repeated performances of a skill to determine what parts of the skill need to be fixed. Problems in skill performance usually result from poor or incorrect movement, timing, balance, posture, or position. Usually the skill isn't finished correctly because it hasn't started correctly. It takes a critical eye to assess which part of a skill is being done incorrectly instead of just seeing the finish. How many times have you heard coaches yell "Reach" when a player hasn't drawn her hitting arm back? Maybe this player cannot open her shoulders to draw her arm back because her feet were incorrectly planted before her jump.

Corrective criticism should be positive and form a picture in the player's mind. If a coach yells, "Reach," it makes a player think she should lift her arm straight up. The phrase "swing up" is more descriptive of the movement required. Feedback that is positive is more accepted by the learner. If the player only hears "Don't drop your elbow" instead of "Keep your elbow up," she is only hearing what she is doing incorrectly.

When correcting a player, the positive/fix/positive phrasing works best. An example would be in a passing drill where the player is not angling her platform correctly to the target. The coach could just say, "Angle your platform more" and hope for correction. If correction does not occur, and the player feels picked on by the coach, he can rephrase and say, "You are putting the heels of your hands together well. If you drop your right shoulder more, the angle on your platform will improve, and the ball will go right to the target. Keep up the great effort!"

Phrases such as "nice job" and "good work" should be limited because they are not skill descriptive. A better phrase is "nice release to the outside" or "way to get your feet to the ball quickly." This reinforces key words, too.

That is not to say a coach should never use these phrases that are not descriptive. I have found that my players love to hear me say, "Saa-weet" after an awesome hit or "Key dig" after a player makes a rally-saving dig. I even have a hand signal for the key dig, which is turning my fist (like opening a door) and then digging it down to signal the player on the court after the play is over. Usually, a front row player gets credit for the rally by putting down a kill. Signaling the defensive player, who kept the rally alive, shows that her miraculous play has not gone unnoticed.

When a coach wants to give feedback to a player, it is best if the coach asks the player, "Do you know what needs to be changed?" If a coach is aware of the mistake, it's half the battle. If the player knows what she must do to improve it, that's great, too! John Kessel calls this *feed forward*. Skill acquisition is dependent on knowing what to do next instead of dwelling on past failure.

Too much feedback can be mind-boggling. For the best learning to occur, the coach should work concisely on one point at a time. If a coach is a megaphone mouth, the players will be turned off. When a coach persistently reexplains, players feel that the coach thinks they have little knowledge of the game. Players lose focus; effort goes downhill!

CREATING GAMELIKE DRILLS

All the sleepless nights over what kind of drill you can find to meet the needs of your team are in your imagination. The recipe I use to make up drills to work on a skill or game portion lies within this step-by-step formula:

1. Identify the skill you need to work on.
2. Go back one play in its gamelike sequence.
3. Start the drill at this phase.
4. Perform the skill that needs to be improved.
5. Perform the next gamelike phase usually performed after the skill.

Many times a skill performed poorly gets the blame. But it is usually what the player did *before* the skill that got her into trouble. This can be poor focus, movement, balance, position, posture, or communication. Practice the skill and fix any part of the skill that is a problem. Finish the drill by doing the next logical outcome from the skill. This final phase will help the players think and react in a game-like manner.

Creating a Solution

I remember the first drill I made up to help my players practice a huge problem we kept having in games. Many times, a player would put down a devastating spike to side out. That same player would be in the rotation order where she had to go back and serve. The serve would be put in the middle of the net! I guess her spiking motion must have carried over to her serve. Taking a deep breath and concentrating on proper serve technique didn't work. So, we initiated the drill to help overcome the problem. I tossed the ball to our setter to be spiked by a hitter. If she solidly put the ball down on the opposite court, she rotated behind the baseline and served a ball into the opposite court. If she successfully served, we had her run into her defensive base and field a setter dump. This combination drill had hitting, serving, and digging within it. We have run this drill in groups of three or more, making the other players set, cover, and move through on the court in support and gamelike movements. We have also assigned points or made the players perform a set number of successful contacts in a row. You will get so good at making up your own drills that your core drills will become your own. Of course, we all like to get a drill or two to keep practices active, fun, and full of razzle-dazzle!

In the following chapters, I've given guidelines on coaching essential skills—posture, movement, serve, serve receive, passing, attacking, blocking, and digging—along with examples of drills for each skill. Having a plan for how you teach and drill makes all the difference in your players' ability to learn and perfect technique.

CHAPTER 8 POSTURE, SERVING, AND PASSING

Posture is a component that is important in every area of the game. All skills need to be learned in the correct posture. Part of attaining efficient movement is mastering the correct posture for all skills. Efficient movement itself also needs to be taught and trained. In this chapter, I discuss these two important skills along with serving, serve receiving, forearm passing, and overhead passing. Beginners often need special attention when learning skills so I've given specific tips for coaching them, too.

POSTURE

Posture plays a major role in efficient court movement. There are three primary postures used when playing volleyball: low, medium, and high (see figure 8.1). Some skills start in one posture and finish in another—for example, overhead passing starts medium and finishes high. Low-posture skills include all forms of floor defense, namely, digging, run-throughs, dives, sprawls, and rolls. Medium-posture skills include forearm and overhead passing and spiking. High postures are used in serving, spiking, blocking, overhead passing, setting, and jump setting.

It is very important to use the correct posture for each skill. Players must be in the correct posture during precontact, contact, and follow-through, and they must be in the correct posture for the next anticipated contact.

Basic ready posture should contain anticipated energy. Anticipated energy means that the player is ready for a quick start and stop. The feet are slightly wider than the shoulders with the knees inside the line of the feet. The knees are bent deep enough to be able to spring in any direction but not low enough to disable agility. The weight is on the inside of the feet centered near the balls of the feet and big toes. It is catlike . . . ready to pounce. The waist, knees, and ankles are at equal angles. The right foot is ahead of the left in a balanced stance leaning forward. This position is called a *stable staggered ready position*. It has to become second nature to a player anticipating passing or pursuing a ball. See figure 8.2.

EFFICIENT MOVEMENT

Basic movement in volleyball is sliding and running. Each volleyball skill requires specific movements such as steps, crossover steps, drop steps, a step and balance jump, jumping, and combinations. Side steps are used in serve receive, defensive positioning, setters' movements along the net, and to cover short distances in blocking. Crossover steps are used

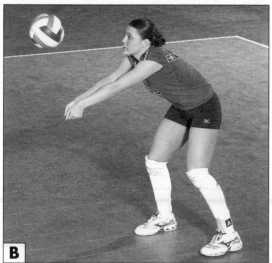

Figure 8.1 Three postures for volleyball skills: (*a*) low, (*b*) medium, and (*c*) high.

Figure 8.2 Basic ready position.

in blocking, pursuit, transition, defensive positioning, and some hitting patterns. Running is used in pursuit to a ball on defense, passing and setting, transition and hitting patterns, and run-throughs. Breaking movements (second to the last step breaks your movement and the last step balances you) are used in hitting, blocking, passing, and setting. These movements will be discussed with each basic skill.

Premovement is a quick movement adjustment that initiates actual direction movement to the ball. During this phase, a player anticipates where the ball is going next and gets her feet moving early. It resembles shadowboxing footwork. When movement in the intended direction begins, one foot starts, but for changing direction and moving forward and backward, two feet have to stop. Movement to the ball usually begins most efficiently with the foot farthest from the ball or from the anticipated direction of travel. If a player takes a step with the foot closest to the ball, this will overbalance the movement. It would be similar to a sprinter stepping off her front foot out of the blocks. This seems basic, but many young players make this mistake when passing. This is especially true if the player thinks she only has to move one step to reach the ball. Remember, volleyball players never take just one step to the ball. During passing, when one foot starts, two feet have to stop.

Other important considerations in movement include these:

- A player should keep the ball between her and the net. Only the setter should be between the ball and the net.
- A player should get to the ball before the ball reaches the ideal contact point. She should try to arrive early enough to be able to make a quick adjustment with her feet.
- A player should keep her weight between her feet.
- A coach should teach movement skills specific to the volleyball skill. She should also teach movement skills from all positions on the court.
- When movement is initiated, it should begin with the middle joint of an extremity, not with the end of the extremity. For example, lifting the arms up should begin at the elbow; moving the feet forward should begin at the knee. This will quicken the movement.
- Once movement habits improve, coaches should train movements at a faster speed than game tempo. This will improve players' ability to meet the ball early and make game tempo almost seem slow.
- When pursuing a ball, if a player cannot arrive early enough to stop to play the ball, she should play the ball and run through it. Otherwise, she will need to slow down to stop. This usually ends up in a lunge for the ball or totally missing the ball.
- Players should focus, adjust, and move two steps (shadowbox footwork) every time the opponents touch the ball.
- Backcourt defense should almost look like a simulated dance routine when the opponents have the ball, with players tracking the trajectory of the ball at all times.

It is important to realize that most of the movement in volleyball is during the anticipation phase and precontact. As a grassroots coach, if I were limited to watching only two movements or skills during a tryout, I would watch two groups of four play volleyball. I

would key in on the side that did NOT have the ball. I would watch to see which players move with the ball and move every time the opponent touches the ball. This shows anticipation, focus, and agility. The other thing I'd do is have each player throw a softball. Throwing is very similar to spiking and serving. If a girl does not throw correctly, teaching these two skills is often quite difficult.

Efficient court movement is one of the three demands I put on my players. Good athletes react to situations, and their movements seem to flow naturally. They tend to have rhythm in their skill performance from precontact to contact and execution. Many trained volleyball players have to be drilled to reduce unnecessary movements and create fluidity. There are ways to shortcut movement and train players to be more efficient to reduce wasted movement.

Balance

One of the most important basic principles in movement is knowing when to be balanced and when to be off-balanced. Players need to be off-balanced when they are ready to move—for example, a player leaning forward in anticipation of moving to pass a ball (see figure 8.3). I make this point because if a player is standing up anticipating movement,

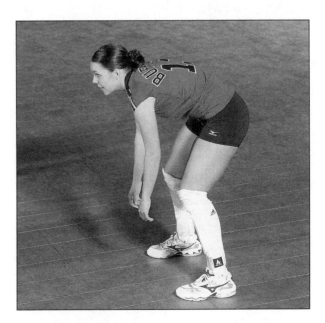

Figure 8.3 Off-balanced posture.

during her actual attempt to play the ball, she will have to lean forward as the first step in movement. So, to shortcut, a player should be in ready position leaning forward. This may seem like it will only save a second or two, but when the ball is dropping, every second counts.

Another important factor is stopping efficiently. When a player is in motion, her second to the last step stops or breaks movement. Her last step is actually a balance step. If a player tries to stop on her last step, momentum will continue in the same direction because nothing has balanced her momentum. Often this can cause trouble, especially if the net is in the way!

Anticipation

To train anticipation movement, grassroots coaches need to instill two principles. One is thinking of the "f" word, and the other is knowing who gets the ball next.

The big "f" word is *focus*. Visually keying in on the ball to determine how to play it and to read the trajectory of the ball provides the player time to get to the ball before the ball gets to her. Focus creates constant movement and adjustment to the flight of the ball. It is the readiness phase. If you ask the players on your team, "Who is getting the next ball?" and their answer is, "It depends," you're in trouble. If they are ready for every ball, their answer will be "ME!"

POSTURE, COMMUNICATION, POSITIONING, AND MOVEMENT DRILLS

Amoeba

Purpose: Nonball drill that allows players to work on positioning, posture, and total court movement

Equipment: Regulation court setup

Procedure: Twelve players set up on two teams on opposite sides of the court in base position (see figure 8.4). The setter runs the drill on each side. Team A's setter calls out "transition." The setter runs to target, the front row transitions off the net, and the back row balances the court. The setter calls out a set or play, and her team runs the play with no ball (pass, set, approach/jump/swing, and cover). At the same time, team B runs their defense to defend the attack (block and digs). Team A returns from cover to base one defense. Team B's setter now runs a no-ball offensive play. The setters may call a dump, free ball, down ball, specific set, or offensive play to run.

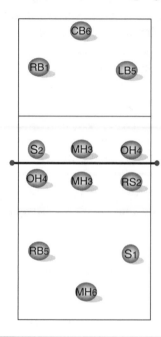

Figure 8.4 Amoeba.

Key points: All players should play all out and not go through the motions! That includes full approaches, full block jumps, and so on. The coach should correct her players in all aspects of court positioning, player posture, and movement.

Variations

- Players must brush the floor with their fingertips to prove they are low on coverage.
- Players must brush the floor with their fingertips to prove they are low on defense.

- Players may take two steps forward, play a tip, and imitate a run-through.
- The coach can add time onto the drill for poor performance.

Tip and Dig

Purpose: To work on run-throughs, approach and tips, ball control, and communication

Equipment: Regulation court setup, volleyball

Procedure: Team A has a setter and two hitters. Team B has a setter and two hitters on the opposite court. The setter starts in between the hitters. Team A tosses the ball to team B. Team B passes the ball to their setter. The setter sets the player who did not pass the ball. The third player on team B must approach the set and tip the ball to team A (see figure 8.5). Team A digs the tip and passes to their setter. Team A's setter sets the player who did not dig the tip. The third player on team A makes an approach and tips the ball back to team B. At any time, the setter may dump the ball. This is a control drill, so the tips and dumps should be in a playable area for the opposite team to dig.

Key points: The passer and setter should cover the hitter. After the ball is tipped, the two diggers should drop step and return behind the attack line in a defensive position, ready to dig the next tip.

Variations: The setter can set second or first tempo balls to the hitters. One setter can be used, and she can duck under the net and set both sides.

Crosscourt Triples

Purpose: To work on gamelike basics and focus (three players defend half a court)

Equipment: One regulation court setup (per six players), one volleyball, center line that equally separates the court in half lengthwise

Procedure: Team A and team B each have three players (on opposite sides of the court). Offensively, a team may use the whole court. Defensively, a team must attack into half the opponent's court. The coach assigns each team a half court to attack into (e.g., crosscourt only). Team A serves the ball into team B's crosscourt (see figure 8.6). The serve must

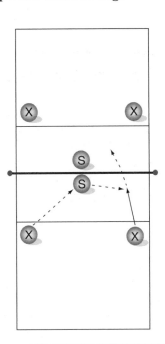

Figure 8.5 Tip and dig.

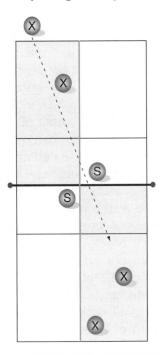

Figure 8.6 Crosscourt triples.

go in the half court or it is out of bounds. Once team B receives the serve, they can spread over the whole court to attack anywhere along the net. But, the ball must be attacked into team A's crosscourt lines. The drill continues like a game, scoring rally points and rotating in order.

Key points: Players should be encouraged to use the total court on offense. One player should stay up to set, and the other two players should dig along the perimeter of the half court. Communication is important with different court lines.

Variations: The opposite crosscourts can be used. One team can use one crosscourt, and the other team has to use the opposite crosscourt.

Michalski 6-on-3

Purpose: To work on pursuit, correcting errors, balancing the court, and communication (a team of three must score against a team of six)

Equipment: Regulation court setup, bucket of balls

Procedure: Team A has three members, and team B has six members. Team A must achieve a set number of points to finish the drill. The coach initiates the drill by sending a ball to team A (see figure 8.7). The coach can toss a pursuit ball, a down ball, a free ball, or attack a ball to team A. Team A must play the ball up and attempt to attack the ball over the net to team B. Team B plays the ball and counterattacks. Play continues until one side wins the rally. If team A wins the rally, they score a point, and the coach initiates another ball to them. But team A must *earn* the point from their attack or block. They cannot score the point on team B's error. If team A loses the rally, the coach initiates a ball to the player on team A who made the error. Once team A achieves the goal score, the drill is over, and another group of three players challenges a team of six.

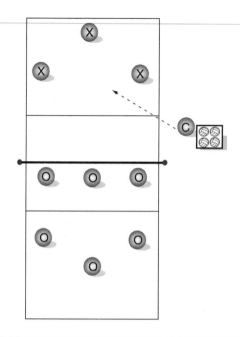

Figure 8.7 Michalski 6-on-3.

Key points: The coach should attempt to initiate a ball to team A in the same manner they erred. The coach should challenge team A but reward them with a down or free ball after they have earned a point.

Variations: The drill can be scored by the number of balls received by the coach. The drill can be scored by timing the drill and achieving a goal score within the limit.

Patriot Games

Purpose: To work on defensive base position and movement to base two position; to work on back row attack; to work on floor defense from a live back row attack; to allow setter to work on a setter dump or setting counter flow; to work on communication skills

Equipment: Regulation court setup, bucket of balls outside the sideline of each court

Procedure: A back row defense with a 1, 6, and 5 player is set up on each court. Each court has a front row setter. The court setup resembles a diamond (see figure 8.8). A coach initiates the drill with a free or down ball over

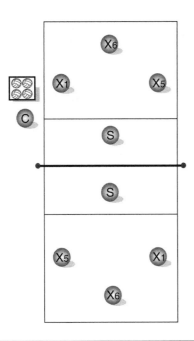

Figure 8.8 Patriot games.

the net to team A. Team A attempts to pass, set, and attack out of the back row or with a setter dump. Team B digs the attack and counterattacks. A point is recorded every time a side wins a rally.

Key points: The back row must call out the name of their set (e.g., 5 calls out red, 6 calls out white, and 1 calls out blue). The defense should read the opponent's setter for a dump, communicate it, and play the ball to their own setter. The defense should not release from base one until the setter sets the ball to her back row. The defense should rotate to a perimeter base two and face into "help" position when digging the attack.

Variations

- The coach or player can initiate the drill with a serve.
- The drill can be scored by total points or by wash scoring.
- A middle hitter can be used to add a hitter.
- A back row setter can be used in conjunction with a right-side player to practice right-side defense and interaction between the setter and help.

Duck Under Drill

Purpose: To work on transition and focus; to work on back row transition from base one to base two

Equipment: Regulation court, two buckets of balls

Procedure: A coach with a bucket of balls is positioned outside the sideline of each side of the court. Three defensive players are in the backcourt of each court. Three front row players start on only one side of the court, which is team A (looks like 6-on-3). The coach outside team B pops a free ball over the net to team A. The six players attempt to pass, set, and attack the ball. As soon as the ball is driven over the net to team B, the three front row players from team A duck under the net and transition behind the 10-foot line (see figure 8.9). They are now on team B. Play continues until the rally concludes. A new ball is always initiated into play over the net to the side the ball was last played on. Wash or yo-yo scoring can be used. The drill can also be timed, or a certain number of balls can be used until the drill is concluded.

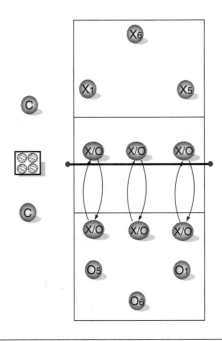

Figure 8.9 Duck under drill.

Key points: Players should run under the net and attempt to get past the 10-foot line before the passer makes the first contact. Back row players must attempt to play every first contact over the net to allow the front row time to transition behind the 10-foot line.

Variations: Middle front can be the setter (4-2 offense). Right front can be the setter (International 4-2 offense). Right back can be the setter (6-2 or 5-1 offense).

USA Drill

Purpose: To work on defense, pursuit, communication, and balancing the court

Equipment: Regulation court setup, bucket of balls

Procedure: Three players set up in the backcourt of one court. One player hands balls to the coach. One player acts as a target near the 4 position (outside), and another player acts as a target near the 2 position (right side). The rest of the team shags balls. The coach sets up anywhere along the net and hits, tips, or tosses a ball to one of the backcourt players. When player A digs the ball, one of the other backcourt players runs and sets the ball up to either target (see figure 8.10). The player who set the

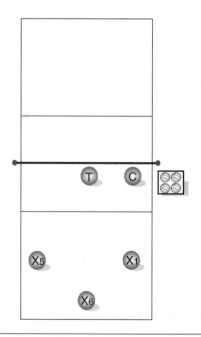

Figure 8.10 USA drill.

ball is out of the drill but is ready to reenter it on the next dig contact. The entering player always takes the place of the player who just set the ball to target. The drill continues and resembles a coach on two diggers. The diggers attempt to balance the court every time a player exits to set to target. The coach attempts to pop the next ball to a vacated area. If the trio fails to play effective double defense, the coach can start the drill again with three backcourt players.

Key points: The coach challenges her players by popping the ball where the defense is not covering. The coach tries to tip when the defenders are on their heels. The coach can send a ball out of bounds for pursuit.

Variations: Instead of starting with three players after an error, the coach can either send a pursuit out of bounds or keep hitting at the player who erred. The drill should be scored by a goal number of digs to target.

SERVE

The serve is the only skill in volleyball where the player has complete control of the ball. The serve can have three main functions:

- It is an attack deployed to score a direct point (ace).
- It is an attack to force the opposition to pass poorly and become predictable in their return.
- It is a method to get the ball in play.

The serve is probably the most frustrating skill for parents to watch. It appears to be simple, but many rallies never start due to a service error. What many spectators don't understand is the pressure involved and the importance of serving strategically. After the referee blows his whistle to start the serve, all focus is on the server. If the server is a rookie, the score is close, or it is a clutch serve, many times the player lets her fear take over.

The coach often signals for the server to use a certain type of serve or to serve to a certain area on the court. This is added pressure to not just get the serve in but also to perform the serve the coach has signaled.

Many teams are very adept at siding out, so when the opponent "just serves it in," the receiving team will often side out with ease. As teams advance in skill and tactics, taking a chance on a risky serve—serving lines or serving the weak areas—is worth the risk to prevent the other team from siding out and getting the emotional high that a kill can give a team.

Serving is about confidence. Serving is as much an attitude as defense is. The server needs to go to the back line and use it as an attack. Many times the server is just hoping to keep it in bounds or hoping not to hit the net. Both strategies are nonaggressive. Drills need to be developed to create gamelike pressure, to practice readiness signals to serve certain ways or to certain areas, and to change the negative mind-set many players have about serving. For younger teams, if the server can serve *in*, it is a real advantage because of the poor serve receive passing of many young teams. If a grassroots player can serve tough (e.g., serve to spots, serve overhead, serve flat and fast), that team is assured a string of points because of the opponent's inability to read and react to the serve's trajectory.

With traditional scoring, if a server missed a serve, the opponent would side out, but no point penalty was awarded. With the new rally scoring, if a server misses a serve, the opponent is awarded a point and the opportunity to serve. This new scoring method has thrown a whole new monkey wrench into the psychological aspects of serving.

There are many kinds of serves. The most common serves are the underhand and overhead serves. Other serves include sidearm, roundhouse, overhand floater, overhand topspin, sidespin (Mr. Twister), jump serve, slide jump serve, and the short serve.

Underhand Serve

The underhand serve is most common for younger players. It is also a skill that all coaches should be able to perform. An underhand serve by a coach or player initiates many drills in practice. It is the easiest serve to teach new players because there are fewer variables. Since it does not involve a toss, it is easier to learn and control.

Here are the fundamentals involved in a right-handed underhand serve:

- Feet in an up-and-back stride position with the weight on the back right foot.
- Ball is held in the left hand in front of the body just below the waist and in front of the right hip.
- Shoulders and upper body lean forward (see figure 8.11a).
- Eyes are focused on the contact part of the ball.
- The server will use an open hand, her flat fist, or the flat area made by the top of the fist at the pointer and thumb area.
- The right arm is swung backward for power and forward toward the ball in a pendulum manner.
- Weight transfer onto the front foot or a step with the front foot is made in the intended direction of the serve as the arm swings to contact the ball.
- Contact is made just below the equator (Australia) in the center of the ball.
- The left hand drops just prior to contact (see figure 8.11b).
- After contact is made, the server continues to follow through with her dominant arm toward the intended target.

Overhead Serve

The overhead serve is the most popular serve in high school and college. The two main overhead serves are the floater and topspin. The short serve and jump serve are becoming tactically very popular, too. An overhead serve is generally faster and more powerful than the underhand serve. The overhead serve technique is similar to throwing a ball (see figure 8.12). A good test to use with a novice player to see if she is ready to learn this serve is to see if she can throw a ball, with good form, from one end line to the other.

For the overhead serve and beginning stages of the floater, two phases are useful in training. The cue words are "toss and draw"

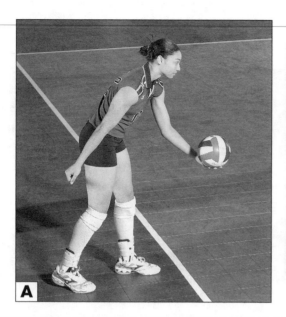

Figure 8.11 Underhand serve.

Figure 8.12 Overhead serve.

and "step and swing." The right-handed server starts in an up-and-back stride with most of her weight on her back right foot. The left hand holds the volleyball extended forward and in front of the server's right side. The left shoulder is forward and the right shoulder is back, with the right elbow bent back ready to draw back.

The server tosses or "lifts" the ball in front of her right side. If the ball were not swung at, it would bounce on the floor in front of the server's right side. The toss is an important training element. It resembles a lower self set. The server should toss the ball in a lifting motion and not lean forward or drop the left hand. The toss should be lifted up just out of reach. A consistent toss will produce fewer variables to contend with when contacting the ball. As a server lifts the ball, she draws her right shoulder and elbow back for power to initiate the backswing. This is the toss and draw phase. Many young servers toss the ball without the draw and lose all the power a swing is supposed to muster. This serve will rely only on a forward, powerless swing with little likelihood of making it over the net. It is also one reason novice servers like to take three or four steps into a serve to gain momentum. I call this approach serving! Taking multiple steps into a serve adds deadly complications to the development of a consistent serve. It also requires a higher toss, which changes the timing element.

After the toss and draw phase, a server steps with her front left foot toward the toss. As a server becomes adept at a consistent toss, she can just transfer her weight onto her front foot. As the server transfers her weight forward, her right shoulder and elbow initiate a fast forward upswing toward the ball. Contact is with a rigid hand and wrist and should be solid, using a firm heel and palm. The fingers are spread but firm and are ball-shaped to support a secondary, solid contact.

The main difference between the floater and topspin serves is the body position on the ball, contact, and follow-through. The floater serve is contacted in front of the right side of the body, and the high hand hits solidly behind the middle, or meat, of the ball creating little or no spin, with a normal follow-through. Its unpredictable path resembles a baseball pitcher's knuckleball. The inconsistent trajectory causes a serve receiver to make poor judgment when moving to the ball. With a topspin serve, the server steps under the toss. The server has to swing up and contact under the ball with her whole hand snapping on top of the ball. The fingers play an important part of the follow-through. The hand follows through with a forward snapping movement causing the ball to drive up but spin down on flight. She must pike forward on follow through to contain the ball in the court and create a topspin flight. The topspin serve is predictable on flight unless the server has put a sidespin on contact. The passer will

perceive the ball to be coming at her chest, but it will actually drop down quickly in front of her. This serve fools less experienced players. A good topspin server should toy with sidespins and start jump serving to add more zip to the ball.

An increasingly popular serve is the short serve. This serve can be confusing because it questions who should be the passer. It is served inside the 10-foot line. Its tactic is to make a probable hitter move forward, making transition to attack nearly impossible. It also creates overpasses by the passer arriving late, a shank, or an ace! It can also force a middle hitter to pass, taking her out of the offensive play.

All kids aspire to be jump servers. A jump serve can also be a great tool to practice one's approach. Any trained attack along the net can be used as a jump serve, including any tempo set or back slide attack. The back line now becomes the center line and resembles a jumping topspin serve with a few differences. The self toss must be high enough for the timing and tempo required by the approach. The server uses one or two hands to toss the ball up high and in front of her body. The toss can have spin or no spin. The toss must help the server to plant and take off behind the back line. The ball has to be tossed in line with the approach and hitting arm. Once again, a consistent toss is critical and must be trained. After the toss, the server uses her approach to chase the ball down. The server must lift and draw up her hitting arm quickly on takeoff. The server must jump under the toss and take off behind the end line. The swing, contact, and follow-through now resemble the topspin serve. The server may land in the court but must be ready to move to her defensive position.

Serving drills for grassroots teams should begin with half court serving. Once a coach sees good mechanics and success in serving from 15 feet over the net, the servers can slowly take steps back. Once the stance is consistent, the coach concentrates on the server generating more power by using a faster backswing. Solid contact and follow-through are essential. The thrill of serving over the net is motivating. Soon the coach will have to develop fun drills with scoring and target areas marked creatively for the age level on the other court.

SERVING DRILLS

Jess' Serving Drill

Purpose: To work on serving under pressure, serving when tired, gaining composure and serving, and endurance

Equipment: Regulation court, two buckets of balls, two cones

Procedure: Buckets of balls are located in two opposite corners of the court. A cone is placed in the other two vacant corners of the court. Players serve a ball over the net and proceed to run outside the court lines to the other end line of the court to serve again (see figure 8.13). Each player must serve 15 balls *in* in 3 minutes by continually running around the court to the opposite end line to serve. Each player must shag any ball to serve. At the end of 3 minutes, if a player has not achieved

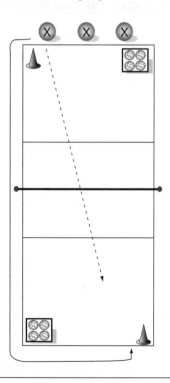

Figure 8.13 Jess' serving drill.

15 serves *in*, she must repeat the drill by serving 8 balls *in* in 90 seconds. The players who achieved the first goal should hand balls to the players who have to run the drill again.

Key point: The players should stop and serve . . . not serve on the run.

Variations: Vary the time for grassroots teams. Challenge higher level teams by making them achieve a jump serve on the final serve. Challenge teams by limiting the area they can serve into on the court.

Fisher Serving Drill

Purpose: To work on serving, serving under pressure, and serving away from a player to an open court spot

Equipment: Regulation court setup, one ball per player

Procedure: Every member of the team stands behind the same end line with a ball in hand. Each player serves one at a time. The server goes where her serve lands on the opposite court and lies down on the court facing the remaining servers. The next server must wait until the server before is on the floor, so players must sprint to their floor position. If a server misses a serve (out of bounds) or hits a person on the floor, everyone returns and the game starts over. The goal is to get everyone on the floor without serving out or hitting someone.

Key point: Use regulation serving rules.

Variations: The coach can assign a consequence for serving out or hitting a player. This drill can be timed, or the number of serves can be used as a scoring method.

Serve and Dig

Purpose: To work on serving, court movement, and digging a tip

Equipment: Regulation court setup, two buckets of balls

Procedure: A server serves to the opposite court and proceeds to her base one position. A coach on the opposite side of the court tips a ball (simulating a setter dump or overpass) for the same player to dig to target (see figure 8.14).

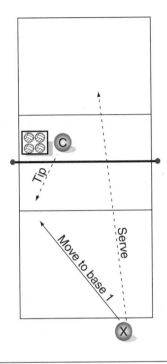

Figure 8.14 Serve and dig drill.

Key points: The server must focus on her serve before moving to her defensive base. This should help the server focus on the next play instead of admiring her serve.

Variations

- This can be done on both sides of the net. The coach can stand on the same side of the net as the server. The coach can tip a ball to the incoming player.
- A "live" setter can position in the target area on the opposite side of the server. When the serve hits the floor on the opposite court, the coach can toss a ball to the setter to dump over the net for the server to play at her base one position.
- The coach can assign court areas for the server to serve into.

Sitting Bulls

Purpose: To practice serving

Equipment: Regulation court setup, bucket of balls

Procedure: Split the team in half. One half serves and the other half are "sitting bulls." The bulls find a spot on the court, at least an arm's length from any sideline, end line, or attack line. No more than three players can be between the attack line and center line. Each server gets three serves (not in a row) to hit a bull. Each hit is a point. Once the team on one half of the court is done serving, their score is recorded, and the team on the other half performs the drill. The team with the most points wins the drill.

Key point: The coach should make sure the server is performing the serve technically correct.

Variations: The coach can assign different areas behind the end line for the server to use when serving. The drill can be best two of three games. Each team can have two serving opportunities.

FOREARM PASSING

Forearm passing is one of the most unusual techniques in all of sports. Volleyball players have to develop an eye–forearm coordination. Many young players struggle with this because they are used to using eye–hand coordination in sports. It is also unusual because it is a rebound skill instead of a catching, throwing, or striking skill as other sports use.

The forearm pass is one of the most important skills in the game. Until recently, all serves had to be received using this skill. Overhead passing is allowed in the game now, but it is risky on a hard serve, because sometimes the officials inconsistently call a held ball. If a team cannot use a forearm pass to receive serve, they can't initiate their offense to side out. It is probably the skill most often taught first and trained the most by effective coaches. Players think it is boring to practice forearm passing unless the coach is creative!

Forearm passing is used for free and down ball passing, serve receive, setting, third ball contacts that cannot be attacked, and floor defensive plays including digging, run-through, J-strokes, emergency techniques, and tip passing. Each use has to be trained separately because each use has different precontact situations, flight velocities and trajectories, court locations, and outcome goals.

Free Ball Passing

A common use of a forearm pass is for passing free balls. A free ball is a ball that an opponent returns easily over the net. It can be a return using a forearm or overhead pass in a nonaggressive manner. A free ball's return usually allows a team a quality first contact to initiate offense. When possible, a passer should use the overhead pass because it is more accurate. If a player does not have good overhead passing skills, she should stick with the forearm pass. It is becoming more acceptable for the first contact to be an overhead pass, especially in junior club and college ball. Many middle and high school players are deterred from using the overhead pass because of the almighty whistle! Remember that it is okay to double contact the first contact.

Most coaches teach forearm passing from a free ball first. It is less threatening to pass a ball from a toss than from a serve because of the slower speed and shorter distance.

One of the most popular coaching clichés in passing is "your feet pass the ball." This could excite a soccer player! The actual meaning of this statement is that the passer must get to the ball before the ball gets to the intended spot of contact. Not only does the player have to get to the spot first—she must be stopped and ready to ensure a successful pass.

A player needs to be in an intermediate ready position (as in figure 8.3 on page 85) assessing how and where the ball is coming on the court. The passer faces the ball with the feet slightly wider than the shoulders and the right foot forward. The weight is balanced on the inside of the balls of the feet and big toe but ready to push off and move quickly. The back is leaning forward. The arms hang down with the hands extended in front and over the thighs. The shoulders are shrugged forward of the bent knees, and the knees are in front of the feet. The passer moves to establish early floor position, usually using shuffle steps in the direction of the movement. If she has to move forward, she takes her steps and jumps into a balanced position (see figure 8.15). If she has to move backward, she uses a drop step, crossover, and jump into a balanced position. Ideally, the ball is kept at the midline of the body. Once floor position is established, the platform is formed by shrugging the shoulders forward, placing the heels of the hands together, and pointing the thumbs down to create a flat platform. The fingers of one hand are placed naturally on top of the others.

The platform is angled to the target. The ball is contacted below the waist. The higher the level of play, the flatter the pass used to expedite the offense. This is created by permitting the ball to drop in a lower zone allowing the platform to contact more behind the ball instead of under the ball for height. If the ball is outside the midline of the body, the passer will have to drop the inside shoulder downward to angle the platform to the target. If the ball is more forward, the platform becomes more parallel to the floor so the ball rebounds up and is contained in the court. If the ball needs some force to help direct it to target, a forward push by transferring weight to the front foot and a forward shrug of the shoulders will add some power on the pass on follow-through.

Novice passers usually learn from a slightly higher ready position (figure 8.2 on page 84). Movement is the same, but beginner passers usually need to pass the ball higher to give the next teammate ample time to get under the ball. To create a higher pass, the beginner passer presents her platform, still angled to the target, just below the waist at a medium zone. The arms are at about 60 degrees to create the proper rebounding angle. The teaching method that young passers have most difficulty learning is maintaining the angle of the platform and not swinging or lifting their arms up. Swinging arms creates more speed on the pass causing overpasses. Lifting arms changes the rebound angle and causes the ball to go straight up or sometimes behind the passer. Once a novice passer has learned to let the ball contact her platform, she can learn to feel if the ball needs more impetus. This can be accomplished by transferring weight from the back foot to the front foot on follow-through.

A player should keep her arms out in front and be ready to make the decision of whether to forearm or overhead pass the ball. The height and speed of the trajectory are the deciding factors in positioning the body away from the ball for a forearm pass or under the ball for an overhead pass. John Wilson, who coached at Duke and Rice, often used this phrase at camp: "Keep your arms available." The arms are out in front, and the elbows are above the thighs and slightly bent, to maintain balance and to execute either passing skill.

This whole scenario must be trained and become second nature for players. I used to take offense when people said, "Your kids look like passing machines." I thought they meant it didn't look like fun. If a player can get into the proper passing posture and position before the ball is played, she has a better chance to create a quality first contact.

PASSING DRILLS

Wilson Passing Drill

Purpose: To work on passing, court movement, support, and communication

Equipment: Regulation court setup, bucket of balls

Procedure: Three players start in the 1, 6, and 5 positions. Two players are out of bounds behind the end line ready to enter the drill. One player acts as a target. The coach pops a ball over the net, and one of the three backcourt players passes the ball to the target. That player leaves the court, and the next player runs in and takes her place (see figure 8.16). The coach continues popping balls over the net as soon as the target touches the pass. The player who passed the last ball always exits the drill, and the next player always enters the drill and takes her place.

Key points: The coach should encourage constant movement, support from teammates, and maintaining proper posture. When the players exit the drill, they use a drop step, crossover, and run movement, keeping their eyes on the ball.

Variations: Players can forearm pass or overhead pass. The pass can be scored 3, 2, 1, 0 for a goal score to end the drill. The coach can hit down balls. The target can set the ball.

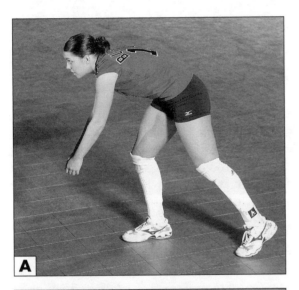

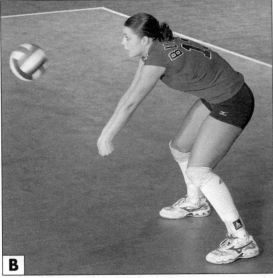

Figure 8.15 Free ball passing.

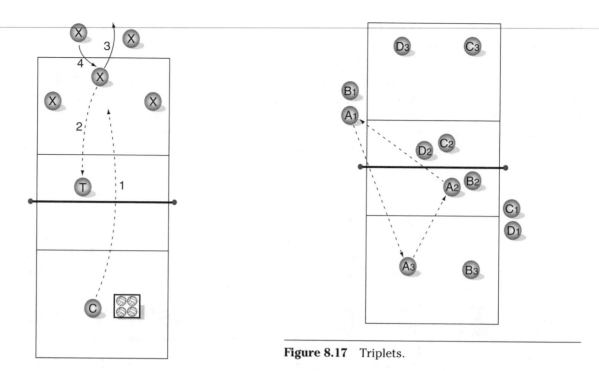

Figure 8.16 Wilson passing drill.

Triplets

Purpose: To practice passing

Equipment: Regulation court setup, eight balls per court

Procedure: Four teams of three players are formed. Each team (triplet) works together independently of the others. Team A has two players on one side of the net—one player in position 5 (passer) and one player in the target area (see figure 8.17). Team A's other player is on the other side of the net out of bounds near the 2 area (tosser). The tosser and target start with a ball in hand. The tosser pops a ball over the net to the passer. The passer passes the ball to the target. As soon as the tosser pops the ball over the net, the target bounces her ball to the tosser. This keeps two balls moving at the same time. The rule for the tosser to remember is she can't pop a ball over the net unless the target has a ball in her hand (the target may have to shag an errant pass).

Figure 8.17 Triplets.

Team B is set up similar to team A except their passer is at 1, their target is behind team A's target, and their tosser is just behind team A's tosser. Team C sets up on the opposite side of the court similar to team A. Team D sets up on the opposite side of the court similar to team B.

When this drill is running, there are four passers and 8 balls in motion. After 2 1/2 minutes, team A and team B switch places (do-si-do) and team C and team D switch places (do-si-do) so the passers can pass different angles. After the next 2 1/2 minutes, the players within their own teams rotate—passer becomes target, target becomes tosser, and tosser becomes the passer. After 5 minutes, each girl has passed 100 balls. The entire drill takes 15 minutes to complete. The coach can surround the court and help the four passers.

Key points: Targets should stay in the setter/target area for the offense the team runs. Passers must call out "mine." Passers should return to ready position in between passes.

Variations: Overhead or forearm passes may be used. Targets can count the number of passes they receive in the time limit.

7 Up

Purpose: To work on pass, set, hit; to work on communication and achieving goals

Equipment: Regulation court setup, bucket of balls

Procedure: Divide the team into two groups. Team A starts out of bounds in a straight line behind the 6 area. Team B and the coach (with a bucket of balls) are on the other court running the drill. The coach sets a goal for the drill (e.g., must pass, set, and hit an outside hitter attack). The coach pops a ball over the net. The first three players on team A run onto the court and attempt to achieve the goal (see figure 8.18). If the first three players achieve the goal, they run to the end of team A's line. The coach pops another ball over the net, and the next three players in the line attempt to achieve the same goal. The drill continues until a trio fails to achieve the goal or the team achieves seven in a row. If team A fails to achieve seven in a row, they run under the net to become the working team. At the same time, team B runs under the net and forms a line behind the end line at the 6 area. The coach now repeats the same goal for team B. The competition is to see which team can achieve seven in a row first. Once a team wins, a new goal is set by the coach.

Key points: The first player who runs out from the end line should run to the target area to set. The second player out should pass the ball. The coach should include communication in the drill (e.g., the player who handles the first contact must say "mine").

Variations: The coach can develop endless goals and change the scoring method to number of successful repetitions. This drill can be used by grassroots and the highest level teams by adjusting the goals.

Queen of the Throne

Purpose: To work on passing to target and communication

Equipment: Regulation court setup, bucket of balls, chair (throne)

Procedure: The coach stands on court A with a bucket of balls. Three players split the backcourt on court B. A chair (throne) is placed at the target area on court B. A fourth player sits in the throne and is the queen. The coach pops a ball over the net from court A. One of the players passes the ball to the queen on her throne. The queen attempts to catch the ball but must remain seated with her back on the chair when she catches the ball. If she is able to catch the ball, the passer becomes the queen, and the queen runs to the end of the court to get in line to pass. If the queen cannot catch the ball, she remains on her throne. If the passer does not pass to the queen, she must shag her errant pass, hand it to the coach, and run back in line to pass again.

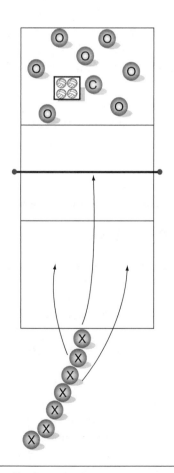

Figure 8.18   7 up.

Key points: This drill is fun for younger teams. The coach has an opportunity to coach posture, movement, and technique. Two players should move to the ball. One player should call "mine" while the other players support her on the court.

Variations

- The coach can pop down balls.
- The drill can be done with two players.
- The drill can be done on both sides of the court if the coach or player pops the ball over the net from out of bounds.
- This can be a serve receive drill. The queen is allowed to take her back off the chair but must stay seated to count a good serve receive pass.
- This can be a two-team drill with one team passing and one team shagging.

Pass and Swing

Purpose: To work on passing and transitioning to attack

Equipment: Regulation court setup, bucket of balls

Procedure: A coach starts on court A with a bucket of balls. On court B, a setter is at target. Another player is positioned at 4 ready to pass. The coach pops a ball over the net to court B for the 4 player to pass to the setter. Once she receives the ball, the setter sets an outside set. After passing, the 4 player swings outside a cone placed at the sideline and 10-foot line and hits the outside set (see figure 8.19).

Key point: The passer must focus on passing first before transitioning to attack the set.

Variations

- A back row player can be added to create decision making and support within the drill. The setter could set the back row player if the front row player passes and vice versa.
- Another front row player can be added to pass and swing to a different area

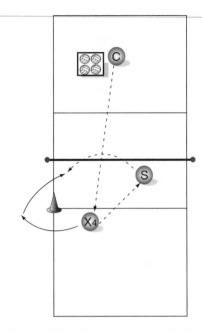

Figure 8.19 Pass and swing.

on the court. The setter could set the passer or set away from the pass.

- For a higher level team, two passers could be used. The player who does NOT pass the ball runs a first tempo attack, and the passer runs a second or third tempo set.
- A blocker or blockers can be added.
- The coach can send down balls over the net.
- This can be a serve receive drill.

Serve Receive

The primary function of the forearm pass is serve reception, although with rule changes the overhead pass is becoming popular for better control and to quicken play. For success, serve receive first has to be individually taught and then integrated into team serve receive training.

Some main differences between free ball passing and serve receive are the distance and speed on the incoming ball. A serve receiver needs to let the ball rebound from her platform and, if needed, put more impetus on the ball. Serve receiving a powerful serve such as a jump serve may even require cushioning some force off the ball. This can be done by shrugging the shoulders forward, allowing the arms to relax to absorb some heat off the ball. A free ball usually needs forward motion to add push on the ball so it reaches the intended target. A serve is traveling 30 feet just to get to the net. Obviously, a higher serve may require some forward motion to add force on the pass.

Ready Position

The ready position for serve receive is similar to that of the free ball ready position, as shown in figure 8.20 for novice players and figure 8.3 (page 85) for flatter passes.

Figure 8.20 Serve receive ready position.

Premovement

Premovement is extremely important in serve receive. The primary passers should focus on the server, reading what cues she may offer, including the direction her front foot is pointing during serving and her hand's contact on the ball. The servers should make a quick adjustment to these cues and it will put them in motion. Nothing is sweeter than watching two, three, four, or five receivers make a premovement to the ball in unison. As they read the flight of the ball, they continue their move-

ment quest to their intended floor position. The goal is to be stopped by the time the ball reaches the net. This still gives them time to make a quick adjustment if needed, making sure the ball is at midline. More importantly, it allows them time to angle their platform before the ball arrives.

Serve receive movement is usually accomplished in one of three ways: (1) using a side or diagonal shuffle step, (2) using a forward step and quick jump into a balanced base, or (3) using a back slide step. To move backward, it's best to use a drop crossover step, but time rarely permits it. Some very successful athletic serve receivers move backward, as the ball comes at them, by shuffling back but maintaining forward lean and shrugged shoulders. No matter what movement the serve receiver uses, the basic principle of beating the ball is important. The goal is to position the ball in the body's midline and present a stable platform angled toward the target. Otherwise, the receiver has to adjust her platform by dropping her inside shoulder, creating a shield to stop the ball from passing her. The bottom wrist is turned toward the target and the top arm forms the shield. The shield platform must be presented in front of the body line or between the body and target to contain the ball on the court. Otherwise, the ball will bing off the arms and off the court.

The side step is the most common movement in serve receive (see figure 8.21). It is commonly used because most movement is done laterally to get behind the ball. The term *side step* sounds like it is only done to the side. For that reason, some people call this movement a *slide*. A side step can be performed laterally (sideways), and it can also be performed backward or forward. To go backward, a player has to perform a drop step, and then she can sidestep backward. To go forward or diagonally forward, a player has to take a step forward and then sidestep in the intended direction.

Another common movement is to take a step or two forward and then jump into a balanced stance. This is used when a passer has to move forward to get to the ball. It is very important

Figure 8.21 Side step.

that the passer ends up in a stopped and balanced position before the ball arrives.

The third movement is a drop step or back side step. This is used when the passer has to move backward because the ball is coming at her too high. Of course, the other option is to overhead serve receive. But if the velocity of the ball is too fast or there is a spin on the ball, it would be a risky method to employ. It would be risky because the speed of the serve or the spin on the ball could force a passer's wrists to "give" backward. This would be construed as an illegal contact because of the amount of time the ball rests on the passer's fingers. Therefore, a back side step is used to move backward. Time is of the essence. It is difficult to move backward and stop in a balanced position to pass. The passer drops her foot back, preferably her left foot because it is already slightly behind the right foot. She could then sidestep easily backward (see figure 8.22). Her position is similar to a left-handed hitter up to bat, with her right shoulder forward to the net. It is very important for her to get back square to the net, facing the incoming ball. She must also have her arms out ready with her platform facing the target.

With each movement, the serve receiver must use her second to last step as her breaking step so her last step balances her stance. Balance is key in passing. Quick feet (agility),

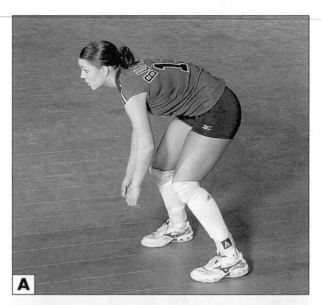

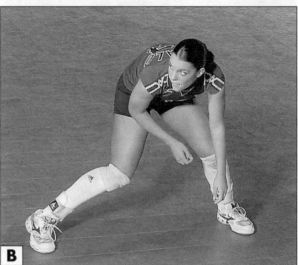

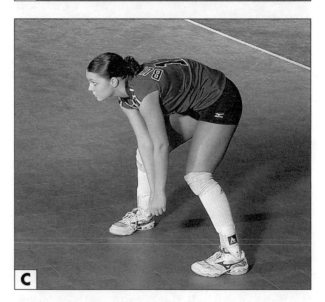

Figure 8.22 Drop step.

balance, and reading and adjusting to the ball are key to staying in focus and beating the ball to the spot. As stated earlier, if players think the next ball is coming to them, they will be ready.

Precontact Position

When the receiver can, she should always make a third and final, small, quick adjustment to the pass. This is similar to a shadowboxing move and also similar to the premovement just described. This time it is a fine-tuning movement to be in the perfect place to have a perfect pass.

Just before contact, the passer will usually spread her feet wider. The passer's arms are hanging down straight, and her thumbs are pushed down to ensure a flat platform (see figure 8.23). The passer is still facing the ball ready to put her arms together, so her platform is angling toward the intended target. Her arms are also out at an appropriate angle to allow the ball to rebound off her platform to the target instead of over the net or above her own head. This is the angle of deflection—the angle needed for her platform to rebound and direct the ball.

Lastly, the passer puts the heels of her hands together and places her fingers on top of her other fingers. Again, it is important that the thumbs are pointed down through this movement. If the passer is not behind the ball and she has to reach to a side to play the ball, she must make sure that her inside shoulder drops in proportion to the angle of deflection to the target. Her inside knee should turn in a bit more, too.

Contact

Players need to contact the ball below their waists (see figure 8.24). The ball should be deflected off outreached forearms. The player should contact the ball as far away from her body as she can comfortably reach. The angle of the arms should remain constant to deflect the ball to the target. If force is needed to propel the ball off the arms, usually the back foot is used to give the ball more thrust. Some players maintain a constant angle of their arms and push forward with their shoulders and their back foot. This will usually push the ball faster and lower to the target, as long as the passer doesn't lower her hips or raise her shoulders or head. If the velocity of the oncoming ball is extremely fast, the passer may have to take some "heat" off the ball by absorbing or cushioning at contact similar to digging a hard driven spike.

Figure 8.23 Precontact position for serve receive.

Figure 8.24 Contact.

At the high school level, many players have to receive a topspin serve. If a receiver is moving forward but is arriving late, she may have to lift her thumbs at contact to prevent the ball from careening straight ahead under the net. This is similar to the J-stroke used when digging tips or arriving late to digs. This will contain the ball on the player's side of the court. The downside is that it will usually create a backspin on the ball that makes it difficult for the setter to handle. Another technique used to play a ball close to the net is for the passer to jump low in a squat and present a platform parallel with the floor. This will create a platform where the ball will rebound straight up with no spin. The passer must use her legs for power, to maintain her platform.

A passer must pass cleanly. This requires her to maintain the integrity of her platform by not changing the angles of her body. Changing body angles will change the angle of the platform.

Follow-Through

Every movement should have a follow-through. In serve receiving, it is often necessary to maintain the same angle of the platform until the ball is on its way off the arms to the target. The passer must maintain her position until she is sure the ball is passed. Only then should she start her next movement in the intended sequence of the play. The following are tips for serve receive follow-through.

- Posture and arms stay true.
- Put platform behind the ball.
- Swing to get ball to target after push.
- Only swing to get impetus on ball.
- Only time you change posture is if you are unable to "mold" or feel the pass.

Common Serve Receive Errors

While coaching different levels from grassroots to college, I have studied serve receive errors. These tend to be related to one of three major problems. One is poor trajectory reading, another is lack of focus, and the last is poor movement.

The most difficult to correct is lack of trajectory reading or tracking. If a girl has been raised only playing with Barbie Dolls throughout her formative years, she probably lacks it. But a girl who has played softball, thrown Frisbees, or played touch football probably has good ball flight recognition. This is important because the serve receiver has to read the flight of the ball as it is served. If she can envision herself as a wide receiver, she will be able to get to the ball. But remember our goal is to have her there *before* the ball arrives. Again, she has to beat the ball. So she must move faster than the velocity of the ball and get herself set and balanced to pass.

The next problem is focus. A player has to have a set routine of being in ready position before the whistle. She then needs to visually study the server, reading clues the server will give her. One important clue is the server's lead foot. Where she steps is normally the direction the serve will go unless it is a mis-hit or she puts a spin on the ball. The other clue to watch, of course, is the hand contact and follow-through. This is especially true of intermediate servers who have not learned to put the ball in specific places on the court. Many young servers are happy to keep it inside the antennas and on the court! Another important fact to know is if she has a consistent serve placement.

The last problem is movement. Receivers with little formal coaching or background in the sport often use incorrect movement to the ball. Some even use the no-movement-to-the-ball-and-reach method, too. Those passes usually end up in the bleachers knocking off someone's glasses. Following are some of the most frequently used poor movement methods:

- Taking a step forward with the front foot to pass a ball. This is a poor foundation and resembles a lunge, balance beam, or skateboard base. The passer is off balance, and the pass generally is an overpass that causes the opposing blocker to lick her lips.
- Taking one step sideways to the ball with the foot closest to the ball. This overbalances the passer so she can't adjust.

- Running forward to the ball with the arms low. This usually ends up with the ball being passed into the net and the stomach of an opposing blocker.
- Backpedaling and taking a ball in the chest . . . a double hit no matter what!

Despite all of these variables, if girls can track a ball, focus, and have good premovement, they have a much better chance to become a good serve receiver. Another important factor is to make sure her body is facing the incoming ball.

Wasted movement errors are also common. Here are some of these:

- Putting fingers on top of fingers first. This often causes a passer to bend her arms at the elbows or "pray." This is one of the toughest bad habits for intermediates to break. Also, some players "pray" as a method of trying to move their body backward. They end up backpedaling, which is inefficient and unbalanced movement.
- Not pushing the thumbs down. This can result in a wrist snap as the ball is being played. This adds to the impetus put on the ball and sometimes causes overpasses or passes that are too high.
- Putting the hands together at the shoulder level and then dropping the hands below the waist. It looks like a butterfly stroke. Many players learn this from free ball passing where they usually have time to drop their platforms before the ball arrives. It is another wasted movement that can be risky when the velocity of the ball increases; if the passer is not ready, she takes a ball in the front of the elbows.
- Putting her hands together at the midline of her body but realizing late that the ball is on her side. She then swings her platform outside her body without dropping her inside shoulder to contain the ball on the court. The ball ricochets into the back wall or knocks over the linesman!
- Not keeping her arms out in front of her. Many young players do this. They should be taught that their arms are like measuring sticks. Keeping their arms out in front helps them know how far they need to travel to get

to the ball and maintain an arm's distance away from the ball. It also provides some direction because it gives the illusion that they are closer to the ball.

- Swinging the arms too high or too fast while passing.
- Changing body angles. This includes squatting, pushing the hips forward, straightening the back, straightening the knees, lifting the head, or raising the shoulders. All of these changes will change the angle of the platform.

Tips for Teaching Beginners Serve Receive

The forearm pass is a tough skill to teach children. The skill usually hurts the arms of young players because they have a tendency to swing too fast at the ball. Here are some tips for teaching young players this skill:

- Use a light volleyball, beach ball, or large balloon (no helium).
- Have them wear long sleeves in the beginning.
- If a player is swinging too fast, tell her to "bunt" the ball instead of trying to hit a home run.
- Keep in mind that most young players have difficulty serve receiving because of poor trajectory tracking. They usually reach or fall forward because the ball beats them to the expected point of contact.
- Add movement requirements to teach serve receiving early in instruction. Don't toss all balls at them. Tossing balls at them will result in their thinking that the ball has radar so they don't have to move.
- Add another passer to help develop communication and decision making early in the learning process. How many times have we coaches heard, "Whose ball was that?" after the ball has hit the floor between two mute passers?
- Many new players reach up to pass a ball. Keep demonstrating the low contact point of the ball. It takes patience to let gravity do its job. I have found the

use of "start here" and "finish here" good visual cues in a demonstration.

- Make sure their ready position is proper. If they don't start right, they won't finish right.

- Make sure they practice receiving the kind of serve they will be passing. It may be macho to jump serve some balls to a sixth grade team, but few opponents will actually serve them in a game.

- Start with drills that have a higher arc and slower velocity. As movement and passing improve, lower the serve arc and quicken the velocity.

- Make sure their arms are out. David Beiter, our modified coach, tells his players to pretend they are carrying their school lunch tray to help keep their arms out in front of them...don't spill the spaghetti! If the novice passer's arms are out in front, the ball will rebound higher. It also gives the younger player a "measuring" stick to determine how far the body has to be away from the ball to acquire eye–forearm distance.

- Make sure they understand that the faster the speed of the serve, the less impetus they have to give the ball. Many times in fear or in self-defense, young serve receivers will swing fast to receive a hard driven serve. They will often reach up at a tough serve to shield the incoming blast from their bodies.

- Teach the forearm pass as just that . . . a pass. Young players like to call the forearm pass a *bump*. It is a cute name but does not describe that the action has a purpose. In our middle school, we had the young players call it a *forearm pass* or a *bump pass*. A player who uses a forearm pass to put the ball over the net is really using an *emergency skill*.

A Purpose for Everything

One of my favorite stories is of an opposing coach who finally decided she had discovered the secret to my success. She said she knew that I coached my own "farm team" in the middle school. So the next year . . . sure enough . . . she was coaching her middle school's volleyball team, too. Her team kept passing the ball over the net to us on the first contact. However, our team would receive her kids' free ball and convert it to a pass, set, swing attack. It wasn't always a devastating attack, but we were playing real volleyball. After the match, she came up to me and said, "How do you get your kids to pass to your setter? I have had enough trouble teaching my kids to just pass it over the net." So, you can see, you need to play the game and use the skills the way they were intended. A forearm pass is just that . . . a pass to a teammate.

Tactical Tips

- When players are younger, they should all be given an opportunity to serve receive. As the level increases, primary passers are usually selected to increase the percentage of good passes. Use statistics to identify the best passers. But, all players should still serve receive in practice. The primary passers should drill together in practice so they can become familiar with each other's habits and learn to pass as a unit.

- Depending on the type of offense used, it is beneficial to try to keep the ball passed at the same tempo. An example is if a ball were passed near the back line, the pass would be flatter. The closer the passer is to the net, the higher the pass. We call this *tempo passing*. It helps the running of multiple attacks by keeping the timing consistent.

- If a front row player is required to serve receive, she must pass high enough to give herself sufficient time to run her hitting route. A smart setter will see that this hitter has taken herself out of the offense to play a tough serve. In turn, a smart server will try to take out a great hitter by serving to her.

- At intermediate levels, serve receivers should be cognizant of a back row setter versus a front row setter. A ball passed too tight to the net can cause havoc for an inexperienced back row setter, especially a setter with a low vertical reach.

- If a player has to receive a tough serve, she should worry not only about passing the serve but also containing the ball in her court. It is better to pass the ball safely off the net than to set up the other team's blockers for an overpass kill. Perfect passes are not always going to happen.

SERVE RECEIVE DRILLS

Basic Serve Receive Drill

Purpose: To work on individual serve receive

Equipment: Regulation court, two buckets of balls (one behind each end line)

Procedure: From behind the 1 area, player A serves a ball down the line and over the net to player B. Player B is on the other side of the net receiving in the 5 position. Player B passes the ball to player C, who is at the target area along the net (see figure 8.25). Player D serves a ball from behind the 1 area on the opposite end line. Player D serves down the line and over the net to player F, who is on the other side of the net receiving in the 5 position. Player F passes the ball to player E, who is at the target area along the net.

Key points: Passers must start in proper posture and execute proper premovement, reading the server. Passers must establish a good base with their platform facing the target. Passers must communicate "mine" every time.

Variations

- Players A and D serve from different areas behind the end line.

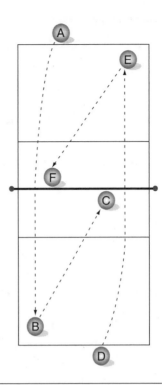

Figure 8.25 Basic serve receive drill.

- Players B and F serve receive from position 6 or 1.
- Vary depth of serve.
- Add another serve receiver behind players A and D and rotate serve receivers every five passes.
- Score the pass to target as a 3, 2, 1, or 0 value.
- Count the number of successful passes within a specific time limit.
- Start with a set number of balls and count the number of balls that go to target (ratio).
- Competition between the two sides.
- Competition between server and passer (e.g., ace = 1 and bad serve = -1, good pass = 1 and shanked serve = -1).
- Use overhead pass to serve receive.
- Have the target become a setter—she runs under the pass and self-sets it to practice movement to a second ball. Or she runs under the pass and sets it outside or back sets it to a target.

Serve Receive, Hit, and Cover

Purpose: To work on serve receive, preparing to attack after serve receive, and coverage court movement

Equipment: Regulation court setup, bucket of balls

Procedure: On one side of the court, player A serves to the opposite court. On the other side of the court, a serve receive team is set up in a two-, three-, or four-person pass system. The setter is at target position along the net on the same side as the passers (see figure 8.26). Players serve receive the ball to the setter. All players on the receiving team communicate and ready to attack. The setter sets against the flow (opposite side the ball was passed from) to a player who attacks the ball. The remaining players cover the hitter in proper court positioning.

Key points: The passer executes proper premovement reading the server's tendencies. The passer establishes a good base with her platform facing the target. Passers communicate "mine" every time. Nonpassers support teammate by communicating direction of serve and location on court (e.g., short, long, out). Nonpassers and passer ready themselves to attack the ball and communicate with the setter about set selection. Nonattackers cover the floor around and behind the attacker in low posture.

Variations

- Setter sets the serve receiver.
- Only back row attacks.
- Setter is front row and allowed to dump or attack.
- Setter penetrates from the back row.
- Setter sets a front row attacker.
- A middle hitter is added to the drill and attacks quick sets.
- Rotate receivers in by removing the player who attacked the ball.
- Rotate receivers in by removing the player who passed the ball.
- Score the drill by awarding different points for running certain plays (e.g., quick attack = 3 points, back row = 1, ball in play = 0, shank = -3).
- Score the drill by awarding different points for directing attacks into various court areas (e.g., 3 points down the line, 1 point crosscourt, and so on).
- Have coverage lightly touch the floor to prove low posture.
- Have coverage return to defensive base with proper posture and court movement.

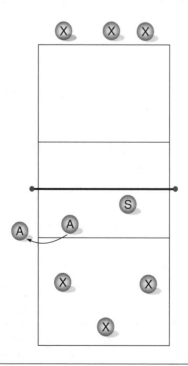

Figure 8.26 Serve receive, hit, and cover.

One-on-One Serve Receive, Set, and Attack

Purpose: To practice individual serve receive, basic skills of set and attack, footwork, and court movement

Equipment: Regulation court setup, two buckets of balls (behind each end line)

Procedure: Two players work together. Player A serves to player B on the opposite court. Player B is allowed three contacts: serve receive, self-set, and attack. Player B changes postures and sets the ball up in front of her attack pattern. Player B approaches her self-set and attacks the ball.

Key points: The passer executes proper premovement reading the server's tendencies. The passer establishes a good base with her platform facing the target. The passer communicates "mine" every time. Player B self-sets the ball in front of herself to allow for an approach.

Variations

- Put up an antenna in the middle of the net and use long half court boundaries to accommodate four players in half court games.
- Play the ball until the rally comes to a natural gamelike conclusion. Award a point for winning the rally. Rally winner gets to serve next.
- Play continuous singles awarding a point for winning a rally. Winner stays on court, and a new challenger serves to dethrone the winner.

Multiperson Serve Receive Drill

Purpose: To work on decision making when serve receiving, balancing the court, court movement, and support between serve receive system

Equipment: Regulation court setup, two buckets of balls

Procedure: Same procedure as basic serve receive drill but a player is added to each side so there are two serve receivers on each court. Receivers split the court to cover assigned areas.

Key points: The passer starts in proper serve receive posture, executes proper premovement reading the server's tendencies, and establishes a good base with her platform facing the target. The passer communicates "mine" every time. The nonpasser supports

her teammate by communicating direction of serve and location on court (e.g., short, long, out).

Variations

- Vary depth of serve.
- Have the passer change positions with other receiver to change the angle of pass to target.
- Add another serve receiver behind players A and D and rotate serve receivers every five passes.
- Score the pass to target as a 3, 2, 1, or 0 value.
- Count the number of successful passes within a specific time limit.
- Start with a set number of balls and count the number of balls that go to target (ratio).
- Competition between the two sides.
- Competition between server and passer (e.g., ace = 1 and bad serve = -1, good pass = 1 and shanked serve = -1).
- Use overhead pass to serve receive.
- Add a third, fourth, or fifth passer.
- Create movement in the drill by removing the player who just passed the ball and replacing her with a player waiting out of bounds.
- Have the target become a setter—she runs under the pass and self-sets it to practice movement to a second ball. Or she runs under the pass and sets it outside or back sets it to a target.

OVERHEAD PASSING

Overhead passing is used most commonly for setting. It is also a skill used to pass the ball to the setter as the first contact. This would include an overhead pass from a serve receive, a dig, a free or down ball, or a tipped ball. It is also used as an offensive weapon to attack an opponent's open or weak area on the court.

Setting is only one of the functions of an overhead pass, but most people use the words synonymously. For years the overhead pass was a basic technique to play the first ball. When the open hand underhand pass was banned from modern power volleyball, the overhead pass lost its luster. The forearm pass was instituted. Currently, volleyball organizations are trying to promote longer rallies, so overhead passing is becoming popular again as a first contact. It is allowed as a method of serve receive and digging. Double contacts are not called on the first contact, which allows more latitude to the old adage that only the pure setter could use her hands without being called by an official.

Every player on a team needs to know how to overhead pass and set. Even if a passer feels more comfortable using forearm passing, there will be times in a game that require her to overhead pass or set an attacker on a "help" call from the designated setter.

Movement to the Ball

The ready position for overhead passing is similar to that of the forearm pass. Training players to be ready to forearm or overhead pass with a similar ready position will cut down on training methods. The main difference occurs in the movement to the ball. For the forearm pass, the body stays in a lower intermediate posture and stays an arm's length away from the ball.

For the overhead pass, the body stays in a higher intermediate posture, and the passer's feet must move *under* the ball . . . like a soccer player getting ready to head the ball. The passer should be in a stable stance (with feet staggered), ready to take the ball above her forehead. There is one other main difference in the precontact positions for the two kinds of passing. In the forearm pass, the passer faces the ball, but for the overhead pass, the passer faces the target. In the overhead pass, the passer forms a ball shape with her hands, and her hands are raised above the hairline. A window or triangle is formed by the relationship between the thumbs and pointer fingers. The elbows are bent at the correct angle if, when the hands are drawn together to touch, both thumbs and pointer fingers touch at the same time. The wrists are cocked back, simi-

lar to chugging back a pitcher of soda pop, to receive the ball with the fingers and still be able to spring-load (absorb some of the ball). The passer uses all her fingers. The pointer and middle fingers absorb more of the shock. Actually, the "fingerprints" are the contact point while using the outside edge of the fingerprints for spring. The thumbs add control and stop the ball from falling through the window! Be sure the thumbs are not spread too wide from the fingers or the ball will fall through. The thumb pads are facing each other with the tips pointing toward the eyes. The hands are strong and the fingers are comfortably spread. The pointer and middle fingers are used for direction, and the ring and pinkie fingers help control the ball. The correct hand, wrist, elbow, and arm position are the same as those used to catch a ball above the forehead.

Contact and Follow-Through

As the ball drops into the waiting hands of an overhead passer, the arms and hands move forward through the ball. As the fingers handle the ball, both the fingers and wrists absorb some of the weight of the dropping ball. The rebound effect from the fingers and wrists occurs simultaneously with the extension of the elbows through the ball. The finish or follow-through is an arm extension with the palms pushing toward the ceiling. It is similar to the "raise the roof" gesture commonly used today. John Kessel uses the cue "fly like superman." See figure 8.27 for the overhead pass sequence.

The legs can extend through the ball simultaneously with the arm extension. Young players need to use their legs to add power. As a player becomes stronger, she can tap more strength from her arms, which will help her sets become more consistent because she is using fewer levers for power.

The ability to set from a consistent point of release is important for a young setter to develop so she can become steadfast in delivery. Consistent point of release demands efficient movement to the ball. Once a setter has developed this skill, most of her training to acquire other types of sets will be centered on her follow-through. As a setter becomes

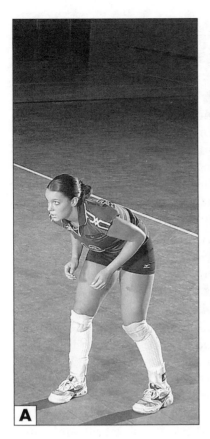

Figure 8.27 Overhead pass *(a)* start, *(b)* movement to the ball and contact, and *(c)* follow-through.

stronger, she can use firmer wrists and a higher point of release to quicken the play.

Tips for Teaching Beginners Overhead Passing

Teaching young players how to set can be a challenge. Once again, using the correct ball is crucial. When my son was a toddler, we started with large round balloons. This was ideal because it gave him plenty of time to move under the balloon. There was no fear of a ball falling on his face. We also put up a streamer in our family room to act as the net. I kept the streamer high so he had to follow through high to get the balloon over the streamer net. As soon as he could "bump pass" and set, we changed the rules and allowed three hits on a side. We played this game for years. Even with overhead serving, spiking, and digging, we had the extra time to play the ball. The balloon rebounding off lamps and chairs was, of course, legal! By the time my son was ready for preschool, he was in the back row of my practices digging real volleyballs.

Many kids overhead pass by extending their elbows too soon. This leaves them with no power to put on the ball except to slap the back of it with their hands, and practice begins to resemble gym class volleyball. This usually occurs because the kids fear allowing the ball to drop close to their faces. So, developing the skill requires overcoming the fear factor.

• Start with the appropriate ball. Rookie players can start with balloons, Nerf balls, and "volleylites." New players, even adults, have the fear factor of the ball falling on their faces.

• Start with a two-hand catch and throw. The catch will automatically put the hands around the ball successfully. The throw should be directed up to the ceiling so a high follow-through is taught. The wrists should not flex forward on the follow-through. As the player's movements and positioning improve, direct the player to hold the catch for a shorter amount of time.

• Demonstrate a bounce and set. Toss the ball high so the rebound from the floor is high enough to run under. Have the player move under the bounced ball, set, and follow through (toward the lights) so that the ball will bounce high enough to repeat the drill. Assign a goal to this drill. The goal could be a number of successful sets in a row or in the amount of time allowed. Make sure the player starts over if she gets out of control or handles a ball illegally. This is good for movement under the ball, for contact, for follow-through, and for tracking the ball. It is not very gamelike, but there is little fear factor. The rebound from the floor causes the ball to be only 3 to 5 feet above a player's head. This causes less fear than handling a ball tossed 10 to 20 feet above the player's head. This drill can be used as an individual warm-up that challenges the player. It is also fun to add a partner. The players alternate contacts. The rule is a player MUST overhead set the ball because kids will become lazy and forearm pass a low bounce. It can be challenging because the kids need to drop to knees or butts to set a ball. It also tests their limitations.

• Use wall volleys to practice proper hand contact and proper wrist action. The player should be about three feet away from a wall and should volley the ball against the wall just above her head. She needs to make quick adjustments with her feet so she can keep a consistent *point of release*. Make sure she does not take just one step to the ball, but rather at least a two-step adjustment to keep herself balanced. The real key in this warm-up is to make sure her hand and wrist positions are correct and her follow-through has no wrist extension.

• Start tossing balls over the head of the player. Toss it high enough that she can get under it but not high enough to create fear. Make sure the passer adjusts her feet first to achieve positioning for consistent point of release. If she doesn't start right, she won't finish right. As she becomes more successful at handling higher tosses, have her start redirecting the ball to a target (instead of a straight-ahead target). Remember to make sure she now adjusts her feet to face the target and NOT the ball. This will be a major step in teaching her how to overhead pass correctly. The point of contact is the same; the body will just be positioned at a different receiving angle.

• Remember that young players need to use their legs more because they need added power. Make sure the elbow and knee extension occurs simultaneously. Discourage players from arching or lunging as they set. It is fine to follow through and end on the balls of the feet, but arching or lunging will produce uncontrolled power.

• To teach correct setting positioning, have four players form a square on one side of the court. Start with a toss and set counterclockwise. This will teach a player to receive the ball over her left shoulder, face her target to the right, and follow through. Common pitfalls are facing the ball and twisting to the target or facing halfway between the ball and the intended target with a side set. Again, make sure the feet are facing the target and the player is adjusting to the toss sideways. This drill should be started with a toss and catch to ensure proper footwork and correct point of contact. After this has been achieved, start with a toss, catch, and throw. Then go to a toss and set in a counterclockwise square. If the drill goes out of control, have the players start over with a toss. It's great to challenge players, but don't allow players to practice illegal contacts.

SETTING

As soon as players become proficient with the square drill, position the setter at the target area along the net according to the offensive system used. It is important to establish the position along the net because the setter only has 180 degrees to gain position under the ball. Have the setter open up, or face, the incoming ball. She is in a *setter's lean*, or leaning forward slightly ready to move. The setter readjusts and moves under the incoming ball. The setter *squares to target*, or faces her shoulders and hips to the outside hitter (4) attack area on the court. This is an area setters need to establish as a neutral body position. It helps keep sets consistent and later adds to deception when setting other areas. It is a position where the feet and hands are ready at the same time.

Movement to the ball is still in a beat the ball tempo or beat the ball to the spot of contact. A setter wants to overrun behind the ball and step into it. Movement to this area is usually trained as a left-right movement off the net. If the setter only has to move left-right off the net, she turns on the toe and ball of her right foot to square to target. The setter will have to add steps the more the ball is passed off the net but finishes so the last steps are a left-right step through the ball. This will allow weight transfer, pivoting the hips up through the ball, finishing with a follow-through on the left foot. If the player has to play a pass past her ability to stop, she may have to play a ball while moving. She spins off her right foot and turns to set, finishing facing the target. To play a ball behind her, she drop steps with her left foot and moves behind the ball to set. How far the setter has to move back will determine if she can establish a left-right movement through the ball or must spin set.

If the setter cannot get under the ball or has not learned to spin set, she should use a forearm pass to set up the attacker. Every player should be trained to forearm set an attacker since setters call "help" and may need to use this secondary skill to create an offensive play. Tactically, a setter should contact a ball as high as possible. Out of system, a setter should take the ball lower to gain power. As a setter increases in skill, she wants to set counter-flow, set hot hitters, set against weaker blockers, and acquire the ability to check out the blocker before setting her hitter. A setter follows her set to cover the hitter.

The next set to learn is the back set. A back set is taught from neutral position and point of release is established, but follow-through is different to propel the ball backward. Some coaches have the setter arch back, push her midsection forward, or throw her head back on follow-through. At some point, the palms must face up and the arms follow through backward. The force, angle of release, and follow-through will determine the speed,

height, and direction of the set. The setter turns toward the net to cover the hitter.

The jump set is also important to learn. It allows the setter to save a pass or dig from hitting or going over the net near the tape, to speed up an attack, and to dupe the blocker into jumping by making her think she is going to dump. Learning jump setting usually helps a setter's point of release because she must establish firm position under the ball. A jump setter establishes posture to jump, lifts her hands above her forehead, and sets on her way up. Some advanced setters are capable of setting on the way down as a deceptive method.

A front row setter also should learn how to dump as an attack. This is performed most aggressively by showing a jump set before attacking. Usually a back dump is performed with the right hand. To dump into the center of the court, the left hand is used if the pass is off the net and the right hand is used if the ball is tighter to the net. The setter must be trained to show a set first, extend to the ball, and dump with the hand directed to the intended target. A setter does not want to use her arm to dump or follow through or she will rake the net. A back row setter can also dump the ball, but she cannot attack a ball above the net. Most back row setters dump by turning at the last minute using a two-handed overhead power pass to the opponent's donut.

Tactically, a setter cannot dump unless the diggers are on their heels, a blocker is ready to pounce, or an area of the court is unattended. It is a great change of pace but shouldn't be overused. It is a good attack to use when the opponents are moving slowly from coverage to base and the setter receives a fast pass near the tape. But the setter should learn how to set tight passes since many opponents key in on a dump in this circumstance.

Grassroots coaches frequently train all their players as setters so they have good overhead skills and can identify potential setters. A setter should be athletic, smart, a leader, and a hard worker. A young setter needs to learn movement under the ball and a consistent point of release. Most novice setters have problems with starting at the net. Since most young teams pass the first contact in the middle of the court, the setter thinks she should start around the 10-foot line. But this causes a setter to move 360 degrees. A young setter also has to learn how to set balls with different heights by adjusting the angle of release and follow-through.

It is important to train setters at every practice. It may take a scheduling wizard to find time to do it in a one- or two-hour practice when you only have one court, but it is worth it in the end. The setter is the quarterback and ideally will touch one of three contacts every time the ball comes onto her court. To be an effective playmaker, she will need many quality touches on the ball. She will have to know how to better the ball and redirect the pass to create a hittable set for her attacker.

SETTING DRILLS

Front Set, Back Set, Long Set

Purpose: To practice setting

Equipment: Regulation court setup, volleyball

Procedure: Three players line up along the net in the 4, 3, and 2 positions. Player 4 tosses a ball to player 3. Player 3 back sets to player 2. Player 2 long sets to player 4. Player 4 sets to player 3, and the drill continues. After a set number of passes or time limit, the players rotate.

Key point: Players work on consistent point of release.

Variations

- Player 4 sets to player 3, who back sets to player 2. Player 3 turns after the set and faces player 2. Player 2 front sets to player 3, who back sets to player 4. Player 3 turns and faces player 4 again, and the drill continues.
- Player 3 must jump set.
- All players must jump set.

Repetition Setting

Purpose: To work on footwork and components of setting

Equipment: Regulation court setup, bucket of balls

Procedure: A target player stands in the outside hitter position on the same side of the court as the setter. The setter is in target position on the court. From the same side of the court, the coach tosses balls to the setter to set outside sets.

Key points: The setter can work on footwork, squaring to 4, point of release, and follow-through.

Variations

- The setter can start in each of the six serve receive positions or at base position to work on movement to the target area.
- The coach can toss balls from different areas on the court.
- The coach can toss balls to target, in front of target, off the net, or behind the target area to work on various footwork.
- The coach can toss tight balls to work on jump setting, attacking, dumps, or other emergency techniques for handling balls in the plane of the net as a front row or back row setter.
- The setter can work on different sets other than outside sets.
- Blockers can be added to help the setter practice decision making on when and where to set or dump.
- Hitters can attack the sets (but this slows down repetitions).
- Other setters can rotate into the drill.
- The setter can set off live passers.
- The drill can be used as a warm-up by having the setter set different heights (arcs) front or back.

4 or 5?

Purpose: To practice setting

Equipment: Regulation net, bucket of balls

Procedure: A player stands at the OH (4) and RS (5) position as targets. The coach tosses balls to a setter (see figure 8.28). Just before the setter contacts the ball, the coach calls out 4 (to signify setting an outside ball) or 5 (to signify setting a back set).

Key points: Proper footwork to target and to the ball should be coached. The setter should always square to 4 to be consistent. The setter should maintain a consistent point of release.

Variations

- The setter can set from a live pass.
- Hitters can attack the sets.
- Blockers can set up on the opposite side of the court and call out (before the set) where they think the setter is setting to learn to read the setter.
- Other sets can be added to the drill.

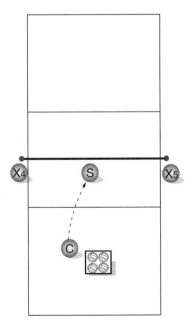

Figure 8.28 4 or 5?

Right-Side Communication Drill

Purpose: To work on communication between setter and right-side hitter

Equipment: Regulation court setup, hitting box, bucket of balls

Procedure: On one side of the court, a coach stands on a hitting box in the right-side position. An extra player hands balls to the coach. On the other side of the court, a setter (player A) positions in the 1 area, a right-side player (player B) positions at the 2 area, and a target (player C) stands in the 4 area at base one defensive position. The coach on the platform slaps the ball to signal to the players to move to base two position. The coach tips or hits the ball toward player A or B. If player A plays the ball, she yells "help," and player B runs under the ball and sets to player C. If player B plays the ball, she yells "mine" and digs the ball up to the target area, and then transitions to become an attacker. Player A runs under the pass and sets to player C.

Key points: Communication is key. Consistent passing in the target area is important. A clear path for the incoming setter must be established.

Variations

- Player B can be the setter and player A can be the backcourt player.
- The backcourt player can pass a tighter ball for the front row player to attack on the second hit.
- The front row player can set the backcourt player to attack out of the backcourt.
- Player C can attack the set.
- A middle blocker can be added as player D to transition, set, and attack.
- The coach can hit off the hands of the blockers to work on defending errant balls. This usually works better with two blockers and an additional digger in the 5 position to make it more gamelike.

Setter Help

Purpose: To work on communication and out-of-system play; to allow nonsetters to practice setting

Equipment: Regulation court setup, bucket of balls

Procedure: On court A, six players set up in base one defensively. The coach is outside the sideline along court A. The coach tosses a ball to emulate an errant pass on or off court A. This is their first contact. It should be a toss that forces the setter to make a decision on whether she can set it or a toss that she definitely can't get to. The setter either yells "mine" and sets or forearm passes to an attacker, or yells "help." If the setter can set or forearm pass to set up an attacker, the play continues to attack and coverage. If the setter yells "help," the player closest to the ball runs under the ball and overhead or forearm passes the ball up to an attacker in the front row or back row. The other players are readying themselves and communicating that they are ready to attack. If a player has to pursue an errant pass, she passes the ball back into the center of the court and a player attempts to attack the ball. This attack can be an approaching hit, standing hit, or a well-placed free ball.

Key points: The setter must make a quick decision and communicate. The player who plays the second contact on a "help" must communicate to avoid confusion. If a player has to exit the court to pursue an errant pass, a player should follow her (as a trailer) in case the pursuer "just" gets the ball up. This will ensure that a player (the trailer) is close enough to forearm the ball over the net. The coach should make sure the players understand her out-of-system philosophy before the drill.

Variation: The coach can toss balls over any part of the court, off the net, or into the net.

CHAPTER 9

FUNDAMENTALS OF ATTACKING

There are no free balls. That is the philosophy I used at Sweet Home to create an aggressive atmosphere on the court. To create a comfortable atmosphere, I praised aggressiveness and trained my players to be responsible for efficient court movement and posture.

During the first match every year, I realized that I had forgotten to teach the players how to strategically pass the ball over on the third hit. This is an emergency skill, but most of my drills are formulated to create and promote aggressiveness. "Test your limitations" is one of my favorite phrases. If a player is falling backward and takes a swing up on a ball, she will find out what she is really capable of doing. If she doesn't test this during practice, she will play too safe in a game. The coach who supports aggressiveness in practice but changes her philosophy to "just keep it in" during a game is asking her players to change their timing and their mind-set. I am not saying to never use a tip or roll shot. Both these techniques can be used aggressively, too. Strategically passing the ball over on the third hit is a skill that should be trained because it can be aggressive and used as an attack if placed properly. The higher the level, the more the hitter has to be able to recognize whether to take a full swing, vary her direction, or place a controlled shot over the net. This is due

to the increased level of blocking. Beginning and intermediate players need to recognize when to take a full swing or when to place a controlled shot over the net. This is due to poor timing or inconsistent sets. But I still feel that coaches should create a comfortable atmosphere on the court so the players feel free to try different aggressive shots.

PRECONTACT MOVEMENT

Movement is required of the attacker before an approach begins. She may need to transition from serve receive, transition off the net from a free ball, transition off the net after a block assignment, transition after off-blocker responsibility, or transition from a down ball defensive scheme. The back row players need to make transitions from their defensive assignments. These would include from their base position, from coverage, from passing, and from digging. Coaches want their back row players to be ready to attack, too.

Normally, coaches teach young players to make a three- or four-step approach to the ball. But coaches sometimes forget to teach how to get to that starting point. That is why so many hitters hit off serve receive very well but never have a good run on the ball during rallies. Transition footwork is as important as a spike approach.

SPIKE APPROACH

Many times a 3- or 4-step spike approach is taught first. Volleyball coaches have changed the offensive patterns to extend from one side of the court to the other. Actually, what is most important is that an attacker's last 2 steps are dynamic. So we will concentrate on a hitter's last 2 steps. That way she will be able to make a 3-step or even a 15-step approach. The following discussion refers to a right-handed attacker.

A hitter's approach is intended to bring speed and momentum into her jump. Her last two steps convert from a horizontal direction into a vertical lift. Her second to the last step is a broad step. Remember, it is also a breaking step to stop her forward momentum. The hitter must land with her right foot (or the outside edge of the sole of her right foot) on the

floor first (see figure 9.1a). This will help break her forward movement. As her right foot is planted, her left foot simply steps forward as the balance step, readying the hitter to gather energy to jump. As she plants her left foot, the outside of her foot should be almost parallel to the net (see figure 9.1b). This will allow her shoulder to open up easily to the ball. The foot position resembles that of a pigeon-toed person. One of my downhill skiers thought it resembled a beginner "snowplower" skill.

Many coaches are now also teaching players to land on two feet (instead of the quick right then left sequence). This is a great technique as long as the beginner does not jump for height before she plants her feet.

The hitter *must* plant her left foot behind the ball, or in other words, keep the ball in front of the body. As the hitter plants her left foot, the knees are bent deep enough to be able to jump to extreme. If an attacker bends her knees too much, it will break her movement. Conversely, if she doesn't bend enough, she will not be using the strongest muscles to aid in her maximum jump.

Figure 9.1 Last two steps of the spike approach.

ARM MOVEMENT

The arm movement during spike approach should resemble a person walking or jogging. It should be natural and should not be done in unison (resembling a skier or cheerleader). As the hitter plants her last foot down, she has three arm speeds through her attack.

The hitter must lift her arms up quickly. Her arms should be above her shoulders before her toes leave the ground. She should lift from the elbows . . . I usually say "lift from the triceps." This lifts the whole arm quickly.

The hitter should not allow her right arm to come forward of her body during her arm lift. As she lifts her elbows up, her upper body disassociates from her lower body. The left shoulder and elbow lead up toward the ball, and the right shoulder and elbow draw up and back for added power and complete range of motion (see figure 9.2a). Her wrist and hand should be relaxed.

Figure 9.2 Arm movement for the spike.

The hitter should then start the next part of her swing up to the ball. It is important to start the swing up on her way up. She needs to start her swing when the ball is out of her reach. The attacker initiates her swing up with her shoulder and then her elbow (see figure 9.2b). This is similar to throwing a pop fly in softball. As the elbow is swung up, the hand (comfortably open) follows naturally. The heel of the hand hits behind and on top of the ball (see figure 9.2c). The fingers and wrist snap over the ball. The fingers and wrist finish over the ball in the intended direction of the spike.

The final part of the swing is the follow-through, shown in figure 9.2d. The hitter finishes her swing with her arm by or alongside her body in the intended direction of the path of the attack. The only exception to this is if the set is tight and the hitter has to follow through *in* to avoid hitting the net.

TRANSITION FOOTWORK OFF THE NET

There are four transitions off the net that a front row blocker makes to become an attacker. They include free ball, down ball, off-blocker, and blocking.

The footwork for free ball and down ball are similar. Depending on a coach's philosophy, a blocker may stay at the net to see if she can block or attack the ball. If the transitioning player does not stay at the net, she pivots and turns off the net in the direction of the ball. She uses a crossover step and runs off the net to the desired starting location on the court. At the same time, she gets herself ready to play the first ball over the net in case it is in her area of responsibility. If she cannot get to her intended approach start position before the ball gets to the net, she must be ready to play the ball forward in case the ball hits the top of the net and falls down. Once she sees that the ball is clearing the net, she can continue her route off the net. As a free ball passer, she assumes her "arms available" ready position so she can overhead or fore-arm passes. Most coaches' philosophies are to have the back row players play as many free balls as possible so the front row players can ready themselves better for an attack. As a down ball passer, she will assume a lower position leaning forward ready to dig and pass a topspin attack. Great versatile teams also have their backcourt players transition off the 10-foot line for a back row attack. A back row attacker should always get at least a right/left jump into a set.

The transition for an off-blocker is to rotate into the defensive position first. The area of responsibility will be determined by the defense the team is playing. It will either be to stay inside the 10-foot line and play tips (perimeter) or to transition behind the 10-foot line and dig spikes (rotation). The movement off the net to the defensive position is to pivot, crossover step, and run off the net to the area of defensive responsibility.

The next responsibility is to play the ball. If an off-blocker has to play a tip, dig a ball, or perform a run-through, she must then transition again while the ball is in the air to the setter. If her route is to hit a quick, she will probably start her route from her own pass. If she doesn't have to pass, she will start her quick route as the ball is being passed off the arms of the passer.

The transition of a blocker can be two different footwork patterns. One is if the blocker knows she doesn't stand a chance to touch a block (the hitter roll shots or tips, another hitter gets set, or the hit is obviously around the block). This blocker can start turning and pivoting as she lands and run off the net or sidestep off the net. If the blocker stays up solid, knowing she can block or partially block the ball, she comes down solid ready to play a ball near her. Otherwise, she comes down solid and pivots and turns in the direction of the hit. She pivots and uses a crossover and run step or sidesteps. How deep the ball was attacked on the court will determine how much time she has to transition. The quick hitter needs to stop moving off the net by the time the ball is in the passer's arms. See figure 9.3.

This transitioning footwork *has* to be practiced until it becomes as natural as an

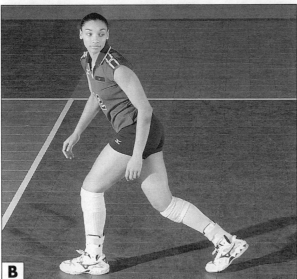

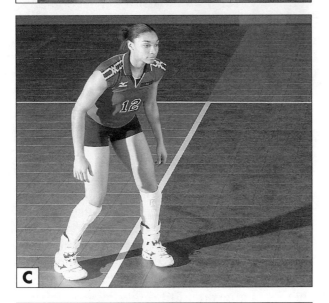

Figure 9.3 Blocker transition footwork.

approach. Long rallies require a lot of transition movement on and off the net. A team that wants to stay aggressive and win the long rallies needs to transition like it is a short sprint off the net every time. It can be tiring and discouraging if you don't get a lot of sets, but good transition will win rallies.

POSITIONAL ATTACKING

Attackers are usually divided into three front row positions. The outside hitter is notorious for being the "go-to" or power hitter who can attack an outside third tempo set using a variety of shots, including crosscourt, down the line, cut shot, outside in, roll, and tip. Also included is "using the block" and hitting through the seam of the block. Hitters want to be as deceptive as possible by starting from a neutral zone, normally off the left side of the court. Outside hitters usually approach showing the strong crosscourt hit. Different shots are achieved by changing hand position on the ball and follow-through. An example is the cut shot used by a hitter if the ball is set outside the antenna and the attacker has to cut the ball around the antenna to keep it in-bounds. It's also used when a hitter is trying to cut the attack around the middle blocker's left hand at an extreme crosscourt. The attacker approaches and hits behind the ball and drives her left thumb down across the inside (left side) of the set ball. Many hitters turn toward the net (away from the intended flight) and end up facing the net on follow-through.

Another example is a down-the-line shot, which is achieved by two popular methods. The first is to show crosscourt as the hitter is lifting on her jump, to square her shoulders parallel to the net. The time it takes to square her shoulders will allow the set ball time to travel in front of her body. Her contact is behind the ball and follow-through continues down the line. A deceptive way to hit down the line is to maintain the crosscourt approach but hit the right side of the set ball and follow through over the hitter's left shoulder. For many novice attackers, hitting down the line is natural because they don't transition off the court and instead make a straight approach to the net. An outside in shot is achieved by combining a down-the-line shot but cutting the ball around an outside blocker's right hand.

A roll shot is used to roll the ball over the top of a block or into an opponent's vulnerable open court space. The attacker uses her approach but instead of swinging fast, she drops her elbow and creates backspin on the ball by driving the heel of her hand under the ball, then snapping her fingers and hand over the top of the ball.

A tip is used if a defense is on their heels, the set is tight, or the hitter is attacking an opponent's court area. The hitter should approach the set and show crosscourt. The hitter starts her swing but slows the speed before contact. The contact involves dropping her elbow and opening her hand resembling a one-handed set. To stay within the rules, the attacker must continue her follow-through in the direction the ball was contacted. *Using the block* refers to an attacker who can exploit a blocker's weakness. The hitter aims her attack at the weak blocker, including a blocker who is jumping off the net with the attack stuffed between her hands and opponent's net. It can also include wiping a ball off a blocker's outside hand to force a ball to rebound out of bounds. Hitting an attack through the seam of the block is a method of exploiting a double block. If a team uses a front row setter, the setter becomes the other front row attacker and should be trained to dump, tip, turn and joust/block, turn and swing, and transition to swing if another player sets the second ball contact.

A middle hitter's popular attack includes a first tempo set. Again, most coaches train their middles to establish a neutral zone from transition to camouflage her intended attack path. First tempo or "quick" sets are set in front of or behind the setter anywhere along the net. The closer the set is to the setter, the quicker the hitter has to be up above the net. A quick hit is supposed to be attacked on the ball on the upward flight of the set. Many hitters attack the downward flight of the ball, which is usually easier to block. A first tempo hit must also be practiced crosscourt, cut back (opposite crosscourt), tip, and dump. Many middles also work on rolling a tip shot to play a low set or if the hitter has late timing. A first tempo dump is very effective because it is hard to defend. The hitter contacts the top of the ball and pushes it down similar to a setter's dump. Some elite teams run a double first tempo attack but an offensive play should always have an "outlet" or safe set in its combination. It might be the best choice for a setter if the blockers stay with the quick hitters, too, which is the purpose of running players on quick patterns.

All hitters should be able to hit second tempo hits. These attacks are usually used in conjunction with a first tempo hit and many times set behind the quick hitter creating tandem action. If the second tempo hitter, or second hitter, runs a path parallel to the quick hitter's path, it is called a tandem. If the second hitter runs a pattern which crosses a quick attacker path, it is called a cross. Many scholastic teams, who do not run quicks, use the second tempo set as a middle hitter's best attack.

Coaches need to train hitters to transition off the net and position in a neutral zone, from which the attackers use their approaches to establish a good jumping base to attack the ball according to the timing and tempo of the set. The hitter wants to establish a good base so she can use any of her repertoire of shots against the block or to attack the ball into the intended court area. A team with outside hitters who can attack first tempo attacks and middles who can attack third tempo sets can wreak havoc on defenses and add many options to their offense. It's wonderful to have an impressive number of combination plays, but without a solid first contact and quality set, the offensive plays are worthless.

Having a lefty on a team can add a power attack to the "weak" side of the court. The left side is generally the power side for a righty. If a righty plays right side, or opposite, it is generally called the weak side. If a team has a strong left-handed attacker, the right side of the net is now an additional power side.

Another popular attack mode is the one-foot takeoff, or slide attack, first used by aggressive hitters who were either late to the ball or had to hit a poorly set ball. The slide attack is now often used by middle hitters attacking behind a setter. It is becoming essential in a 5-1 offense to create an attack behind the setter to spread the offense pin to pin, or antenna to antenna. It can also be set in the zone close behind the setter. It can also be a set hit in front of the setter and hit by a lefty right-side player. Again, a player can jump off one foot and hit any attack, in front or behind the setter. It is easiest taught to beginners from the middle of the court about eight feet off the net and running a path parallel to the net. The coach should first teach and train the footwork without the ball. The footwork resembles a lay-up in basketball, or for a right hander, left-right-left. The hitter plants her first left step parallel to the setter/target after she releases the ball. She uses her right step to chase the ball and plants her left foot (takeoff foot), by toeing in toward the antenna. The player is envisioning takeoff so the ball is in front of the hitter at a distance between her left shoulder and the net. The hitter lifts her right knee to help elevate the jump. The players pump their arms alternately, similar to a running motion.

When the player is comfortable with the footwork, either the coach tosses or the setter sets a second tempo back set to the antenna. This will allow the hitter to hit line or cross-court on follow-through. The arm swing is performed by drawing the right elbow back and up when the left foot plants and the right knee lifts. The right hand is drawn from near the hip with the right elbow cocked back leading the draw. The hitter swings up on the ball, similar to any attacker's swing, as high and fast as possible. The hand contact, arm swing, and body's follow-through will determine the path of the ball. A slide hitter should always land on two feet to balance the landing and prevent unbalanced twisting compression off the hips, knees, and ankles. Once a hitter is adept at a one-foot takeoff, she can use it for a first tempo attack. Usually, a hitter uses a one-foot takeoff for a third tempo attack if she's late to the ball or is attacking a poor inside set.

The back row attack was once perceived as an option set from a poor first contact. The back row attack can add two or three hitters as options in an offense. Many hitters are just as effective out of the back row because the attack can be harder to block due to greater blocking timing. It also allows the hitter a larger angle to hit around.

Training by position must include a player's movement to get to neutral zone, or training the movement from player's responsibility before she becomes an attacker. This would include defense or blocking from several areas depending on the net or court area assigned to the position and the opponent's attack position. From these court positions, the hitters need to know how to get to neutral and ready to start their attack patterns. Training by position should be done individually, with players adjacent, and then within the team infrastructure.

Training by position is not just about offense. It is about defense to offense to defense if your team is serving and offense to defense to offense if you are serve receiving. The better a team transitions, the more likely the team can continually attack during rallies from quality first contacts.

Lastly, a team practices in-system more than out-of-system—the percentage breakdown of these in a match is a useful stat to keep. It benefits coaches and teams alike to practice out-of-system play to prepare the team to attack in different situations. Communication, overhand and forearm setup skills, and aggressiveness are keys in training out-of-system offense.

BREAKING BAD HABITS

A lot of our efforts, as coaches, are given to breaking bad habits. That is why it is important to put the best technicians on the grassroots teams! Following are some common errors along with methods of correction.

1. *Double pump/cheerleader.* This attacker was taught to bring her arms, swing-

ing simultaneously, in front of her body once or twice during approach. First of all, you want to break the habit of her arms swinging simultaneously. This is a deadly habit for any approach and for the back slide. In addition, it makes the hitter lift her hitting arm in front of her body. The result is the attacking arm never gets back in time to swing forward.

One way to correct this habit is to have the hitter run her attack with her arms behind her (like Superman's cape) until both her feet plant to jump. Another way is to have the hitter hold onto her shorts/spandex until both feet plant to jump.

The hitter should let her arms hang and move naturally.

2. *My fingernail polish is drying!* The attacker, who swings her attacking arm in front of her while jumping (with her fingers pointing up), will lift her elbow forward and her hands back as if she is touching the label on her shirt. This creates the second half of a swing (elbow swing up) so the hitter never gets to drive up to the ball. The attack will be lower and at a downward angle only. If the blocker is weak, the hit can be devastating. Put a real blocker against her, and she is shut down.

There are different ways to attempt to break this habit. This worked with Maria Gurreri, later an NCAA All-American, when she was in middle school. We had her make a fist through the whole approach. If your wrists are down in a clenched position, you can't raise your fingers up. The fingers up position is what makes a hitter's elbow lead and fingers draw back. After she became accustomed to the fist routine, we let her open her hand just prior to contact on the ball.

3. *"Throws like a girl" arm swing.* It's difficult for me, as a female physical educator, to even say it like this. I should say, "throws incorrectly," but you all know what I mean! This is the girl who throws off her wrong foot. Her arm swing is either initiated with the elbow starting forward or she throws with a straight arm. Many young hitters swing with a straight arm. Many young hitters initiate their swing with their hand first, instead of from the shoulder and then an elbow swing up to the ball. Many high school players are good hit-

ters using the straight arm method until they meet a "real" blocker. Again, this is actually swinging down on the ball, which is the third phase of a complete arm swing. The hitter is not using the levers in her arm to swing up and over a ball. She will never develop good shots. Diggers and blockers can read early where she is hitting, too. This is the hitter who develops rotator cuff problems. She probably serves incorrectly.

- Have her throw some pop flies with a tennis ball. Make sure she doesn't drop her elbow below her shoulder.
- Have her hit some standing attacks to work on the swing up to the ball. This way, she doesn't have to worry about approaching and jumping. If she is taller, raise the net.
- Make sure she is planting her last step, her left foot, parallel to the net. She can't draw her arms back if her toes are pointing to the net. Actually, guys can do this because their center of gravity is higher than that of girls. Girls need to plant left and rotate their nonhitting shoulder to the ball to open up their shoulders. Instead of drawing back with their right arm, they must turn their left shoulder/elbow to the ball; this is the way gymnasts do twisting movements more fluidly.
- Make sure she is not swinging her right arm in front of her body on her lift from the floor. As she starts her jump, the hitter's arms should be behind her. In one movement up from the elbows, the right elbow draws up and back, and the left elbow lifts up and rotates in the direction of the ball. It should resemble a softball catcher throwing down to second base.
- For the seriously "throws like a girl" challenged player, pull out a stacked gymnastics mat. They fold to 18 inches, which is the average jump for a high school player. Put the mat at an angle to the net around the 10-foot line. Put your hitter on the mat with her feet planted like she is ready to jump on her

approach (left foot parallel to the net). Her left shoulder should be forward with her arms up over her head. Her right arm should be in the ready attack position. Basically, she should look like she has jumped up and her arms are in the perfect position. Have someone toss a second tempo ball in front of the hitter's arm (this may be the hardest part!). Instruct the hitter to initiate her swing with her elbow first. Keep repeating until you achieve success or you are eligible for retirement. Make sure her shoulders are open. She cannot swing up on the ball with her shoulders forward and her chest high.

- Have this player swing on a higher net to force her to swing up to the ball with her elbow. If she initiates her swing with her hand and a straight arm, the ball will bury into the net.

4. *Early and under (dreaded back bump attack).* If I had a dollar for every time I have told a player "E + U," I'd be rich. Early and under the ball is either a timing, poor transition, or footwork problem. An approach is used to help accelerate before the jump. A player who approaches and stops is gaining nothing out of her approach.

As a timing problem, the cause is the hitter starting her approach too soon. If an attacker is hitting a third tempo ball, she must read the depth of the set off the net as the ball is on its way up out of the setter's hands. She has to judge where the ball is going to be on its way down when the ball is still on its way up. Many rookie hitters just start their approach when the ball is in the setter's hands. This early timing problem will cause the hitter to guess where the ball will be, or the hitter will go where she wished the ball would be set. Since she is early, the hitter has to stop her approach and wait for the ball. If the ball is off the desired course, the hitter has to figure out a way to propel the ball over the net. The safest way to execute the contact is by turning her back to the net and back bumping it . . . or as I call it, the *dreaded back bump attack.* It is very common in young teams whose hitters approach early. It is also common for a hitter

to get stuck under a set when she has poor transition during rallies.

- Try having her start her footwork to the ball when the ball is at the height of the arc on a third tempo ball when the setter has just released the ball. This gives the hitter a visual cue.
- Many hitters make a three- or four-step approach to a third tempo ball. Have her shorten her first step on a three-step approach or shorten her first two steps on a four-step approach.
- Give her a verbal "go" when she should start her approach.
- Hold her shirt from behind (tough to do in a match).
- Look to see where she plants her second to last (right) *breaking* step. Many times this step IS behind the line of the set. It is the last step—the balance step (the left step)—that really gets her under the ball. This is a tough concept to get across. It has been a comfort zone for the attacker to be too close to the ball rather than out of swinging distance.
- Work on her transition and make sure her steps are long enough, or add a step. She should know visually where her minimum starting area should be relative to the 10-foot line. This can be determined by putting her back to the net with her feet starting where a set trajectory's path would intersect, and having her make a full approach. Where she lands should be her minimum start area.
- Have her work on repetitious rally drills. Have her hit, turn, transition, approach, and swing, and keep repeating this. So many hitters get stuck at about six feet off the net during transition. This will promote a good, healthy back bump attack.
- Remind her the tempo is run-jump-swing *not* run, stop, jump, swing.

5. *Fishy in the net.* This is the hitter who consistently falls into the net or rakes the net on her follow-through. The general causes are

usually jumping off her toes and not breaking properly during her approach. This is common of the younger player who jumps too close to the net because it is safer and spiking means hitting down. This is a common problem when sets are tight. Most beginner teams think it wise to set tight so the hitters can hit down. Blocking is poor at this level so a reason to hit around a block is not needed. But we want to teach hitting from a set off the net so a hitter will learn to swing around blocks eventually and so she can have a full follow-through without getting her arm caught in the net.

- Start by having this fishy hitter hitting out of the back row. Set her behind the 10-foot line so she sees and feels what it is like to have a full follow-through.

- Have the setter set or toss balls off the net instead of over the net to hit.

- Check out her feet. Is her second to the last step in her approach (the right, breaking step) placed down using the heel of the outside of the foot to break her forward momentum?

- Check to see if the hitter is approaching the net instead of the ball. Again, make sure the ball is set off the net. Many hitters, especially E+U hitters, just run to the net instead of reading the set.

- Make sure she isn't goofy footed. This is reverse footwork where the last two steps are left then right. Usually, the right foot ends up in front of the left. This will also cause hitters to run off the toes or maintain a forward momentum through a jump.

6. *Goofy footed and she has no tempo.* Goofy footed is reversed footwork. It means a player's footwork is backward on takeoff. Instead of a right/left finish, the hitter plants left/right. It is difficult to change, and many just let it go and hope for the best. When the hitter jumps with her right foot forward, it screws up her arm swing. With her right (hitting) shoulder forward, she can't open up her shoulders to the net. Therefore, she has no backswing. She has to resort to swinging down with a hatchet swing. It's like that guy at the carnival swinging the jackhammer down

to ring the bell. It is generally a line shot, but the timing has to be perfect so the hitter doesn't bury the ball in the net. She also has to hope there is no block. Many times goofy footed hitters jump off their toes and also have to contend with not falling forward into the net. They can be effective high school hitters because of poor blocking.

- If the player is younger or the player and coach are confident, this footwork can be broken, but it has to be trained and you have to be patient. Off-season is best. Train the last two steps only because they are the problem. Start by having her hold the hands of two players who approach correctly, with "goofy" in the middle of this chorus line. Work on *right-left* over and over. Use two lines on the floor as a visual cue of how long the right step should be (about three to four feet long from a stand). Make sure their weight is resting on their left foot during the chorus line. Then, just to simulate a step *before* the right (plant) step, have them stomp the floor with a left foot . . . going nowhere. Yes, now you have to make sure she has her weight on her right foot. So the tempo would be stomp left, right, left. After she has accomplished this, have her do it for homework—25 in the morning and 25 at night. This has to become second nature. Once she feels more comfortable with the last few steps of her approach, have her run and approach a tossed ball. Once she can perform in repetition drills, have her use her new approach in a scrimmage drill.

- Use her as a right-side hitter.

7. *Helping the hitter with a 9-inch vertical jump or the vertically challenged hitter.* This is common with many interscholastic squads and younger Junior Olympic teams. If the hitter is small, she can still be a good attacker. If she has a low jump, she can be a good attacker as long as she doesn't have wasted movement. She is only off the ground for a limited amount of time!

- Tactically, set this hitter off the net . . . way off the net!

- Make sure she has no wasted movement. She should plant left so her shoulders are opened up to the ball. She cannot have a forward cheerleader arm swing. She has to make sure her arms lift right up into striking position. She also wants to lift from her elbows since this lifts the entire arm quicker.

- She has to initiate her swing with an elbow swing up to the ball. She cannot swing with a straight arm and initiate her swing with her hand. This hit would just drive down into the net.

- This hitter needs to plant a little closer to the ball so the heel of her hand contacts under the ball to drive the ball up and over the net. She has to create topspin on the ball using a more vertical swing than the average player does.

- This hitter needs to make sure she starts her swing *before* the top of her jump. She has to use all the power she can muster to drive the ball up and over the net.

- She has to develop different shots to hit around blocks or hit toward defensive weaknesses.

- She has to practice swinging tight sets off the outside blocker in hopes of using the blocker in error and driving the ball off her hands out of bounds. If a setter errors and sets the smaller hitter too tight, it is very difficult to tip. She might be able to fist the ball over if the blocker does not penetrate.

8. *Swinging from your ear.* Some hitters have trouble swinging up on the ball because they let the ball drop to their ear and swipe at it. There is no swing up on the ball, and many times the ball gets buried in the net. Coaches constantly yell, "Swing up" or "Reach."

- This is a perception and timing problem. The hitter does start her swing when it is above her so she thinks she is swinging up. The reality is she is starting her swing when the ball is in her reach. By the time she initiates her swing, the ball has dropped to her head level or to her shoulder level. The hitter has to use her hand to hit the ball since the ball is too low. Sometimes she even drops her elbow and it results in a roll shot or resembles a serving action. What the hitter needs to do is to initiate her swing when the ball is higher than her reach so by the time she swings her elbow up to the ball and her hand follows high, the contact is made at her reach. Gravity plays a major part in timing. Hitters have to trust that the ball will really be there if they start their swing higher than their reach.

- Sometimes the hitter does not make sure her elbow is above her shoulders as her feet leave the ground. To use her levers correctly and in sequence, she must make sure that her elbow is above her shoulder, and her wrist is above her elbow. Her wrist and fingers have to be loose enough to finish the snap over the ball and follow through in the intended direction of the hit.

Another mistake many hitters make is planting too far to the left of the ball when they are hitting "on-side." They plant where they think their swinging shoulder is right behind the ball. This is true, but they are setting themselves up for a narrow margin of error. Their right arm is behind the ball right before it is at the lowest part of the arc before it drops below the top of the net. Girls who have a lower jump probably have to plant their feet this way. But, girls who have a good swing up on the ball need to plant behind the trajectory of the set at a higher point. This is why some girls hit better from their off side. They reach across their body and contact the set higher.

A hitter has to time her approach, plant her feet in the correct place along the arc of the set, and swing up when the ball is out of her reach. No wonder this is such a hard skill to master!

Tips for Teaching Beginners Hitting

When teaching hitting, I have found that separating the approach and the arm swing works best, although I also show them the whole skill so they know what they are working toward.

My goal is to try to get them to feel natural and comfortable with their footwork. As described before, we work on the last two steps. Then we add running and the last two steps. Homework is assigned as previously mentioned.

Then I go on and work on another skill, usually forearm passing. After we have exhausted the fun in bumping, we go back and work on arm swing. We work on throwing pop flies while keeping our left hip forward and our right elbow above shoulder level. We do standing hits making sure our left hips are forward and we are behind the ball. We start with our arms already up in hitting position and then advance to working on raising our arms up into a hitting position. We stand on mats and have people toss balls in front of us with our arms raised up in hitting position. Then we practice lifting our arms into hitting position and swinging at the tossed ball.

Then we practice a different skill such as overhead passing. I try to keep arm swing and serving separate from each other, so it doesn't tax the shoulder too much. The other reason is the motions are similar but they differ on swing and contact.

After I start seeing natural movement to the ball, we start putting the whole thing together. Generally, I have attackers hit overpasses first. It is usually instant success! Here are a few points to remember:

- Make sure the hitter starts with her left hip forward and uses her right/left footwork to get behind the ball.

- Have the hitter start from just behind the 10-foot line.

- Make sure the tosser tosses the ball high enough and deep enough so the hitter can swing high and follow through.

- Have the tosser toss balls so that little adjustment is needed by the hitter.

- After the hitter has tasted success, have the tosser challenge the hitter by making her move laterally or varying the depth. This should just be slight so that the hitter learns quickly that she has to go play the ball and the ball is not going to come to her!

After we have done overpasses, we do one of two things. We either have the hitters hit out of our hands or we toss them "one" sets.

Some coaches have contraptions that hold the ball between two foam marshmallowlike compressors. Some coaches stand on a platform and hold a ball above the net. This is all done to isolate the ball so the hitter doesn't have to worry about timing a set. For obvious reasons, we don't want to do this too long. Timing is an important part of hitting successfully. But having hitters hit a still ball can have some merit if done correctly:

- Make sure the ball is high enough to make a hitter swing up on the ball.

- Make sure the ball is off the net enough so the hitter follows through without hitting the net.

- Make sure the hitter plants behind the ball so she doesn't hit the coach off the platforms. Coaches with short arms should not attempt this.

- Make sure the hitter's left hip stays forward. The whole reason for doing this lead-up is to check out the footwork *first*. The hitters only care about how "cool" and vicious the hit is. We, as coaches, must check out the feet, the arm lift, the arm swing, and the follow-through. That is a lot to do when you are in fear of being run over by a 12-year-old attacker out of control.

Some coaches go right to the tossed "one" ball. The timing is "You go, I throw." Again, there are some considerations:

- As a coach, stay off the net so the hitter can follow through.

- As a coach, vary your toss according to your hitter. If she is five-foot-nothing, toss her off the net. If she is taller, toss her a little higher so she swings up on the ball. Make sure the ball is tossed high enough for all the hitters so they swing up on the ball. One of the pitfalls on this drill is if the ball is tossed too low, the hitter will adjust and just swing down. Oops, we don't want to practice a technique incorrectly.

- As a coach, you still need to coach footwork, arm lift, arm swing, and follow-though. This is tough to do when you are timing and varying tosses.

- This is a drill where most kids will plant under the ball. Young hitters do not trust that their arms will reach the ball. They plant so far under a ball that they must think their arms have a reach of three inches.

- To stop kids from jumping under the ball, we have tried to put floor tape down as a reminder that kids shouldn't jump in front of the tape. Of course, we toss the ball between the tape and the net. The main problem with this is it gets the hitter to look down instead of focus on the ball. But, it does work many times. Another thing this helps is to create a visual cue for the hitter *after* she hits. As described previously, many hitters will plant their right foot behind the ball. But then when they place their left foot down to balance before their jump, they have now planted themselves under the ball. Many hitters have trouble comprehending that they really do this. The taped floor will show them. Their right foot *and* left foot have to be behind the tape. In order to do this, the hitter must plant her right foot a step behind the tape.

After the one ball, I like to hit second tempo balls out of the back row because the timing is clearly that the hitter approaches just after the tosser/setter releases the ball. We imagine that the net is the 10-foot line. This allows the hitters to swing up and follow through. It also promotes aggressive backcourt swings! Then we take our hitters to the net and toss "real" second tempo balls. We keep in mind that the toss needs to stay off the net for a decent follow-through. Then we add a setter who can set second tempo balls. Sometimes this is the coach or an intermediate player.

Then we have them start hitting second tempo balls off their own setters. This is always a head shaker. But, we need hitters to realize that sets aren't perfect. It also shows us that we need more setter training! We don't have our hitters hit what our setters can't set.

So, our last grassroots toss is our high outside, or our third tempo set. The timing involves the hitter approaching the ball when the ball is at the height of its arc. This is the hardest set because it involves the most timing. It's funny because kids like to hit third tempo sets the best! We usually start with a toss, then go to an intermediate setter setting, and then their own setters setting.

The most important consideration is to make sure the drill is run so *you* can watch their technique and *coach* it. Don't practice bad habits. It's better to go back and fix it now before it gets too ingrained. My fifth grade teacher, Mrs. Stoddard, used to make us recite, "Habit is a cable. We weave a thread of it every day and at last we cannot break it." I didn't know it then, but it was the first piece of coaching advice I received!

CHAPTER 10 FLOOR DEFENSE AND BLOCKING

If you ask a player what the first rule in blocking is, she would say, "Block the ball." John Kessel, of USA Volleyball, would say, "Keep out of the net!" A tactician would say, "Take away a hitter's best shot or take away court space."

Floor defense, or digging, has one main goal, namely, to keep the ball off the floor. Its secondary goal is to contain the pass over the center of your court. I cover both blocking and digging in this chapter.

BLOCKING

Blocking is one of the toughest skills to coach in volleyball. Of all the skills at the scholastic level, it is probably performed least correctly. At the grassroots level, it doesn't need to be taught until there is an attack that is consistent and is more powerful than a roll shot! Bill Neville made a great point when he said, "Blocking is needed only when an opposing player can hit the ball harder than your team can control in the back row."

Blocking Is Important

One of my favorite stories about the importance of blocking comes from my old buddy, Sid Feldman. He asked me once what I thought were the three most important skills in volleyball. I dutifully replied, "Serving, passing, and attacking." Sid replied, "No!" So I tried again, "Serving, passing, and setting." Again he said, "No!" I said, "I give up!" He replied, "Be lucky, the serve, and the block." I asked for an explanation. He replied, "Win the coin flip, serve every ball in, and block every spike. You'll win 15-0." Point understood!

Good blocking is dependent upon many factors, including jumping ability, timing, lateral quickness, footwork, and the ability to read a set and a hitter. It becomes more complicated as attack patterns become more diverse. Anticipation and vision are two more important qualities a blocker should possess. Blockers should be taught to anticipate, read, and use compact movement. There is no time for wasted movement that delays timing.

Ready Position

In a blocker's ready position, the feet are spread about shoulder-width apart. The knees are slightly bent with the weight on the balls of the feet. The heels are slightly off the floor (see figure 10.1).

Blockers' base position starts about an arm's distance off the net. This base position readies the blocker to attack an overpass. Some coaches prefer to have their blockers start with just their hitting shoulder side angled off the net. In either case, this is to promote aggressiveness and allow space for the blocker to follow through without contacting the net when attacking. Grassroots coaches find this helpful because there are as many overpasses as sets. A word of warning to grassroots coaches: Make sure your blockers do not *approach block* when they return to the net to ready to block (after no overpass has occurred). This could cause the blocker to jump off her toes and end up in the net. Remember that the net is not a hammock! Another common error would be for the approach blocker to drop her arms and end up lifting the net on her swing up.

A blocker's base position is about two feet off the net. This is relative to the length of the blocker's arms. The longer the arms, the farther the blocker is off the net. Many younger players are taught to return closer to the net because their arms are shorter and cannot penetrate the net. But as a player gets taller, she must adjust her blocking base off the net to allow for penetration. A common error for a blocker is to swing the arms forward to penetrate the net. This will surely result in rope burns on the arms and a referee's whistle.

The arms are bent at the elbow and held up in front of the blocker. The elbows can be naturally outside shoulder-width. The hands are spread and should be between shoulder and eyebrow level. The blocker should be able to see the back of her hands. The faster the offense, the higher the hands. Outside blockers generally hold their sideline arm up slightly higher than their inside arm. Middle blockers generally hold their arms up higher for faster penetration on a quick attack. The blocker should minimize dropping the hands before jumping. It changes the timing and increases error. The sideline arm should be strong, and the arm should be locked and extended. The hands should be spread, and the thumbs should be close to each other to maintain a strong and solid rebound surface. The hands are angled down toward the center of the opponent's court.

A ball that is blocked down to the opponent's court is called a *stuff block*. If the blocker jumps late or cannot penetrate the net, she can perform a *soft block*. This is performed by pointing the fingers back toward her own backcourt. It slows the spike and causes it to deflect higher, allowing the backcourt to play the ball easier. If a blocker gets a piece of the ball or a *partial block*, this can be good or bad. The result can be similar to a soft block—slowing the ball down and allowing the defense to pass the ball easier. The ball can also rebound off a hand at a bad angle and deflect down onto the blocker's floor or out of bounds.

Figure 10.1 Blocker's ready position.

Block Jump

Timing a block is instinctive and trained. With most hits, the blocker has to jump just after the hitter. But the distance the set is off the net plays a big part in timing. The speed of the arm swing is the other variable. When the blocker gets ready to jump, the legs bend and then the arms and legs extend in unison. If a blocker drops her arms to help her jump, she is varying the timing involved to block the ball. The increase in vertical jump she will gain in dropping her arms is small. It is more important to lessen the timing variables and get up in proper position to reject the ball from crossing the net. If she can keep her arms up and steady, just using them to push and penetrate, the timing is easier. The blocker's main goal is to time the hands to penetrate the net before the ball reaches the tape. The arms diagonally extend forward to penetrate or seal the net (see figure 10.2).

Figure 10.2 Block jump.

Since the hands are in front of the body, it is easy to push the palms forward to penetrate. The thumbs close in within an inch of each other to surround the ball. The hands and wrists are firm and strong. When a blocker lands, she should flex her knees to help prevent injury and athletically ready herself to make her next move. Her feet should return to the same position she took off from. She should be ready to pivot, turn, and step in the direction of the ball. She may have to play the next ball or transition to attack. When a blocker lands, she can come down one of two ways. From an aggressive blocking situation, she should come down strong on two feet. To transition, she can either jump sideways to the net and sidestep off or turn and run. If she goes up to block and knows she is not even close to blocking the ball, she can come down in a "step-step" tempo. It is a quick landing where one foot lands just before the other, but the blocker starts her next movement in the next intended direction. This could be a blocker transitioning off the net. This could be a middle blocker who has just been duped into jumping with the first tempo hitter when the ball is actually being set outside.

Sequential Movement

The blocker starts at base position and watches the opponent's play develop. A blocker's eyes must stay ahead of the ball and assess the action. Being able to see around the direct visual focus requires the use of peripheral vision. The only time the blocker and her defense focus directly on the ball is on contact. The coach should face the blocker to watch her eyes refocus on proper read sequence.

A blocker first reads the flight of the pass. She should be able to watch the beginning path and read its intended direction. She should get her focus off the ball early and assess the information and cues or tendencies the setter reveals. This includes assessing a possible setter dump. The blocker must know if a hitter is in her area or zone. The blocker can read the path of the set but must take her focus off the ball before the set is at its peak. She must then focus on the hitter's path and read where the ball is traveling and what eligible hitters are in her zone. If she is the blocker closest to the attack zone, she will generally be the player to set the block. Usually, the blocker who sets the block lines up to *front the hitter*, meaning she moves so she is in line with the hitter's follow-through or where she assesses the ball will cross the net. Many young players line up chest to chest with an attacker and end up watching the ball fly outside their shoulder. If the ball is set in another area, the blocker has to make the decision to move and form a multiple block or transition and play floor defense as an off-blocker. The blocker now focuses the hitter's contact on the ball. In general, the blocker must get over the plane of the net before the ball is contacted. This will vary with the distance off the net the ball is set. In review, the blocker's visual sequence is ball-setter-ball-hitter.

Young blockers and defensive players focus too much on the ball. This eliminates the opportunity to read how the player is going to play the ball. An example of this is the opponent's attacker who is approaching the set looking like the Statue of Liberty, and everyone else knows she is going to tip. Since the grassroots team is focusing on the ball, they rotate into a blocking defensive scheme instead of transitioning and digging a tip.

Push-Step-Close-Step/ Sidestep

This footwork is used when a blocker has to adjust up to eight feet. The ability to travel this distance using this footwork pattern is dependent on the length of the legs and the agility and power of the blocker. It is movement done by an outside blocker to adjust to her blocking assignment. A middle hitter who does not have to travel too far along the net also uses it. It is a safe movement because the shoulders and hips face the net throughout the movement. It is quick footwork and adds momentum to the blocker's jump. The weight has to be on the inside of the feet with more

weight on the foot opposite the intended direction (the trail foot). As the blocker gets ready to step with the foot closest to the intended destination (the lead foot), she pushes off her trail foot first. Then the trail foot closes next to the lead foot and stops the lateral movement (see figure 10.3). Lastly, the lead foot takes one more step to balance and ready the blocker to jump. The feet should be slightly narrower than the ready position so she is ready to gain her maximum jump. Weight should be distributed on both feet with slightly more on the leg closest to the sideline. This will give the blocker more stability to jump up. It will also give the blocker more strength to defend against the *wipe*. Many times hitters try to *wipe* the hit off the block if they know the blocker has a tendency to drift. This could also happen if the blocker has her blocking hands facing out of bounds (usually the feet are planted incorrectly, too). Sometimes the hitter can wipe when the outside hand and arm are not strong and turned inward. Having more weight on the sideline leg will build power and strength toward the middle of the court. The sideline leg should also be slightly closer to the net with the foot slightly toed in toward the center of the court.

Pivot Step Crossover

This is the footwork most commonly used by a blocker who has to travel over seven feet away. The middle blocker often uses it to close a block with the outside blocker. It covers more distance because it is basically a turn and run movement. The blocker first pivots and pushes off the trail leg. At the same time, the lead leg takes a step in the intended direction (see figure 10.4a). The trail leg then crosses over the lead leg (see figure 10.4b). This step is the break step so the blocker must plant her foot to stop the movement. That trail leg must be planted with the toes facing back toward the net. The lead leg then balances the movement and readies the jumper (see figure 10.4c). Make sure the lead foot is planted facing the net slightly forward of the trail foot. This will help keep

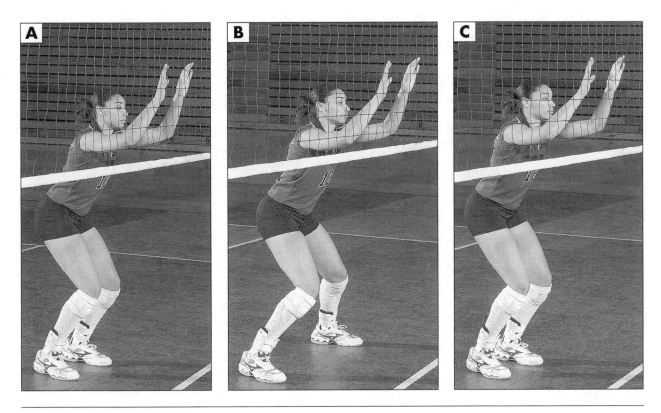

Figure 10.3 Push-step-close-step.

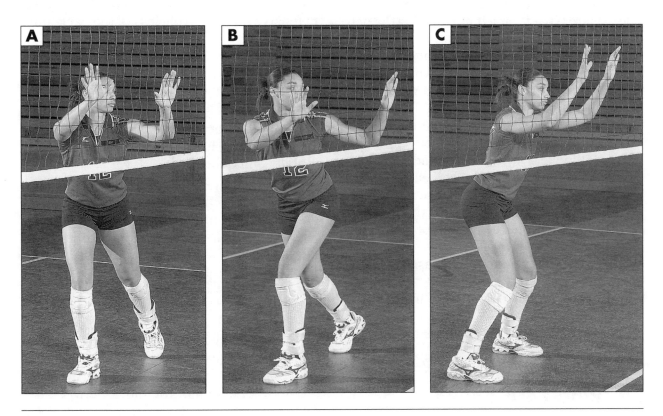

Figure 10.4 Pivot step crossover.

her outside shoulder forward and stronger so it won't be "used" by the attacker. The feet should be planted at a distance that supports maximum jump. It is usually slightly narrower than the ready position.

Transitioning off the Net

For transitioning off the net, blockers need to practice their landing and footwork. When a blocker lands on two feet, she has to pivot, turn, and step in one movement. After this initial move, the hitter runs off the net. This is consistent and easily trained from every attack point on the net. Blockers who know the ball is not even close to being blocked can come down "step-step" as previously explained. Some hitters, especially middles, find it easier to land more flexed on two feet. Then they do a quick jump (90 degrees flexed) and start sidestepping off the net. They can watch the ball back over their shoulder so they know when to stop and how to time the start to their attack pattern. Some middles always come down with their left hip facing the net. This ensures that their left hip is facing the net during their attack pattern. They only have to plant right-left or jump off two feet as a finale in their approach. But blockers who execute this method cannot play balls defensively to their left when they come down. The coach would have to put this responsibility onto the outside blocker or off-blocker (left front player). Blockers who are trained to come down in the direction of the ball can execute this technique, too. It seems more natural to turn in the direction of the ball. If the blocker comes down with her right hip forward, she sidesteps off the net watching the ball over her left shoulder. Then on her last sidestep backward, she steps her right foot behind her and uses it as a push off for her first step in her forward approach to her attack pattern. This puts her left hip toward the net, ready to plant and jump.

Blocking Formations

There are four kinds of blocking formations, namely, one person, two person, three person, and none (otherwise called *nobody home*). There is a particular time when each system is usually used, and each has its advantages and disadvantages. Chapter 12 discusses the four formations in more detail.

Blocker Responsibilities and Tactics

The responsibilities and tactics of blockers will vary according to a coach's philosophy and game plan, but the following are some guidelines.

- Many people say that a blocker is the first line of defense. The blocker is also the first line of offense when attacking an overpass.

- Take away the hitter's best shot. In high school, it is usually a crosscourt shot. But I have seen line hitters destroy a team who does not adjust. Force a hitter to use another shot. Many intermediate hitters do not have one, so they tip. Also, a hitter will divert back to her favorite shot, especially in long rallies.

- One of the blocker's responsibilities is to block an area of the court. This will allow the defensive players to dig less of the backcourt around the *shadow of the block*. The shadow of the block is the area behind the blockers that does not have to be defended from a spike. Of course, this means that every block is successfully timed and executed!

- Middle blockers are usually involved in every attack. They must be smart, laterally mobile, and quick.

- On a perimeter set, the sideline blockers usually set the block and the middle blockers close the block. The outside blocker must set the block early enough to give the middle blocker a target to get to. The outside blocker does not want to adjust out toward the antenna again. This will cause her to drift out and weaken her block. It will also prevent the middle blocker from closing the block. Having a hole in the block ruins the shadow of the block. It causes havoc with your backcourt and invites the hitter to put a ball to the floor. The area of the block between the blockers' hands is called the *seam of the block*. Many hitters aim for the *seam* knowing that it can be a weak area of the block.

• If the sideline blocker takes away a cross-court hit, the middle blocker is taking up space. This is a tough concept for the middle blocker to accept. The middle blocker needs to understand her responsibility. The middle blocker must be ready to block the ball in case the sideline blocker does not set the block properly or the hitter cuts the ball around the block.

• Generally, the sideline blocker blocks crosscourt and invites the hitter to hit line. This is good percentage play for the blocker because the sideline limits the amount of useable court space. A defensive team can also position a backcourt player to dig a line hit.

• The farther out the set is, the more the block is set in. Kids want to do just the opposite. They love to set a block at the antenna when the set is outside the antenna. Players have to see that the antenna cuts the possible angle the ball can legally be hit into. The whole team, including the diggers, can defend just the crosscourt area. This is a blocking tactic that has to be visualized and trained.

• The farther off the net the set is, the more inside the block should be set. It is more difficult to hit a set off the net down the line than a tighter set.

• Train your players to read the whole play. If the set is off the net, the middle blocker should shift her weight onto her left foot to get ready to push off to block an opponent's probable outside hit. A poorer pass usually means another outside set, and the left front blocker should get ready to become an off-block digger in the defensive scheme. A bad set could also mean a higher outside hit. A higher outside set usually means a powerful crosscourt hit or mistiming by the hitter and a possible tip.

• A high outside set that is not pushed out to the antenna is usually hit at a lower part of the set by the hitter. She is looking for a ball pushed out and is ready to make a step to the ball near the sideline. The hitter has to adjust in, and many times does not adjust enough. This is a hit that many blockers can *stuff block*.

• A blocker should be careful not to *reach away from help*. This means that the outside blocker should not reach with her outside hand for the ball. If the ball diverts from her hand, it will be hit off the court and away from the defense. This is also true of the middle blocker. Many times we train our middles to "get out and close the block." If they don't get there, many times they reach out. This drops the height of their block. It makes more sense for the outside blocker to close a bad block. She would be reaching in toward the court where her help is.

• If the middle blocker is having trouble planting her feet and keeps colliding with the outside blocker, she may be overzealous and is trying to block a ball instead of close a block set by the outside blocker. At a USA CAP clinic, Joel Dearing suggested the blocker "sneak a peak" to help while training.

• After a successful block, expect a tip. After a successful block, expect the setter to set a different hitter.

• During long rallies, expect the other team's hitters to transition less. This can result in the hitter being under the ball. Hitters who are under the set will hit the ball higher with more of a chance to hit the top of the block or go over deep. Some hitters tip or roll shot more.

• If a hitter has an error, expect her to change her shot the next time she is set.

• During practice, a coach can observe blockers from behind, in front, or from a referee stand. When you face the blockers, you can see their faces and head level well. You can also see where they are looking through the entire play. From the referee stand, you can see how much the blocker's hands penetrate the net. From behind, you can see how well they close the block and the footwork. You can also check out where they jump from and where they land.

• Train your blockers to come down from a partial block or tip and play balls within reach of them.

• It is equally important to train your players when NOT to block. Train your blockers not to jump when they recognize a free ball, tip, or roll shot. Some blockers fake a jump to scare an opponent so they will send the ball deeper. Some teams still have the blockers jump to try to either block, force the opponents into a deeper third hit, or to attack a ball. A coach has to decide what her philosophy is and what the success percentage is in these situations. I have had great middle blockers who I have sent up to defend the low topspin standing hit. I have had others that I have trained to transition off the net because they end up causing more errors.

- Tighter sets are easier to block because the timing is easier. The farther the set is off the net, the more patient the blockers have to be. If it is a double block, the blockers have to be trained to jump in unison.

- Make sure the middle blocker is trained to travel from the middle to the outside with her hands high. Many net touches are made when the blocker lifts the arms to jump.

Tips for Teaching Beginners Blocking

- At the grassroots level, blocking can be the last skill taught. You know it is time to teach blocking when the diggers can't handle the heat of the spike.

- Blocking should be taught on a net relative to the appropriate age level. The Canadians have several different net heights, which encourages realistic hitting and blocking. The only drawback to using a low net is that overhand serves zoom in faster.

- The rookie blocker needs to see a good role model executing the ready position and block jump. Also point out how the feet come down in the footprints of where they took off from.

- The players should work on good ready position first. Hands held higher, hands in front of the face, and weight on the balls of the feet with the heels up are very important keys.

- Once the coach feels the blocker has good ready position, the jump needs to be added in the drill. Make sure hands are held high through the jump and hands push diagonally forward for penetration (or to seal the net). A bad habit many young blockers acquire is dropping the hands low when coiling to jump and swinging the arms forward to penetrate the net. Lastly, the head level should be checked. Blockers should watch the ball with their eyes, not by picking up their chins. If the blocker lifts her chin, her arms will lift up instead of press forward to seal or penetrate. This is one of the common reasons blockers get stuffed.

- Once the blocker has achieved a good ready position and block jump, the coach can stand on a hitting box and hit balls into the blocker's hands. This should be done repetitively to help the blocker develop penetration and "mold" around the ball. The blocker should practice ready position, coil and jump, penetration, and pressure around the ball. The coach can see if the player is a "peakaboo" blocker. In other words, if the blocker just gets her hands up above the net with no penetration, the coach will teach this blocker to *seal the net* to effectively stop or slow down attacks.

- Movement should be added as soon as the blocker has demonstrated good stationary blocking technique. The first movement taught should be side step (two steps) to the ball. Teach and train the footwork first and then add the jump. Keep in mind that the ready position and stop/jump position feet are slightly different. Remember, if you don't start right you won't finish right! Keep the player on the block with the ball. Have the blocker start off two steps to the right or left of the stationary ball. The blocker can then practice footwork adjustment and block jump to the ball in each direction.

- Once the blocker can adjust a few steps and block a stationary ball, it is time to practice stationary blocking technique against live attacks. Have a capable player or coach stand on the block and hit self-tosses into a jumping blocker. Start by having the hitter face and swing into the same direction (e.g., cross-court). This will give the blocker a chance to feel the impetus of the hit and how strong the blocker's arms must be to reject the ball.

- Once the blocker has attained this goal at a reasonable level, the blocker needs to make adjustments to the hitter's approach. This is a great time to teach blockers how to read approaches and arm swings. Blockers can also start learning how to front the hitter. This is taught by having the blocker adjust in line with the attacker's hitting shoulder to intersect her direct angle of approach and follow-through.

- Many blockers have a bad habit of just watching the ball and not reading the attacker. The blocker needs to learn how to read the approach *and* front the hitter. The front the hitter drill below can help in training the blocker.

- The next progression is training the crossover step. This is usually a middle hitter course, but some perimeter blockers use it as a movement to multiple block in the middle.

- Another aggressive block technique is to attack an overpass or a set in the plane of the net or over the net. If a blocker reads that the pass or set is coming over the net, the appropriate blocker must readjust her feet behind the path of the ball and ready herself to jump. By assessing the height and depth of the ball, the blocker has to decide whether to seal the net, attack block, or spike the ball. If the ball is falling near the top of the net tape, the blocker may choose to block straight up and seal the net allowing the ball to fall on the other side of the net. This is a wise choice when the setter is playing the ball at the top of the net on her side and the blocker can't interfere. She may also choose to penetrate the net and block the ball down as a stuff block by propelling her hands and wrists forward to direct the ball straight down to the opponent's floor. This is a wise choice if the ball is in the plane of the net or an opponent is not attempting to play the ball. If the path of the ball is high and deep enough, the hitter can drop step and spike the ball. The attacking blocker rarely has a block and can hit.

BLOCKING DRILLS

Front the Hitter

Purpose: To work on blocking and focusing on the hitter's path

Equipment: Regulation court setup, bucket of balls

Procedure: One player, who will hit a toss, stands near the attack line on court A. An opposing player, who will block the hitter, starts in a blocking position on court B. A coach or player stands behind the blocker at about midcourt. The coach tosses the ball over the head of the blocker (she can't see it) so the hitter can approach and hit (see figure 10.5). The toss should simulate a high outside overpass. The hitter approaches the overpass and tries to hit the ball versus the one blocker. The blocker reads the hitter's approach and positions herself to block the attack. Score can be kept by awarding one point for an attack into the court and two points for a block.

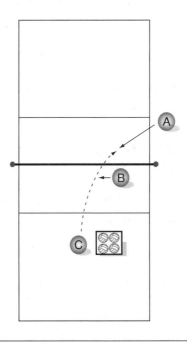

Figure 10.5 Front the hitter drill.

Key point: Proper blocking movement and technique should be coached.

Variations: A middle and an outside blocker can block a hitter. Scoring should be one point for a block and two points for an attack.

Joust

Purpose: To work on blocking, coverage, playing tight balls in the plane of the net, digging balls near the block or around the block, and digging balls stuffed in front of the blocker

Equipment: Regulation court setup, referee stand, bucket of balls

Procedure: Team A and team B are set up in base one positions on each side of a court. Blockers are facing each other at the net. The coach is standing on a referee stand attached to one standard. The coach tosses a ball in the plane of the net between two opposing blockers. The blockers are only allowed to attack block, tip, or joust the ball. No spiking can occur. The rest of the players on the court move from base one to cover the blocker as they would a hitter. Whatever side the ball is propelled to after the joust, that team plays the ball out as they would in a game. Gamelike play continues until one team wins the rally. A point is awarded to the team who wins the rally.

Key points: Coverage must be low. The first pass should be coached to be played up to the center of the court or near the target according to skill level. Blockers must keep their hands in front of them to stay strong through the joust.

Variations

- The coach can toss the ball between two sets of blockers to create double blockers on the ball.
- The coach can occasionally toss the ball into the backcourt to make sure they are focused on playing the first ball.
- Scoring can be wash, rally, or yo-yo.
- After one team reaches the goal score, the coach can have the front and back rows flip-flop positions or rotate.
- A lead-up to this drill is conducted by tossing the ball up between two players.

- The next lead-up to this drill would be to toss a ball up between two players and have one player behind each blocker to help with coverage.

Empire Drill

Purpose: To work on blocking and transition

Equipment: Regulation court setup, two buckets of balls

Procedure: Two coaches are positioned on each side of a court in the deep 6 position with a bucket of balls. Team A and team B are made up of five players in the other positions at their base one position defensively. The coach on team A's side slaps a ball to signal her front row to transition off the net, and the setter goes to target to receive an incoming toss from the coach (see figure 10.6). The setter runs an offensive play. Team B forms a defense to stop the attack. If the ball comes on team B's side, they dig the ball and counterattack. Play continues in a usual manner. If a ball is attacked in the 6 area, the coach tosses another ball to the target area. If the ball hits

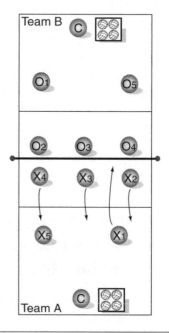

Figure 10.6 Empire drill.

the floor on one side, in or out of bounds, the coach on that side slaps another ball and tosses it to target to continue the drill.

Key points: This is a continuous drill that is tiring because it demands constant blocking, transition, attack patterns, and coverage. The coach needs to maintain correct tempo by requiring the front row to transition in a timely manner. The coach needs to make sure the back row defense does not rely too heavily on the coach at 6 and plays as many balls as possible in their positions.

Variations

- Scoring can be plus or minus points for winning a rally or successfully running set plays.
- If a team has numerous setters, the coach should make sure the setters have a chance to set different hitters.
- The setters can be front row or penetrate from the back row.
- The coach can dictate any set play to run offensively or let the setters call their own plays.

Lateral Blocking Drill

Purpose: To work on blocking and movement

Equipment: Regulation court setup, volleyballs, hitting boxes

Procedure: Two players stand on hitting boxes on one side of the court, one at the middle (3) and the other at the left-side (4) position. Each player holds a volleyball above the net. On the other side of the court, a blocker stands opposite the middle position in block ready posture (see figure 10.7). When the coach says "go," the blocker jumps up and attempts to block the ball. It would resemble "surrounding" the ball. The blocker comes down, performs her blocking movement footwork toward the outside, and performs a block on the other ball. The blocker repeats this drill, going back and forth between the two balls, until she has

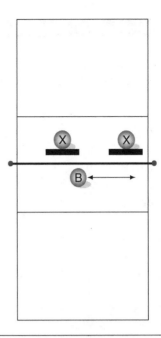

Figure 10.7 Lateral blocking drill.

performed the set number of blocks assigned by the coach.

Key points: The players on the boxes holding the ball must extend the ball high enough for the blocker to use her individual maximum jump. The coach can instruct the blocker technically throughout the drill. The players holding the ball should feel some pressure over the top of (behind) the ball to prove penetration.

Variations

- The same drill can be set up with the blocker moving toward the opposite direction.
- A second blocker, on the outside, can set up to simulate a double block.
- The distance the blocker must travel can be lengthened to work on a crossover step or shortened to work on a side step movement.
- The coach can count the number of reps performed in a set amount of time.
- The player holding the ball on the platform can perform a standing hit into the blocker's hands instead of holding the ball.

FLOOR DEFENSE

Playing floor defense is like being a hockey goalie. It is your last line of defense before a score.

For a player to be successful at digging, she must have an attitude . . . aggressive! She must always be able to play by the two rules that are posted in every gym. Go ahead, walk into your gym right now. Every coach knows where they are posted.

Rule #1 Get to every ball.

Rule #2 If you can't get to every ball, refer back to rule #1.

This means pursuing a ball in wild abandonment. It means not giving up on a ball until it has bounced twice (the ref may not have seen the first bounce).

Great defensive players keep rallies going and help win that big volley that can emotionally swing the momentum to your side. The crowd oohs and aahs great digs, but hitters get the all-star awards. You know your kids really love volleyball when you watch them mature and go from loving to serve, then hit, and finally to loving to play defense. That's when you know you have a complete player.

Floor defense is used in digging spikes, tips, touches off a block, roll shots, and well-placed returns by the opponent. It is any ball that cannot be played in a balanced forearm or overhead pass. But the rules have changed to where floor defense can be played with an overhead pass or a forearm pass technique as long as the ball is not held too long. Double contacts by a player are allowed on the first contact on a side. Floor defense can also include a ball rebounding off other body parts including the feet.

Traditionally, most defense is played with a forearm contact. The game is moving toward training overhead contacts. These are becoming more and more popular on the first contact because of increased control, the ability to play in the middle of the court instead of perimeter, the ability to have more range in a play area, and the ability to play touches off blocks deeper behind the court. All of these plays would have been whistled illegal contacts a few years ago.

Ready Position

From her base position, the defensive player establishes her floor position. The defensive player is in a low, ready floor position at base one. After reading the set, blocking scheme, and hitter's approach, the digger adjusts to the correct floor position while maintaining her low posture. Her feet are pointed in the direction of the middle of the court, and her upper body is turned toward the attacker. This is called *facing on help*. This will allow the ball to be dug in the direction of the middle of the court and in the direction of her teammates in case help is needed. It will also prevent the defensive player from digging a ball back up to the attacker to smack back on her! After the digger has established her floor position, she realigns her posture and is ready to dig the ball. She was already in a low position but must lower it more and lean into the line of attack. This is achieved by bending forward so the shoulders are in front of the knees and the knees are ahead of the toes (see figure 10.8). The feet are wide and the weight on the balls of the feet with the heels up. The right foot is slightly ahead of the left. The back and shoulders are

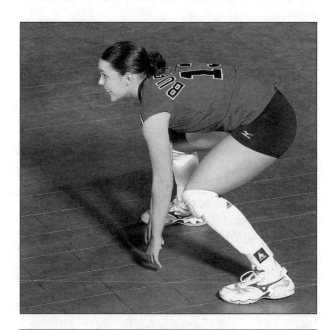

Figure 10.8 Ready position for the dig.

rounded close to parallel to the floor, and the head is up watching the ball. The arms are relaxed over the thighs, ready and available to dig a ball using the forearm or overhead. The body is leaned forward, and the center of gravity is low. If a person were to push a digger from behind, she would have to step forward with her left foot to stop from falling on her face.

Individual Defense

The digger must assess from the hitter's arm swing the speed of the attack. If the hitter is swinging full force, the digger has to present her digging platform to dig the attack. This may require a quick foot adjustment and platform change. As the ball hits her platform, she has to feel how much impetus or absorption to put on the ball to contain the ball on her court.

Sometimes the digger has to adjust the platform rebound angle toward the target. If the ball is hit outside the line of the body, the digger has to adjust her feet and body position to dig the ball. Many times she has to change her posture and drop her inside shoulder. By dropping the inside shoulder, she will help ensure that the ball rebounds off the arms into the middle of the court instead of into the side wall. When reaching to play a ball, the top arm shields the ball from going back, and the bottom arm is pointed to the intended target (see figure 10.9).

If a digger has to move forward to play a ball, she can rush under the ball and squat down presenting a platform parallel to the floor. This pass will ultimately be a higher pass but will allow the setter to move under the ball effectively.

If a digger can't get to the ball and must play a ball on the run, she may have to J-stroke her platform to contain the ball into her own court. This is accomplished by lifting the thumbs up and bending the elbows (see figure 10.10). The bad thing about a J-stroke is it creates a backspin on the ball, making it tricky for the setter to overhead pass.

If the hitter's elbow is dropped or the swing slows down with the hand opening up, the

Figure 10.9 Adjusted digging position to prevent the ball from going behind.

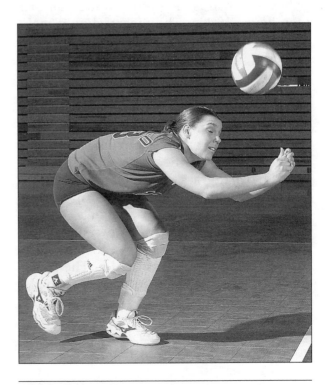

Figure 10.10 J-stroke.

digger knows she has to get ready to dig a roll shot or tip. As the hitter makes contact, the digger would move to the ball with her left foot first and run to play the off-speed shot. If the defender cannot stop and play the ball with a balanced pass, she would initiate a *run-through*. A run-through is executed by playing a ball on the run using a forearm pass. The digger must time the contact, angle her platform to the target, follow through and finish in the intended direction, and run past the contact point. Many times this can be as low as the player's shoestrings or outside her body on the run. If the ball is played laterally, the player must keep her arms and platform in front of the body in order to get the ball to the target. In all digging, the defender must keep the ball between her and the net.

If the ball is coming at the face or overhead, the digger must use a different type of dig. She can use her hands in an overhead dig. The defender must make her hands and wrists strong and push forward with her elbows to stop the impetus of the hit from driving the ball backward. The defensive player might use an overhead dig, or *beach dig*, by interlocking her hands at the thumbs and using her palms and hands as a rebounding platform (see figure 10.11). The digger should make sure the platform is pointing upward. The defender pushes the ball up by straightening her elbows on contact.

The digger may have to resort to using one hand or one arm in a juggling effect. This could be performed underhand, overhead, or by reaching. The ball must be contacted by the fist, hand, or arm in the proper place to ensure that the ball doesn't deflect off the court. The goal is to make the ball propel upward so someone can play the next contact.

When a ball is hit between two defenders, both defenders have to move to the ball in the path of their responsibilities. The trajectory of the spike will determine whose ball it is. When two players, or the diggers, move in the direction of the ball, this is called *meshing*. Usually, the person closer to the ball would go in front, and the one farther from the ball would go behind.

Coaches need to work on good individual technique for each player before developing

Figure 10.11 Overhead dig.

team defensive systems. Players need to be able to read and adjust to various hitting and blocking assignments. Once a player can dig a ball up and contain it on the court, she can start working on developing better ball control. Better ball control will lead her team to better counterattack possibilities, which is a huge step in performing up to the next level of play.

Sequential Movement

Just as blockers have an eye sequence (ball-setter-ball-hitter), the floor defenders have a sequence for movement and posture from base one to base two. At base one the defense watches the passer and on contact leans and readies for an overpass. If the pass is contained on the opponent's court, the defender can read it within the first few feet of the pass. Remember that the defense always focuses ahead of the ball to picture and assess the preparation of the opponent's total action.

The defense now locates the hitters and the speed and direction of their approaches. The defense may make some adjustments to establish net and floor position to ready for a setter dump or a first tempo attack. Still at base one, the defenders focus on the setter and what clues she will reveal. They are in a forward lean ready for a setter dump. Now, focus on the ball and back to the hitter. If the speed and direction of set shows a quick set, the blockers jump and the defenders dig. If there is no quick set, the defenders move to ready position or base two. The block sets up around the intended hitter and focuses on the hitter's actions. The floor defenders are in a forward lean reading the hitter and moving to make a dig.

DIGGING DRILLS

Virginia Tech Drill

Purpose: To work on pursuit, digging, run-throughs, and team spirit and support

Equipment: Regulation court setup, full bucket of balls

Procedure: Three players line up behind the end line near position 1 (see figure 10.12). The coach stands in the 2 area near the net. A player readies to hand balls to the coach. A target stands along the net. All extra players are in position to shag and fill the bucket. One player plays six balls in a row.

1. Player A steps into the court and digs a ball from the coach down the line.

2. The coach tosses a short tip in front of himself, and player A runs forward and digs the tip using a run-through.

3. As soon as player A digs the tip, the coach throws a ball toward the back left corner of the court. Player A turns, runs down the ball in pursuit, and digs the ball back into the center of the court.

4. As soon as player A saves the ball, she turns and gets into defensive pos-

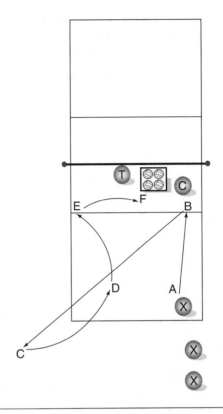

Figure 10.12 Virginia Tech drill.

ture. The coach hits a ball to player A deep in the court, and she digs the ball up.

5. Player A then adjusts to a court position just behind the attack line near the 4 position. The coach hits a ball on player A, who digs the ball up.

6. The coach tosses a tip in front of himself, at the 2 position, and player A runs and plays the ball up.

Player A gets behind player B and C in line. The drill repeats for player B and then player C.

Key points: This is a razzle-dazzle drill, and the team should be cheering for the player. The coach should tip, hit, and toss the ball to challenge the player to test her limitations. The purpose is for the player to dig balls to the center of the court or near target . . . not just touch balls.

Variations: Digs can be rated. The drill continues until a certain number of repetitions take place or until the coach's arm falls off.

Figure 8s

Purpose: To work on run-through defense and pursuit

Equipment: Regulation court, bucket of balls

Procedure: Three players line up behind the end line at the 6 area. A coach sets up in the middle of the same court in the 3 area near the net. A player hands her balls, and another player is the target. The rest of the team shags the balls that do not go to target. The coach tosses a ball toward the 1 area near the deep corner to create a run-through for player A. Player A runs to the right toward the 1 area to play the ball on the run using a run-through motion. Player A loops backward to return behind players B and C (see figure 10.13). The coach tosses another ball in the same area for player B to play and does the same for player C. By the time player C has played the ball, player A should be returning to the line ready to pursue another ball. The coach now tosses a ball to the opposite corner of the court toward the deep 5 area for player A to pursue and dig. Player A digs the ball and loops back to get back in line. The coach creates the same pursuit toss for player B and then player C, who proceed to dig the ball to target and return to line up behind the 6 area. The players should resemble a figure eight movement along the backcourt. The drill continues until a set number of balls are dug to target.

Key points: The coach must toss the ball just outside the reach of the pursuing player to create an effective run-through. The players MUST wait by the 6 area or the coach has to toss the ball farther outside the court (which makes the players have to run a bigger figure eight). The player should angle her inside shoulder down to create the correct angle on her platform. This is a fun drill and is tiring. It is a drill where the players can cheer for their teammates. But the purpose of the drill is to dig to target.

Variations: The same drill can be done with the coach tossing from a platform, which is more gamelike. It can also be done tossing near the 10-foot line. The drill can be timed.

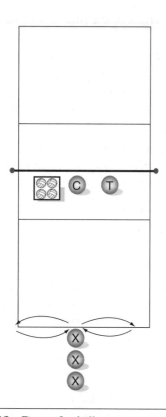

Figure 10.13 Figure 8s drill.

Up and Back Run-Throughs

Purpose: To work on run-through digging and pursuit

Equipment: Regulation court setup, bucket of balls

Procedure: Three players line up behind the end of the court at the 5 area. Another player acts as a target, and another hands balls to the coach. A coach tosses a ball over the net near the attack line area to create a run-through situation for player A. After player A plays the ball up, she returns by using a drop step and gets back in line. The coach tosses another ball to challenge player B and then player C. The drill continues until a set number of balls are passed to target.

Key points: The player cannot leave the back line until the coach has started tossing the ball. The coach must challenge the player to play a run-through. The pass is supposed to go to target or be dug into the center of the court.

Variations: This can be used as a warm-up, using a player to toss the ball and having more than one group on the court at once. To make the drill more gamelike, the group of three players can line up at base one defensively and rotate to base two (in any position) before the coach tosses a run-through.

Mountain Climber Digging

Purpose: To work on individual floor defense, lead-up to dive or sprawl, and endurance

Equipment: Regulation court setup or floor space, bucket of balls

Procedure: Three players perform the drill at one time. Player A starts near the 1 area, player B starts near the 6 area, and player C starts near the 6 area behind the end line. Each player starts performing the "mountain climber" exercise. In this exercise, the player's hands remain on the floor (in push-up position) while her feet run in an up and back rhythm. A target stands in the setter area on the same side of the court. A coach overhand throws (or hits) a ball in front of player A so she must push off and dig the ball in a diving or sprawling manner. The coach must throw the ball in front of the player so she has to play the ball in front of her. After player A digs the ball, she returns to her mountain climber position. The coach continues and throws a ball in front of player B and then player C. The drill can be performed until the group of three passes a specified number of balls to target.

Key points: Players need to push off their front foot and thrust their forearms under the ball. The diggers want to keep the ball off the floor and dig the ball up to the target or center of the court.

Variations: Scoring can be number to target in a row. Scoring can be a bucket of balls using the 3-2-1 target scoring. Scoring can be number of balls to target in a given time.

Out of the Blocks

Purpose: To work on run-through digging

Equipment: Regulation court setup or floor space, bucket of balls

Procedure: Three players perform the drill at one time. Player A starts near the 1 area, player B starts near the 6 area, and player C starts near the 6 area behind the end line. Each player starts in a simulated "track start" with her hands on the floor and feet in an up and back stride. A target stands in the setter area on the same side of the court. A coach bounces a ball in front of player A so she has to run forward and dig the ball on the run. The player should be led into performing a run-through dig. Player A then drop steps and assumes her start position behind the end line. The coach continues the drill bouncing a ball in front of player B and then player C. The drill can be performed until the group of three passes a specified number of balls to target.

Key points: Players should not step and jab to pass a ball. Players should dig to target high enough for a setter to play the ball. Players should maintain low posture throughout the drill. Players should use proper communication.

Variations: Scoring can be number to target in a row. Scoring can be a bucket of balls using the 3-2-1 target scoring. Scoring can be number of balls to target in a given time.

Defense Drill

Purpose: To work on defensive movement and digging; to warm up before a match

Equipment: Regulation court setup, bucket of balls

Procedure: A coach starts in the 4 position on one side of the net. Defensive players set up at base one on the same side of the net, at positions 1, 6, 5, and 4 (see figure 10.14). A setter starts at position 3. The coach pops

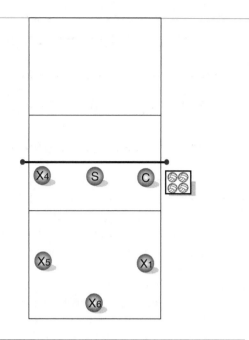

Figure 10.14 Defense drill.

a ball to the defense. The defense passes the ball to the setter. The setter dumps the ball back on the defense or sets the coach. The coach hits, tips, rolls, or passes the ball back onto the defense. The defensive players stay at base one and dig a setter dump. If the setter sets the coach, the defensive players rotate to base two and dig the ball back to the setter, and the drill continues. If the dig goes errant, the team pursues the ball and tries to maintain flow. To keep it more gamelike, if a dig goes errant, the pursuer must set up the coach since she is the second contact.

Key points: The coach should attack the team in the manner its opposition attacks. The defense should stick at base one in case the setter dumps. Once the setter releases a set, the defense should move to base two. The defense should communicate and read the set and the attack. If possible, the setter should back set to the coach. The setter must set the ball high enough to simulate the timing of a third tempo set or it will not allow the defense gamelike time to move to base two.

Variations: The coach can perform the drill from all attack zones on the defense. Another coach or player can perform the drill from an opposite zone to create more gamelike decision making and movement. If a player helps run the drill, she should be a defender (off-blocker) when the opposite coach/player attacks into the defense.

CHAPTER 11

OFFENSIVE STRATEGIES AND OPTIONS

Adopting an offensive team system is like having a physical examination. Just as a doctor evaluates a patient's total health, a coach has to assess a team's strengths and weaknesses. A coach can make rational decisions on an offensive system if he evaluates his player's ball control and setting. A coach who tries to make a team *fit* into a higher level offensive system, without possessing the proper basics, is setting his team up for failure.

BALL CONTROL

A team that has inconsistent passing has not met one of the criteria needed to run a more sophisticated system. If a team cannot pass a ball to the target area, a setter will be continually frustrated by running passes down or always calling for help on the second contact. This is not an offensive system. This is an *out-of-system* play.

Teams who have the ability to pass a ball to the target area instead of just up in the middle of the court can run a more sophisticated offense. If a ball can be passed to a smaller and tighter target area, a three-hitter attack can be used. A team who possesses capable setters and hitters can develop a multiple attack within the chosen offensive system.

SETTING

A coach has to evaluate the strengths of his setters. A setter must have good agility and range. A setter has to be in great aerobic condition, be explosive, and exude hustle. The setter's contact, consistency, and deceptiveness are considerations when choosing an offense. A setter must have perceptive focus so she can read and react to her opponent's plays and counteract them with effective setting choices. In addition, she has to be able to make quick decisions, be assertive, be a leader, and have a great team attitude.

Other considerations are blocking and serving abilities. If a setter is going to play front row, she should be able to block because her primary blocking assignment is against the opponent's power hitter. If she is not an effective blocker, a team may be forced to make adjustments to alter the defense. Some blocking systems have been developed to make the middle and left-side blocker in charge of the entire net. This alternative leaves more court space vulnerable and increases the area the two blockers are assigned to cover along the net. It can wreak havoc on a backcourt defense by creating holes in the block and increasing the area the diggers have to cover.

If the setter is going to play out of the back row, she must be able to serve. If a coach has to make a substitution for his setter, to enable someone else to serve, then another player has to set that half rotation. If a team has limited substitutions to use in a game, a valuable substitution is being used up every six rotations.

A setter is compared to a football quarterback. A quarterback must have the ability to read defenses and direct offenses by passing, running, and handing off. A setter must have the ability to run her offensive power around the strength of the opponent's defense. The biggest difference between the quarterback and setter is a quarterback gets more glory. The setter tends to be humble as a playmaker and allows the hitters to gain the fame.

In scholastic play, setters are generally the shorter and quicker players on the team. These players are usually a team's best athlete and are well respected for their hustle. Scholastic coaches have to use the players within their school to the best of their abilities and within the limited time frame of their season.

Junior clubs and colleges usually seek taller players or players with good vertical jumping ability in addition to all the setter qualities previously described. Club and college programs can choose their players from among many recruits. Taller setters can effectively play balls passed tight or at the top of the net. If the setter is back row, she can jump and set the ball instead of allowing the ball to hit the top of the net and fall down or letting the ball cross the net. If the setter is in the front row, she can set the tight pass, dump it to the opponent's court, or turn and hit it. She can also turn and joust a ball that is tight to the net and be an effective blocker in the front row. If the setter is deceptive, she can isolate a blocker on herself or on a quick hitter by "duping" her set.

Another consideration is choosing a left-handed setter. Most offensive systems require the setter, or passing target area, to be on the right side of the court. If a setter is left-handed, she can be a more effective attacker. Most setters use their left hand to tip with because they can direct the ball into the opponent's court more effectively. If a setter uses her left hand to tip a ball, she can play the ball at a higher trajectory, which makes the dump less likely to hit the net and less likely to be blocked by a defender. Most setters use their right hand to dump with behind their net position.

Lastly, a coach has to assess his number of setters when choosing an offensive system. If a team only has one consistent setter, the choice is easy! If a team has two or three setters, a coach has to make a decision. Are two or three of the setters consistent and parallel in effectiveness? Can the team pass well to target or can it only pass the ball up into the middle of the court? Are both setters excellent attackers? Is one setter an excellent attacker and the other setter too small to play front row? Are three setters effective and needed as attackers? Answering these questions will help a coach choose which system to use.

There are two general types of offensive systems. One is a system using a front court setter, and the other is a system using a back-court setter. The main offensive systems are the 4-2, the 5-1, and the 6-2. The first number in the system name refers to the number of hitters in the offense. The second number refers to the setters used in the system. If the numbers combined add up to more than 6, it signifies that the setter or setters are used as hitters, and the setter penetrates from the back row.

Front Court Setter Offensive Systems

The advantages of front court setter systems are simplicity in movement and less confusion in transition. When a setter is in the front row position, the passers have a larger target area. It also provides a shorter movement to the target for the setter. During transition, the setter is already in the front row so there is no confusion with the hitters. It also adds a passer to the back row so the passing base is more effective. Adding a passer in the back row also adds a back row attacker and a player in hitter coverage.

4-2 Offense

The 4-2 offense is the most basic system. It utilizes two setters who set when they are in the front row. The setters must be arranged opposite each other in the lineup.

When the setter rotates to the front row, she becomes the setter to the two front row players who are the hitters. The setter always sets from the middle front position. When she is in the front right (2) or front left (4) rotational position, she only has to change places with the hitter next to her. In the middle front (3), she is already in the correct position and does not have to change positions (see figure 11.1).

When the setter rotates to the back row, she becomes a back row passer. When she is in the back row, she can help set if the pass is too far off the net. This is an out-of-system help play.

If a team specializes in the back row, many coaches put the back row setter in the middle back position. Since the setter is usually a good athlete with good ball control, the coach wants her positioned in the middle of the court to pass a higher percentage of first contacts.

The benefit of the 4-2 is that it specializes the setter into the middle front position,

which is a larger area that allows a less skilled passing team to run an offense. The other advantage to the 4-2 is it usually is less confusing during transition. The setter is already in the front row. She does not have to deal with the confusion of penetrating into the front row between hitters who are transitioning off the net. Back row players do not have to expand their backcourt responsibilities by covering the backcourt setter's area during transition. The distance the setter has to travel to target is shorter than most backcourt systems, too.

The attack areas are more defined. If the setter is going to set a front row hitter, she either sets the front left or the front right player. Many grassroots programs use a front row setter system because of the complexities of playing a tight pass near the net. This affords the young setter the opportunity to tip the ball over the net before the pass hits the net. This does not imply that running a 4-2 offense cannot be sophisticated. Quick tempo sets, combination plays, switching hitter positions, back row attacks, setter attacks, and the use of a back row fake attacker can make the system more deceptive.

One of the cons of a 4-2 system is it puts more pressure on the hitters. The setter can

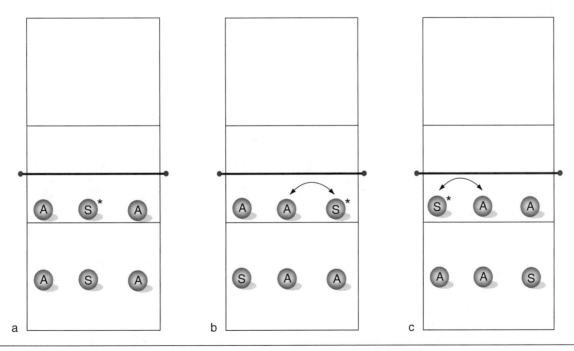

Figure 11.1 4-2 system: *(a)* Setter in middle front position—no setter switch needed; *(b)* setter in front right position; and *(c)* setter in front left position.

only set one of two front row players. The opportunity for the hitter to attack against two blockers occurs more often. Hitters need to be able to use a variety of shots to counteract the double block, including line, cut, roll, wipe, or tip shots. In scholastic play, where blocking is the weakest skill, hitters usually blast through the *seam of the block*, or between the blockers, hoping for a hole or mistimed double block. Some hitters try to hit at or over the small or weaker blocker. They have to learn to identify which middle blockers are slow so they can hit through the seam. They have to recognize when the opponent's outside blocker is small and take advantage of her height. Another effective play is to set lower sets to the *pin*, or antenna, hoping to split the block.

Since many setters are smaller, a coach needs to consider that with a 4-2 system, the setter becomes the middle blocker on defense. This can be a huge disadvantage if the team plays against an opponent who has a strong middle hitter.

For the setter, the 4-2 also involves more movement demands off the net to pursue bad passes. She has to move 180 degrees forward, backward, and off the net. The other offensive systems have more forward movement since their target passing area is off center of the net.

Another disadvantage is the setter should be able to back set the right front (2) hitter. Back setting is a blind set and takes practice to become consistent. Of course, the setter could turn and face her right-side hitter. But this telegraphs to the blockers where the set is going to be delivered early in the offensive play. This would allow the opponents to set up a more effective block.

International 4-2 System

This system is a variation of the basic 4-2. The main difference is the setter sets out of the right front (2) position (see figure 11.2). The 2 area is the passing target area on the court. When the setter is in the left front (4) and middle front (3) position, she has to switch to the right front position (2). When she is in the right front position, she does not have to change front row positions.

The International 4-2 has some advantages over the 4-2. A setter does not have to rely on the back set to deceptively set the right front (2) hitter because there is no right front hitter. Also, it allows a team to use a middle

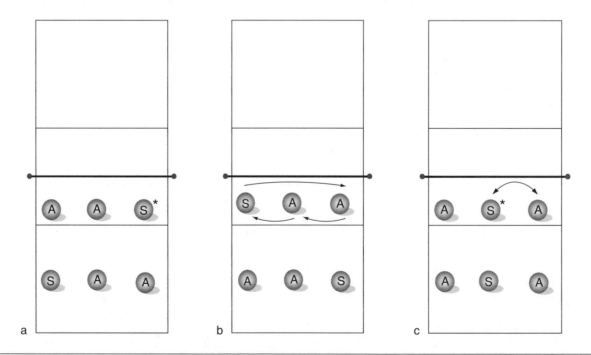

Figure 11.2 International 4-2 system: *(a)* Setter in front right position—no setter switch needed; *(b)* setter in front left position; and *(c)* setter in middle front position.

hitter/blocker. The middle area is a very effective area to hit from in an offense. The team can also use combination plays easier. The middle hitter (3) has the option to hit on the right side, especially if the pass goes in the middle of the net area. So, if the setter is capable, she can use her back set and attack the right side of the court.

The setter also has more area to tip into. If a setter is capable or is left-handed, she can turn and swing at tighter passes. If a pass is tight to the net, she does not have to joust against the opponent's middle blocker.

Many grassroots teams use this offense. It is the starting progression in developing a back-court setter system. It is easier to advance a team from an International 4-2 to a backcourt setter system (than from a basic 4-2 offense) because the net target area is similar.

Some grassroots teams put their best hitter in the middle, closest to the setter, so the delivered set is more accurate. This offense also allows the setter the choice to set a ball to the middle hitter who is closer to the setter. It is an easier set than the high outside set. As the setter develops a consistent outside set, she can be utilized.

If a coach specializes his backcourt players, many times he specializes the setter, after she rotates to the back row, into the right back area (1). This situates both the front and back row setters on the right side of the court. It allows the setters to move only into the center of the court, unless the pass is poor, so there is more efficient court movement.

If a coach is working toward developing a backcourt setter system, the International 4-2 system can be used to teach the passers to dig and pass right to the target. This is consistent with the 5-1 and 6-2 systems.

This system still allows the backcourt setter to help the front row setter's help call in an out-of-system play.

The disadvantages of the International 4-2 are few. One is the setter has to be able to push her outside set. This is the toughest set for a setter to become consistent in performing. In a basic 4-2, both her hitters are next to her so the setting areas are closer to deliver.

If the middle hitter is not trained to move out of the path of an errant middle court pass,

she is taken out of the offense. Many times, middle hitters set the second ball because they are in the way because of poor transition. This telegraphs to the defense that the middle hitter is not the setter and the ball is going to be tipped over the net or set to the outside (4) hitter. With proper training, the middle hitter can transition and hit behind the setter if the setter can back set. The setter can also run a combination play. If capable, the middle hitter can back set to the setter, who becomes a hitter in this out-of-system play. If the outside hitter sets the second ball, both the middle hitter and setter (who has called for help) now transition and become attackers.

Back row passers from the right back (1) or middle back (6) areas find it easier to pass to the target area (2). Right back (5) players have a bigger adjustment to overcome to pass or dig at a smaller angle to the target.

3-3 System

The 3-3 system uses three setters. The setters are set up in a triangle between the hitter's triangle (see figure 11.3, a and b). All six players are attackers. The designated hitters hit three times (rotations) in the front row. The designated setters only hit once in the front row when they are in the left front (4) rotational position. When the setter rotates to position 3 and 2, she is the primary setter in the offense. The system can specialize with the setter in a target area similar to basic 4-2 or like an International 4-2. When the primary setter rotates to the back row, she becomes a passer and only sets in out-of-system plays. This system allows a team to develop three setters and play them in competition. It also provides a larger target area for passers who are still developing consistency. To run a 3-3, a team must have good focus and communication.

The most elementary offense is setting by rotational position. This is common in recreation leagues, grassroots programs, and physical education classes. The variations are as follows:

- Whoever is closest to the second pass becomes the setter, and the rest of the players become attackers.

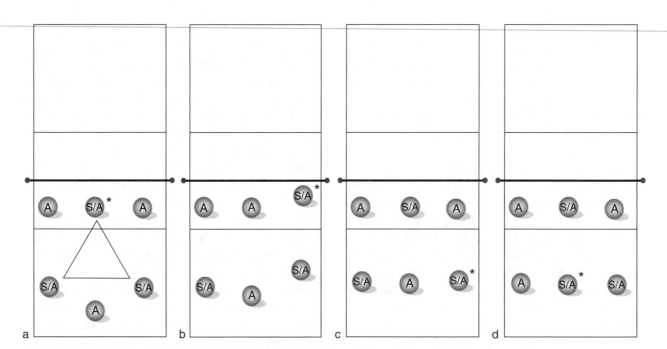

Figure 11.3 3-3 system: *(a)* Basic serve-receive lineup with primary setter in middle front; *(b)* primary setter in right front; *(c)* primary setter in right back; and *(d)* primary setter in middle back.

- Whoever is the middle front player (3) in rotation is the setter.
- Whoever is the right front player (2) in rotation is the setter.

The value of any of these systems is it allows all players the opportunity to learn and set all the positions. Sometimes when players are specialized too early in their development, they do not have the opportunity to acquire all the skills needed to be a total player. It also provides the opportunity for a player to better understand game situations and be exposed to all the positions.

Backcourt Setter Offensive Systems

The advantage of a backcourt setter system is that it adds one hitter to the offensive system. It gives the setter three attackers to choose from when running an offense. It isolates the opponent's block longer, therefore providing the opportunity to attack against a poorer formed block.

The use of backcourt setter systems depends upon the quality of a team's passing and setting. If both the setting is good and the passing is consistent, it is an easy choice. The system can also be used if the passers are excellent and the setter is average. The opposite is also true. If the setter is great and the passers are average, a backcourt setter system can still be used. Of course, the best scenario is to have good setters, passers, and hitters! Here I discuss the three main backcourt setter systems, along with some variations.

6-2 System

The 6-2 is three hitters attacking out of the front row using a backcourt setter. All six players get to hit when their rotational position is in the front row. The setter penetrates from a backcourt position.

The 6-2 backcourt setter system positions two setters lined up opposite each other in the lineup. When the setter is in the back row, she is the primary setter. In a basic 6-2, when the setter is in the front row, she becomes a hitter. See figure 11.4.

As previously stated, the greatest advantage to using a 6-2 is that it uses three front row attackers. The setting options increase, and the opportunities to create different play options and combinations are endless.

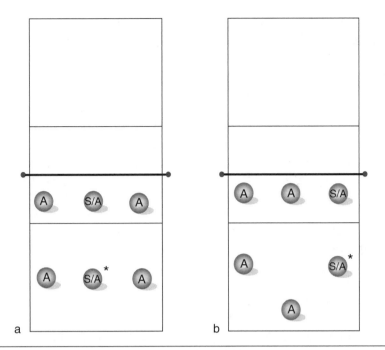

Figure 11.4 6-2 system: *(a)* Serve-receive rotation to *(b)* 6-2 base.

This can baffle the best blockers. If a team's passers are consistent, the hitters will have the opportunity to time their attack paths in combination plays. An added bonus in confusing the defense is deceptiveness on the part of a setter.

This is a common offense for a high school varsity team to use. Many teams have a few great athletes on the team. These athletes are a team's best hitters, passers, and setters. Sometimes it is difficult to decide if the athlete should pass and hit or be the setter. If a team is fortunate to have at least two good athletes, this could be a good system to use.

A disadvantage of the 6-2 is that it requires excellent passing. The target area is between the middle front (3) and right front (2) positions. It requires good communication to avoid confusion within the system. This can be an advantage in developing focus and teamwork!

The 6-2 requires four players, the three hitters and the backcourt setter, to be around the net. If the pass is errant, it can become very crowded along the net. The hitters have to trust that the setter can get to the pass, and the hitters have to transition themselves to line up on an advantageous attack pattern. The reverse is true. The setter has to be able

to read the trajectory of the pass early enough to communicate her intentions in case she needs to call "help." There are emergency situations where a poor pass is ricocheting off the passer's arms to the net so quickly that a front row hitter has to instinctively play the ball.

Another problem with the 6-2 is that the setter, who penetrates from the back row, cannot attack a ball above the height of the net and send it over to the opponent's court. This includes tipping, hitting, jousting, and blocking. If the pass is tight, she must be able to jump set the pass before it penetrates the net. The setter must be able to distinguish a bad pass from a settable pass. Sometimes this system requires setters, especially ones who are smaller in stature, to dig balls out of the net.

A setter has to have a variety of sets if she is going to run combination plays. Even if a team runs a basic offense, the setter must be able to run an outside, middle, and right-side set in order to use the three-hitter attack effectively along the entire net from pin to pin. Of course, the beauty of a 6-2 is to move three hitters in different patterns. But to run a 6-2, a coach needs to assess if a setter is capable of setting different options.

Setter training must include penetrating movement from the backcourt as well as movement along the net. Setter training must include defensive training for a backcourt setter to recognize when she has to play backcourt defense and when she can release to the front row to set. Setter training must include backcourt defense from every position an opponent attacks. Setter training must include good communication with the *off-setter*, or the designated setter in case the backcourt setter handles the first ball. As previously stated, setter training must include a variety of sets, jump setting, passing balls tight to the net, recognizing overpasses, and digging balls out of the net.

The two setters must deliver the ball in a similar manner so they don't confuse the timing of the hitters. Some setters have quirks that change the timing of a set. An example of a setter quirk is a setter who squats when she sets quicks or a first tempo set. Both of these examples take extra time and confuse the timing of the quick hitter. So, if one setter sets correctly and the other setter has quirks that confuse the hitters, the 6-2 may not be the best offense for the team. Both setters must have leadership and good communication skills in the backcourt.

Another disadvantage of the 6-2 is that the rest of the backcourt must cover the vacated setter area (1) when the setter penetrates to the front row on transition. Having two players cover the entire backcourt instead of three makes for a weaker passing base. The backcourt should always pass as many balls as possible to allow the front court the time to transition off the net and ready themselves for their attack approach. The entire team must understand *tempo passing*. Tempo passing is the ability to pass the ball so the air time of the pass is consistent no matter where the ball is passed from on the court. Therefore, a ball passed from the back line would be a flatter, faster pass. If the ball was passed from inside the 10-foot line, the ball would be passed higher. This will help the timing of the hitters when attacking the ball. Tempo passing is especially advantageous to the timing of first tempo balls. Passers must

assess whether the opponent's return is in the direction of the setter's position (1) or on the opposite side of the court (5). A backcourt setter's first responsibility is defense. Many setters "cheat" and release early. Smart opponents return tips, free balls, and down balls in the setter's backcourt area (1) to find open floor or confusion if the setter transitions too early. Otherwise, a pass from the setter forces the right side (2) player into a setting role. This would nullify the three-attacker advantage. An exception is the backcourt setter passing the first contact directly to a front row hitter to attack. This is called a *two-hit* or *two-touch* attack since the first contact becomes the setup. If the right-side hitter (2) is a lefty, this can be a great play. Obviously, this play has to be trained in practice.

A last disadvantage to discuss is poorer hitter coverage. The team is running an offense with three hitters, and the setter has transitioned to the front row. Setters do cover hitters, but they cover an area closer to the net. The backcourt hitter coverage is diminished by one player. The attacker on the opposite side of the play is supposed to cover some backcourt. Depending on the pattern used, this coverage can be less effective. But, if a team is playing against stuff blockers, having another player (back row setter) in the front row will help cover the area closest to the net.

Many disadvantages have been pointed out. A coach may ask, "Why would a team ever use this system?" If a team has the player and skill requirements to effectively run a 6-2, it can be the best system to effectively use a three-hitter attack on every rotation.

5-1 System

The 5-1 is the most widely used offense among higher level teams. The system uses one setter, and the other five players are hitters. When the setter is in the back row, the play is the same as the 6-2. When the setter is in the front row, the play is the same as the 4-2. Generally, when the setter is in the front row, a team plays an International 4-2. Although a basic 4-2 can be used in the front court, it changes the target area on the net. See figure 11.5.

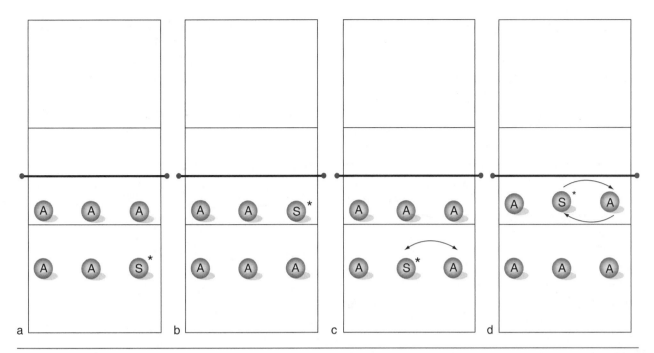

Figure 11.5 5-1 system: *(a)* Setter sets from back row—no setter switch needed; *(b)* setter sets from front row—no setter switch needed; *(c)* setter in middle back position; *(d)* setter in middle front position.

The advantages of the 5-1 are consistency in setting and leadership by one player. Even if a team possesses a few setters, usually one player is superior in skill, movement, and leadership capabilities. The 5-1 allows a coach to develop one player more effectively to set the offense. Teams who hit off one setter are more likely to have better timing when they hit. Using one setter is less confusing to a team and can decrease the number of unforced errors in transitional play. Players respond better to one leader.

When the setter is in the backcourt, a three-hitter attack is in play. This is a huge advantage. Conversely, when the setter is in the front court, a two-hitter attack is in play. This can be a disadvantage, as will be pointed out. A system that uses both a three- and two-hitter attack can be confusing to an opponent.

One advantage of the 5-1 is that the opponents must keep track of the setter's position. For three rotations, the setter is in the backcourt. The opponents know they have to defend three hitters. The setter cannot tip or attack the second contact above the net. For three rotations, the setter is in the front row. When the setter is in the front row, she can attack the ball above the net. A setter who is effective at tipping can become an attacker on the second contact. If the setter is left-handed (or a right-hander has been trained), she can swing at the second contact.

Another advantage is a team can utilize a great right-side hitter, or an *opposite*, in the lineup. An opposite is the hitter lined up opposite the setter in the lineup. Sometimes this player is a lefty or an effective blocker against the opponent's power hitter.

Other advantages of the International 4-2 and the 6-2 also apply to the 5-1 according to where the setter's rotation is on the court.

The disadvantages of the 5-1 are few but have impact on three rotations. When the setter is in the front row, she only has two attackers in the system at the net. The disadvantages of a 4-2 have been discussed. A higher level team must depend on better back row attack, the deceptiveness of a setter, the setter as an attacker dumping and setting, fakes, an effective lineup, serve receive formations that camouflage the position of the setters and hitters, and creative plays. It also helps if a team's best middle hitter and outside hitter surround the setter.

A 5-1 setter's team has to be aware of the position of their setter. If the setter is in the backcourt, the two remaining passers must split the court and take on the setter's defensive responsibilities when the setter penetrates to the target. A team's quickest and best passers must surround the setter in the lineup.

Another disadvantage of a 5-1 has been cited as an advantage. It is training one setter to be the quarterback. If the setter becomes ill, injured, or mentally "loses" it in a game, substituting affects the whole team. Even though coaches train a backup setter . . . "it just ain't the same." A smart coach not only trains a backup setter but also gives her game time.

In scholastic play, many setters are shorter. During the three rotations, a small setter is in the front row. She can be ineffective as a net player as previously discussed. A shorter setter can be effective if she has good timing and a decent vertical jump.

The opposite, or the player opposite to the setter in the lineup, must be trained to take second contacts if the setter passes the first contact. This requires specialty training. The opposite must be trained to do this when she is in the front court and backcourt. Sometimes a different back row player is substituted for the opposite. This player also needs to train to set for when the front setter calls for help.

6-3 System

The 6-3 system uses three different setters. All six players are hitters when their position is in the front row. The setters are set up in a triangle between the hitter's triangle. This is similar to a 3-3 except the setters set out of the back row and there are always three front row attackers. The setter sets the offense when she is in the back right (1) position and the middle back (6) rotational position (see figure 11.3, c and d, on page 154). Therefore, the setter never has to penetrate the front court from the farthest left back (5) position to the target. This is a good offense to try if a team has three good setters who are also good hitters. It still requires good passing but even better communication. It is commonly used by younger teams that have good ball control and whose coach is developing different setters. It gives more players a chance to set in competition. It has all the benefits of the 6-2 and is usually used as a lead-up to playing a 6-2 or 5-1. Its biggest disadvantage is splitting the leadership and setting tasks between three players. It is rare that a team has three fairly evenly effective setters. But, it can be confusing to an opponent . . . as long as it doesn't confuse its own team!

4-2/6-2

In the late '80s, our Sweet Home team used the 4-2/6-2 (see figure 11.6). I had devised it because it met the requirements my team needed. We had just lost a great, tall setter in a 5-1 system and three primary passers to graduation. We had two smaller athletic setters (one being a lefty) and an average passing team. Our digging skills were questionable! I noticed that we didn't use our right-side hitter in counterattack because our digs were usually off target. To increase and balance our passing and digging stability in the backcourt, we decided to keep the backcourt setter in the back row during defensive plays. A defensive play was defined as any time our team set up a blocking defensive scheme. Any time the opponents sent a free ball, tip, or down ball return over the net, "free" would be called, the setter penetrated, and all three front row players transitioned to become attackers. The only glitch was if an attacker tipped and our defense didn't read it and formed a blocking defense, we treated this as an attack. So, reading early and communication were key. At first, my varsity team thought I was treating them like babies and regressing to a JV offense. Eventually, they bought into the system because of its stability, success, and deceptiveness.

Many modified teams use an International 4-2. As previously stated, it is a great lead-up to use before a 6-2 or 5-1 offense is taught. Many grassroots teams are eager to try a multiple offense. Their passing base, from a free ball, produces a better pass than their dig produces. Also, many younger teams do not counterattack as aggressively off a dug ball as they do off a free ball. In addition, the biggest confusion in a backcourt setter system is *setter release*. A great way to start

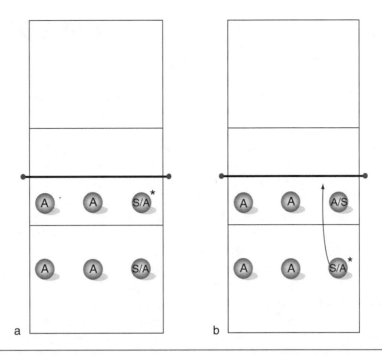

Figure 11.6 Sweet Home's 4-2/6-2 system: *(a)* Front row primary setter sets on the opponent's attack. *(b)* Back row primary setter sets on free balls and down balls.

using a 6-2 is to add it as the free ball offensive system when a team uses an International 4-2 on counterattack.

It is performed by good communication. If a setter and team recognize a free ball return by their opponent, "free" is called, and the back row setter releases to the net; the three front row hitters transition off the net. If a setter and team form a defense against an attack, the front row setter sets the dug ball in a counterattack. This formation keeps a stronger backcourt defense and still allows the front row setter the opportunity to tip, dump, attack, or set a front or back row attacker.

Once a coach observes better digging off an opponent's attack, she can switch over to a total backcourt setter offensive system. This is also a good offense to use with any scholastic team or club team that is still working on digging to the target. Most scholastic teams do not back set off counterattack. So, running an offense off a backcourt setter is sometimes a waste of an attacker and not worth the risks that accompany setter penetration.

This offense also helps the younger setter who is still learning to play balls at the net. If she panics on a ball dug tight to the net, she can always dump the ball because she is front row and is allowed to attack.

This can also be a decent offense to use if a team has two smaller setters. The controlled free ball pass can be accurately passed off the net so a smaller setter is not forced to play tight passes. On counterattack, if the smaller setter needs to dump the ball, the setter is in the front row.

As long as the team possesses good focus and communication skills, the offense can be deceptive. The first time our Sweet Home junior varsity team ran this offense, they not only confused the other team but also the officials!

6-2 Variations

At Sweet Home, many times my best setter was also my most effective hitter. For one of my teams, I toyed with the idea of running a 5-1, but we also had an excellent second setter. Sometimes I would run a 6-2. Other times I developed the lineup so my number one setter set four rotations and my number two setter set two rotations. This allowed my number one setter the opportunity to hit out of the left front (4) and the middle front (3) rotational position. My number one setter was very deceptive and tipped effectively. She could also jump set any tight pass at the top of the net. To accomplish this variation, my lineup did not position the setters opposite each other, which is usually kosher in most systems. Instead, the two setters were two rotational positions from each other. Of course, a lineup could be developed where one setter sets five rotations and another setter sets one rotation!

When specializing, a basic 6-2 positions the setters on the right side of the court, the middle hitters in the center of the court, and the outside hitters on the left side of the court opposite each other in the lineup. For two years at Sweet Home, my two setters were my best middle blockers! So, my setters set out of the back row from the back right (1) position but played middle front (3) in the front row.

A more common specialization is the setters playing outside hitter (4) in the front row and setting out of the back row from position 1. Both of these lineups allow the setters to hit from their power side if they are right-handed. It also allows a team who has lefties to position them on the right side of the net on their strong side. The disadvantage of this is that the off-setter, or opposite, must be trained to handle a ball passed by the backcourt setter on the first contact. It does allow the lefty to two hit, swing, or dump second contacts more effectively than most right-handers.

The basic 4-2, the International 4-2, and the backcourt setter systems provide a target area in the middle front position, the right front position, or in an area between positions 3 and 2. An offense can be developed that changes the target area to the left front (4) position or in between the 4 and 3 front row positions. Why would a coach consider this offense? Perhaps a team has five lefties and a right-handed setter. Perhaps a team has four lefties and one or two right-handed setters or hitters. Creating an offense that best fits a team's talents and needs is most important when considering which system to use.

HITTER COVERAGE

If a team attacks against a blocking defense, the offense must cover the court area behind the attacker in case the ball is blocked in their court. Most teams try to position three players closely around and behind the hitter and two players deeper on the court. Coverage includes all the players who did not attack the ball. They become diggers in a low position ready to play a blocked or partially blocked ball. The setter, the back row player behind the attack, and the hitter closest to the attack usually form the threesome closest to the hitter. Some coaches use the Libero to cover the attack. Coverage is an important skill and position to train. If a player is in doubt where to cover, the best rule of thumb is to fill an open space around the hitter. On a blocked ball, the next phase to train is coverage, dig, to counter attack. If a ball is not blocked, the next phase to train is to move efficiently from coverage to base one.

SPECIALIZATION

When training his players and pondering on an offense and defense, a coach must think about specializing his players by position. It is easier to train and become adept at one front row and one backcourt position. Most agree that grassroots players should play all positions to learn and understand the game, and to allow the coach to assess each player's abilities at every position.

Once a team is ready to attack, some grassroots and modified teams start specializing by identifying the setters from the hitters. The next step of specialization is for a coach to specialize players by position in the front row—namely, outside, middle, and right side players. Next, back row specialization is taught by having specific players play left, middle, and right back. Lastly, a coach specializes *primary* passers, or positions a limited number of players to pass serve receive.

Specialization involves a player moving to the same position when she is in the front row and moving to the same position when she is in the back row. Obviously, the player must start in her serve rotation position until after the serve. So, on the serving team, each player can move to her specialized defensive base after serve contact. If a team is serve receiving, except for the setter, they wait until after the serve reception attack play is complete and the ball crosses the net deep enough on the opponent's court. This allows each player time to move to her specialized base. During serve reception, specialization involves adhering to the overlap rule. Since a team does not want the setter to pass the first contact, she is hidden from the play but positions herself as close to her base as possible. As soon as the serve is contacted, the setter runs to target area and readies to set the first pass.

Teaching specialization from both serve receive and service is one of the most mind-boggling experiences a coach endures. It requires the patience of Job! Here are a few tricks to help in training. Have the players wear pinnies with their positions written on them. Color-coded pinnies work, too. I have also had the setters wear baseball caps. Another key is to make sure the players know that two positions should never be in the front row or back row at the same time if using a 4-2, 5-1, or 6-2 offense. For example, two middles should never be in the front or back row together. The middles should always be opposite each other in serve receive rotational order. Once the coach has gone through each rotation, the only way to really learn specialization is to scrimmage and give it a try! A few gray hairs and a few practices later, it will be second nature for the team.

CHAPTER 12   DEFENSIVE ALIGNMENTS AND MANEUVERS

Adopting a defensive system involves putting players in their best defensive positions and blending them to counteract an opponent's attack. A coach who can position her players on the court according to their strengths will build an impenetrable fortress. A coach must know her opponent's strengths and must be able to alter her own team's defensive system to frustrate and stagnate the opponent's attack system. If she can do this, her team will be able to score on defense by blocking the ball or forcing the opponent to send a non-aggressive predicted return. That is the goal of defense—to force the opponent's offense to attack your strongest defensive scheme, giving you a more aggressive counterattack.

A coach has many questions to answer before deciding on a defense. Just as in choosing an offense, she must assess her players' strengths. The coach has to know which players are effective blockers and which players can dig a ball. A coach also has to know her opponent's probable strength and attack mode. With this knowledge, she can develop a defense to counter her opponent and strengthen her own team's counterattack. Therefore, a team needs to know their opponent well to be able to adjust their defense. If she chooses, a coach can use just one system and then adjust the blocking scheme or dig-

gers' positions to strengthen that defense. A coach wants to put her best blockers against her opponent's best hitters and position her best diggers in the area most attacked or where the blockers have channeled that attack.

In a volleyball defensive system, there are two primary lines of defense. One is the blocking scheme at the net, and the other is the digging formation that covers the court around the blocking design. Included in the digging formation are players who are responsible for tips, roll shots, or rebounds off the net or the block. Other players have backcourt responsibility to cover deeper driven shots, balls off the block, or well-placed attacks where diggers are not located.

BLOCKING

The primary goal of blocking is to redirect the opponent's attack back onto their court floor. The secondary goals are to slow down, weaken, or change (or channel the hitter to change) an attack toward the best diggers. A complete sequence of eye movement for blockers and floor defenders to use within a defense is discussed in chapter 10.

A blocker who merely gets a piece of the ball slows down attacks. This is called a *soft block*, where the ball hits the top of the blocker's hands, usually changing the trajectory of the ball to an upward arc. This kind of soft block also slows down the flight of the ball to resemble the high arc of a free ball. However, if the ball rebounds off the blocker's hands at a less advantageous angle, it may have to be pursued by another defensive player.

At times, a blocker redirects the ball back into the opponent's court area, but when the opponent has good spiker coverage, they can still play the ball and counterattack. In many of these cases, where a ball is played by a coverage system, the result is a weaker attack because all of the players had been hovering in one area. This makes transition awkward and it usually limits and telegraphs the next attack.

A well-formed block can weaken an attack by forcing an opposing hitter to tip or to hit a roll shot. As long as a defense is adept at read-

An effective block can disable an opposing hitter's strong attack pattern.

ing an attacker's mechanics and reacting to the change in her attack, they can dig a tip or roll shot and can easily form a good counterattack. A block must be strong or an opponent can hit through the seam of the block, can overpower the block, or can possibly wipe a ball off the block.

Lastly, a well-formed block can take away a hitter's strong attack pattern. For example, when a team knows that a hitter is a strong crosscourt attacker, the block can take away the crosscourt angle at the net. Conversely, if the hitter can read the block, she can swing down the line, use a tip shot, or use a roll shot. A team that takes away a hitter's intended attack at the net must arrange its best diggers in the channeled court area created by the blockers.

Blocking Formations

A coach has to select one of the four kinds of blocking formations: one-person, two-person, three-person, or nobody home. He must consider how many of his front row players are effective blockers. He must also evaluate any given opponent's attack and decide how many blockers are needed to be effective at the net against that attack.

One-Person

The single block has its pros and cons. The positive side of a single block, or one net player assigned to block an attacker, is that the blocker needs to time only the opposing hitter instead of coordinating her timing with another blocker. The blocker usually takes the "whole ball" instead of taking away an area of the court. Using a single blocker also adds a digger in the defensive system (see figure 12.1).

If the other team does not deliver devastating blows, it is a good defense. It can also be a good defense if the hitter is easy to read, is easy to block, or tips frequently. Simpler is sometimes better. Lawrence High School, in Kansas, won many state championships using a single block system. You can be sure that other teams in Kansas know how to deliver devastating blows! So use what works best for your team.

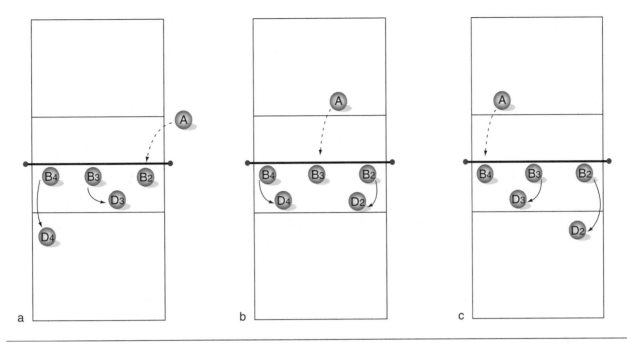

Figure 12.1 Single blocker setups with *(a)* outside attacker, *(b)* middle attacker, and *(c)* right-side attacker.

At Sweet Home, our offensive goal was to create a one-on-one or one-on-no-blocker scheme along the net for our hitters. I felt if my hitter could swing against one blocker, she could be successful at hitting around that blocker (as long as the set wasn't too tight). Joannie Wells, a former National Coach of the Year, was the coach of those championship teams from Lawrence High School. She and I always said it would have been fun if our teams could have competed on court instead of only "in theory"!

Two-Person

An outside blocker and the middle blocker normally form a two-person block. The pros are that the blocking surface is wider and the *shadow of the block* takes up more backcourt area. Therefore, the diggers have to be responsible for a smaller area of the court. It is an intimidating block for a hitter to face. The cons are that it requires good footwork and timing, and it can create a seam between the two blockers.

Normally, each of the three front row players is a blocker, depending on the area of the attack. When an opponent sets the ball to a given area, two of the net defenders become blockers (see figure 12.2). The third front

row player, who does not block, becomes a digger. This digger is called the *off-blocker*. The off-blocker is responsible for digging tips and off-speed shots around the block, or she moves to an assigned backcourt area to dig deeper attacks.

Three-Person

In scholastic play, a triple block is only used in the middle of the court to stop or scare a devastating middle hitter (see figure 12.3). Some higher level teams also use a triple block to shut down a great outside hitter. This block is expected to take away most of the court area. The biggest problem with a triple block is it creates two seams and requires the coordination of three players to time their jumps together with the hitter.

Nobody Home

This is a blocking system where no one blocks. A team might use it if they do not have anyone capable of blocking, or it might be accidental because the blockers have been duped by a multiple attack system. Either way, it requires great floor defense. The players who would have blocked should drop into a low position to play tips, and the other four or five players

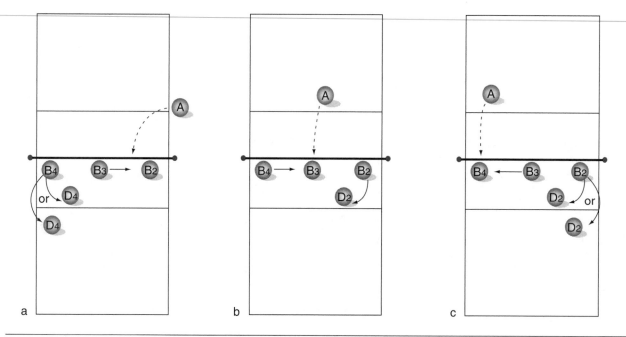

Figure 12.2 Two-person block with *(a)* ouside attacker, *(b)* middle attacker, and *(c)* right-side attacker.

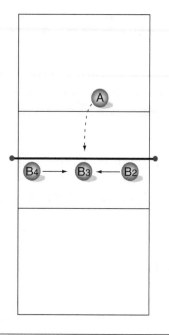

Figure 12.3 Three-blocker setup with a middle attacker.

should rotate to balance and cover the court as effectively as they can (see figure 12.4).

Base One

At their starting base position, the three blockers should be tactically positioned to stop the attack tendency of the opponents.

The basic *base one* blocking position defends second and third tempo attacks. This is a common position for teams who don't need to defend setter dumps and quick or first tempo attacks.

A team that defends higher tempo sets and uses a single or double block usually places the middle blocker midcourt and the perimeter blockers near each antenna one to three feet in from the sideline (see figure 12.5a). If an opponent's setter does not push the ball to the antenna, the perimeter blockers can start pinched (closer to the middle blocker) along the net (see figure 12.5b). Sometimes, teams have a "go-to" hitter. If this is their tendency, it is smart to position the blocker who must move in to create the double block closer to the attacker (see figure 12.5c).

A common base one blocking position that defends first and second tempo sets in the middle third of the court is one where the perimeter blockers pinch in toward the middle blocker. This provides the blockers an opportunity to form a double or triple block on a quicker tempo hit.

If the opposing setter pumps the ball to the outside, the right-side blocker (2) is still close enough to adjust quickly to line up and front the hitter. The middle blocker must move

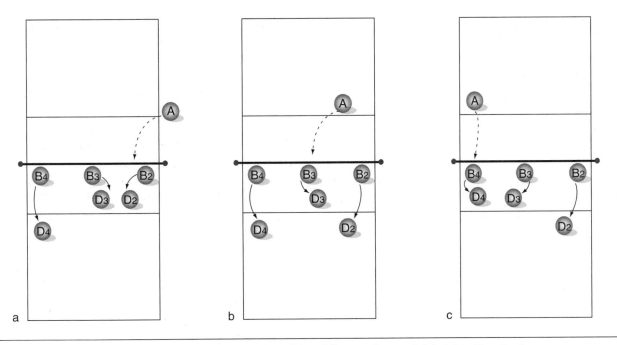

Figure 12.4   No blockers, with *(a)* outside attacker, *(b)* middle attacker, and *(c)* right-side attacker.

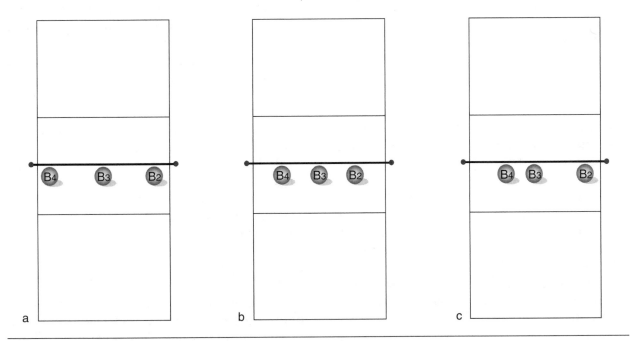

Figure 12.5   Common base blocking positions: *(a)* spread, *(b)* pinched, and *(c)* one outside blocker pinched.

quickly to form a double block. This can be difficult if the right-side blocker (2) moves late, causing the middle blocker to wonder where to end her movement or creating a hole in the block.

The coach can position the blockers at the most advantageous net position to defend an opponent's recurrent attack. The two most popular blocking systems used in scholastic play are *read* and *commit*.

In read blocking, the blockers are positioned at the net to read the setter and react to the set. Blockers do not move until after the ball is set but prepare for one set at a time according to tempo order (base one to base two sequences). Most teams use this basic defense where the blockers read and react, and the backcourt defense reads, reacts to the blockers' movement, and digs perimeter.

In commit blocking, the blockers are positioned to defend a specific attacker based on tendencies. A coach can commit a middle blocker or an outside blocker to an attacker, but most commonly the middle blocker commits to an attacker and relies on perimeter blockers to take on a secondary attacker one on one. If a middle blocker is committed to a middle hitter, she jumps with her and does not worry about double blocking on the outside. If instead the ball is set outside, the middle blocker transitions off the net and has the responsibility to dig tips. The outside blocker is one on one with the attacker, but the backcourt does not need to release to play a tip.

Another scenario is if an opponent has a strong right- or left-side attack, the middle vacates her area, pinches in, and commits to double block the perceived attacker. This could occur when an opponent has a strong slide attacker, lefty, or outside attacker. One more common commit block involves blockers switching places, to match up blockers with hitters. If the outside blockers switch, this can cause havoc if the new right-side blocker has to set the second ball. A third example is a middle swapping with a right-side blocker if the right is an ineffective blocker. The middle takes the hitter one on one and the right-side player either switches to the middle or drops off the net to dig tips, especially when a small setter is in the front row. Teams who swap blocking positions often play read defense after the change.

BACKCOURT FORMATIONS

After deciding on a blocking formation, the coach then has to choose or create a system to dig around the block. These are the players who are not involved in the block at the net

and play floor defense. As the net players read and move to create the block, the other players read and move into positions to dig around the block. This floor defense must be ready to dig an attack that goes around or through a block or a ball that is partially blocked.

Just as the blockers start at a base one, the backcourt defenders also have a starting base. If a team plays a man-up defense, one backcourt player starts in the center of the court behind the 10-foot line. The other two backcourt players start near each corner of the backcourt about three feet in from the side and end line.

If a team plays a man-back defense, the center back (6) player starts in the middle of the court but usually deeper on the court. The coach can tactically place the 6 player anywhere to defend an opponent's tendencies. Many scholastic teams place their 6 player about three feet into the court from the end line. This positions the defender to read and adjust easily; she will also know that if the incoming ball is above her waist, it will be out of bounds. More experienced teams sometimes position their 6 deep player on or behind the end line so she can adjust and dig perimeter into the court. The other two backcourt players, positions 1 and 5 (which I like to call the *wings*), are positioned either pinched in three to six feet behind the 10-foot line or wider to the sideline, if they are more experienced, so they can read and adjust. This base protects against the overpass, the setter's dump, and the sharp angle quick attack.

Base One

Once a team has driven the ball to the opponent's side of the court, they position themselves from coverage (if in-system) to base one, or home base. The front row players rush to their blocking positions at the net; the back row players move to their back court base positions, remaining in low posture. Their defense is in a read position.

The defense anticipates, reads, and prepares to react if an opponent overpasses the first contact. The blocker blocks, attacks ball, or transitions off the net to pass the ball to her own setter, depending on the height of the overpass and her aggressiveness.

If the ball is passed to the front row, the next sequence to anticipate is a setter dump, setter attack, or a tip by a front row player who has played a ball passed too tightly to the net. In any case, the blocker opposite the play must have her hands higher, ready to reject the attack. If the opponent's setter is in the front court, she may play the ball above the net, creating the opportunity for a vicious dump. If the setter is in the back row, she can also dump but must remain below the height of the net. The blocker opposite the opponent's setter position (usually 3 or 2) must block the setter's dump. The backcourt defenders, who are still at base one, ready themselves to play dumps the block may miss. The dump is usually driven to the donut area of the court or tipped toward a sideline over or around the blocker assigned to the setter. Advanced setters can attack deep corners. The setter may also two-hit or turn and block the ball down toward the opponent's floor.

The next progression to focus on is a first tempo attack. The blockers assigned the quick hitters keep their hands higher, ready to jump before the ball crosses the net. There is little time for adjustment by the blockers or floor defenders. Again, communication is essential during read. Players should call out the anticipated quick set, still watching for a setter dump. The coach has assigned (and trained) specific blockers to the attacker. The blockers are positioned at base one to block the quick. The floor defenders are also at base one at a predetermined position around the block, low and ready to dig, play floor defense, or pursue. Most first tempo attacks are hit at extreme angles. If an attacker sprays a first tempo set, it is usually a power tip around or over the block. A defense must have a defender ready to play the power tip near the block since this will be a fast, downward attack. A first tempo ball that is tipped usually requires a lurching dig or a run-through dig to play the ball up and facilitate a counterattack.

If the ball is not passed to the setter, the defense stays at base one and reads a ball not passed to the intended target player. The defense anticipates an out-of-system play or a free ball return. If the second contact is a plausible setup to a viable attacker, it should warrant the defense to move to base two. If the defense anticipates a free ball return, they transition off the net from base one to pass and set up their own offense.

Base Two

Movement from base one to base two occurs after the options that justify base one have been eliminated, including no overpass, no setter dump, and no first tempo attack. Since sets that create the next option of attacks have more "air time," the reading defense has time to move to a more advantageous court position. The next sequence to read includes a second tempo set, a third tempo set, or a back row attack. It can also include an out-of-system play that is a successful attack or that creates a down ball needing a block to help defend. A predetermined number of front row blockers set up on the attacker. Front row players who are not part of the blocking scheme, which we call *off-blockers,* must now transition and become floor defenders. Sometimes such a player rotates to the backcourt to dig hard-driven balls, or she is positioned inside the 10-foot line to protect the floor from tips, roll shots, or junk off the net or block. The back row players adjust to dig hard-driven balls, tips, roll shots, and balls off the blocker. This, again, is predetermined and trained in practice.

Players must be trained at their starting base position, and they must be trained to understand and communicate when it is necessary to adjust and rotate to their base two read position. When practicing backcourt defense, players must maintain low posture and use efficient movement. The defense must be low and maintain a forward lean toward the person who is contacting the ball so that defenders are ready to move to play a well-placed ball out of zone or play a hard-driven attack near the floor. In base two, a floor defender usually moves near a court side or end line in read position to help her relate to the court boundaries and facilitates movement to 180 degrees to dig. The exception is possible movement to play a ball off a block.

In the case of an opponent's poor pass that creates an out-of-system play, if the failed out-of-system play is read early, the defense can transition to play the ball from base one. If the play is read later, the movement to base two has already occurred but the defense can still transition to a no-block defense. A block is not required, the setter moves to target, and the front row transitions off the net while the backcourt balances the court to pass the ball. If the setter is back row, it is important for the back row to balance the court to cover the vacated setter's position. The front row must pass any ball returned in front to them unless a back row player calls them off the ball. Reading, communicating, and adjusting are keys to making transition smooth and error free.

If the opponent does not attack the ball but uses a forearm or overhead pass to send the ball over the net, the defense does not need to set up a blocking formation because there is no attack! "Free ball" should be called, and the defense should move to pass the ball. It is important for the front row to transition off the net ready to pass the ball and ready to set up for their attack formations. The setter should run to target, and the backcourt players should balance the backcourt as if they were playing doubles or triples.

A coach must choose a defense to use when an opponent drives a down ball or sets a back row attack. On a down ball, he may decide to have his team transition as if it were a free ball. If he has good blocking, he may create a defense with a predetermined number of blockers at the net ready to pounce on a low-driven ball. An attacked down ball is usually driven deep into the court, in the backcourt setter's position, or in the middle of the court, sometimes called the *donut*. The ball usually has topspin, which creates a fast downward spin to wreak havoc with the defense. The backcourt defenders usually transition to balance and cover the perimeter

so they can move into the court, stay low, and be ready to perform a run-through or play floor defense. Back row setters are generally instructed to play defense. Some coaches instruct back row setters to transition and allow the remaining two defensive players to cover all deep attacks. If the opponent sets a back row attack, the defense usually either treats it as a down ball or considers it a viable attack and sets up its normal defensive formation. The drawback to sending a block up to defend a down ball or back row attack is the ball is usually set off the net and requires more timing when jumping to block. This can result in more errors and the back row could have "just" passed the ball—especially with a down ball! The coach has to assess where his defensive strength lies. Lastly, if the coach is going to train different defenses with a down ball, a free ball, and a back row attack, communication is imperative during training and must be clear during game play. All the players must understand and know how to react to the call "down ball."

Down balls and free balls are created by an opponent mishandling a ball, a shanked pass that requires pursuit, a poorly set ball that is too difficult to attack, a player set who is not a proficient attacker, an attacker who wants to mix up the offense, or a hitter's poor timing that makes her chicken out or turn around a return into a "back bump attack." In any case, a defense must train to read, verbalize, and move into position for a quality first contact to initiate offense.

Meshing

Defenses are designed to create court areas to defend. All the floor defenders should make an initial movement toward the path of the ball. Since there are no actual floor lines to define these areas, some attackers are unclear on who should pass the ball. If all players have a great defensive attitude, they are ready to dig all balls. But, realistically, if a ball is attacked in the perimeter of two zones, both players must move aggressively to play the ball. This entails movement by one player who is deeper on the court than the other player, creating a *mesh*. The height or depth of the ball's trajectory will determine which player should actually dig the ball. Sometimes this is not determined until both players nearly arrive at the ball. Therefore, it is important to stay true to the meshing movement. A ball hit in the seam of two defenders will more likely be dug if both players are moving toward the direction of the hit. If the ball is hit sharply, a player whose responsibility is to play the center of the court or sharp angles will dig the ball. If the ball is hit deeper, a player who is responsible to dig along the end line will be responsible to dig the attack.

When both defenders look in the direction of the attack and don't move, this is called a *visual mesh*. This is *not* good and usually ends up with the defensive players lunging out to dig or the attack hitting the floor between them. Visual meshing is common when defensive players have not read and adjusted, have not been trained in proper individual defensive movement, or have not been trained in defensive court responsibility.

Beginning level teams usually do not need to employ a blocking defense until opponents start attacking balls that have been set. These teams usually use five diggers and one setter or even six diggers to counteract an opponent's return.

Man-Up Defense

Coaches who want to position one athletic leader in the middle of the court to defend tips, off-speed shots, and maintain clarity use a man-up defense, also called *setter-up* or *red* defense. It involves a backcourt player playing up behind the block. The coach can decide tactically which player should play up. He may decide to use the same player all the time to keep it simple. This is common of young teams who use the 6 player up, and she rotates behind the block where it is formed along the net (see figure 12.6, a and b). Another common man-up defense involves the backcourt player who plays behind the block on offense staying up and playing behind the block on defense. If a team is playing a backcourt setter offense, a coach may tactically decide to have his setter

play the right back or center back position and play man-up defense. This would keep the setter closer to the target area on transition.

Next, the coach has to decide whether he will use a one-, two-, or three-person block, or even a no blocking system.

In a single blocking defensive scheme, one or two players defend the center of the court, and three or four players dig in the backcourt, creating a 1-2-3 or a 1-1-4 court arrangement (see figure 12.6c). This is a common defense used by modified and junior varsity teams who may only have one blocker in the front row but do not defend too many hard driven spikes.

In a double block defense, one player defends the area behind the block, and three remaining players dig in the backcourt to create a 2-1-3 arrangement (see figure 12.6d). This is used by many junior varsity and varsity teams who defend a variety of shots but have effective double blocking skills and need three backcourt defenders. See figure 12.6e for a setup with three blockers. Within each man-up defense, the coach can choose different tactical systems to use different players to defend the system. Within each blocking scheme, the coach can tactically rotate diggers around the blockers to protect perimeter and sharp angles. It is important to place the team's best defensive player in the area the block is trying to funnel the attack to.

Many youth coaches like the man-up defense because it places a digger behind the block where most attackers place their tips. It also has less backcourt movement, which allows the entry level player less responsibility to read and adjust, and allows her to just dig in a prearranged area on the court. Once used as an elementary defense, man-up defense is making a comeback as a viable defense option in competitive volleyball.

Man-Back Defense

The man-back defense is sometimes called a *perimeter* defense. It relies on the block to protect the center of the court and the backcourt defense to read and move perimeter to play the ball. It always involves three players

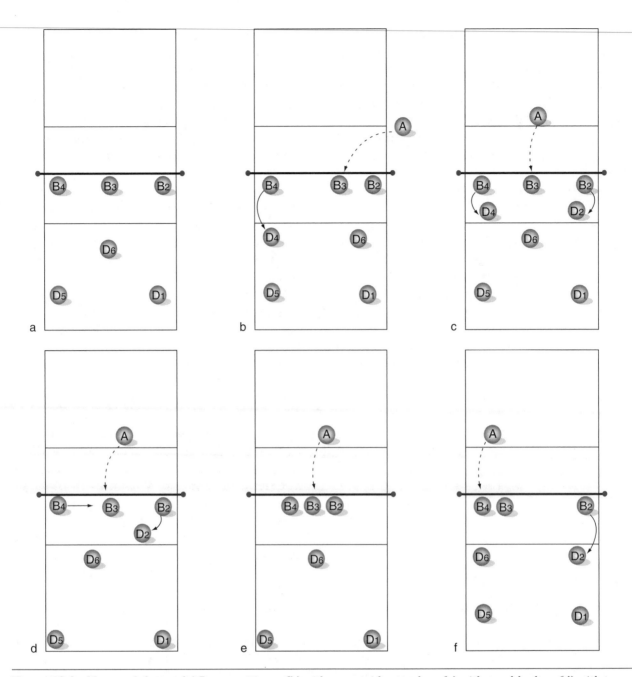

Figure 12.6 Man-up defense: *(a)* Base positions, *(b)* with an outside attacker, *(c)* with one blocker, *(d)* with two blockers, *(e)* with three blockers, and *(f)* with a right-side attacker.

digging the ball outside the block along the side or end line (see figure 12.7a). The defense reads (assesses) their opponent's intentions and adjusts (moves) to a more advantageous position around the block near the side or end line to dig the ball into the court.

The floor defense sets up around the block to cover vulnerable areas not protected by the block. The block sets up to take away either the line shot or the crosscourt shot.

The backcourt defense rotates four defenders to dig the attack. If the block is blocking line, the back right position usually plays balls off the block and plays tips and rolls. If the block takes away the crosscourt shot, the off-blocker rotates to play balls off the block, tips, and rolls.

The area behind the block, which is the block's responsibility, is called the *shadow of the block*. Usually, a floor defensive player

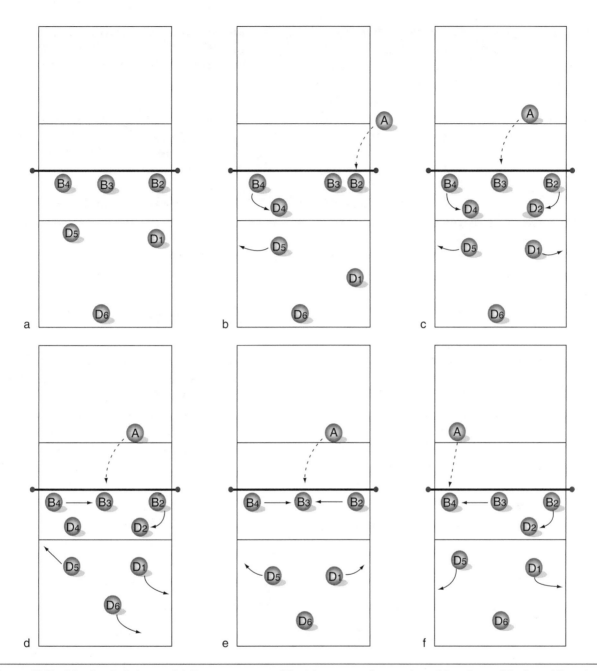

Figure 12.7 Man-back defense: *(a)* Base positions, *(b)* with an outside attacker, *(c)* with one blocker, *(d)* with two blockers, *(e)* with three blockers, and *(f)* with a right-side attacker.

is not assigned to this court area because the block should be effective at protecting this section of the court. It is also important for the floor defense to set up outside the shadow of the block so each player can see the attacker.

The floor defense starts at their base position either pinched in or on the sidelines and on or near the end line. The start position will be determined by the ability of the defenders

to read early and react properly. From here, they read the attack, and then move into the court to dig balls.

The defender should also set up facing *on help*. On help means if the defender digs the ball, it will be rebounded toward the center of her own court. Many diggers err by facing their attacker and digging the ball back to the attacker. This usually results in an overpass kill or a six pack! Since the block is responsible for an area on the court, the floor defenders may not look like they are balancing the court. As long as the block is an effective tool, this is a common look for a defense.

Once a block is formed, floor defenders must be aware of the ranked order a ball will travel according to speed of execution. The fastest attacked ball would be one that is hit around the block or through a hole in the block. This could be a spike or a tip. The next fastest attack is one that is partially blocked. This could be done on purpose by the block, which is called a *soft block*, or it could be just a partially deflected block. Some adept attackers are capable of deflecting balls off the block on purpose. This is called getting *tooled*. If a ball is soft blocked, it usually changes the trajectory of the attack and slows it down. If the attack is partially deflected, it could be sprayed anywhere on or off the court. Many times, this causes panic and havoc with the floor defenders. A partially deflected block can still be good if it slows down the speed of the attack and the defenders read it and move efficiently to the ball. If an attacked ball can effectively tool off the block, it is usually driven off the blocker's hands, and the ball careens at a sharp angle.

In a single block defense on the left or right side, the middle off-blocker plays the tips, and the other off-blocker rotates and plays floor defense in the backcourt. In a single block defense in the middle, both perimeter off-blockers transition off the net to play tips or rolls on both sides of the blocker. In a double block defense, the other four players dig, starting from the outer lines into the court. To play off-speed shots, the floor defense must read and then move into the court. Usually, the off-blocker or player behind the block must be responsible for off-speed shots and be ready to play balls cut around the block. See figure 12.7, b-f, for different situations.

Combinations

Rotation defense is a combination of both defenses previously mentioned. In rotation defense, players rotate to the corners of the court, and the middle back player rotates to the corner down the line from the attacker (see figure 12.8). Instead of the 6 area player staying up to play the tip, this defense uses the 1 area player to stay up and play the tips. Most teams that use this defense do so

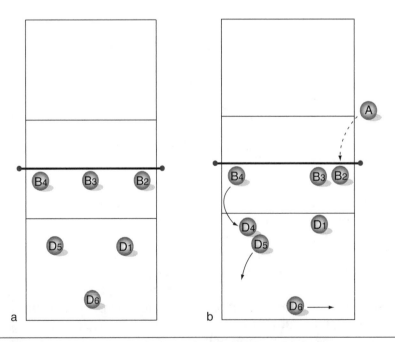

Figure 12.8 Rotation defense: *(a)* Base positions and *(b)* with an outside attacker.

because their backcourt setter is in the 1 position and does not have to dig in the backcourt on an attack by an opponent. When the setter has to move from the backcourt during transition, it creates a longer path to the target for counterattack. Also, when the setter has to cover a tipped ball, it destroys her team's counterattack because the off-setter must run the offense and will not be part of the attack scheme. Rotation defense is also used to protect the court from "line" attacks because the block takes away the line shot. The 6 area player is assigned *down the line* or outside the right-side blocker. Some teams position the 6 player in the seam or behind a shorter outside blocker resembling the defense in a "cup" formation.

Very few teams use rotation defense to defend against an opponent's right-side attack when their setter is in the 1 area position. This would force the setter to be the primary crosscourt defender in the defense and push her deep into her own court.

Variations of perimeter defense can be used to protect the end line and sidelines while still keeping one or two players to protect against tips and off-speed shots. These variations are combinations of both defenses, depending on how a given coach chooses to defend the middle of the court, and are often used by scholastic teams. At the scholastic level, it is common for opposing attackers to drive off-speed shots into the middle of the court.

In this scheme, the middle blocker moves back to the sideline at the 10-foot line; the off-blocker turns off the net and is responsible for tips and off-speed shots near the block. Players 1, 6, and 5 are in charge of harder driven shots. This is a good defense to use when the setter is in the front row.

With this variation, the 1 area player plays the tips and off-speed shots around the block. This is similar to rotation defense.

Junior varsity teams and freshman teams commonly play this variation because it is common for these teams to receive many tips and deeper hits from hitters who stand rather than jump. These players are still learning to read and react to off-speed shots and standing hits, so there is a need for two players to be in charge of the middle of the court and two or three players to play the deeper standing hits.

A defense that uses just one blocker makes provision for either three or four backcourt diggers and one or two shallow position defenders. When a team uses two blockers, two or three players defend the deep shots, and one or two players protect against the tip and roll.

Actually, the first line of defense is covering your hitter in case the opponent blocks the ball back into your own court.

LIBERO

The Libero position (pronounced lee-bah-ro) is the newest position to volleyball. It is a defensive position that was developed to strengthen a team for counterattacking and make our sport more enjoyable to watch by creating more ball control, which will create better offense and longer defensive rallies.

The Libero must wear a numbered uniform jersey of contrasting color to her teammates so the officials and opponents can monitor her restrictive play. Only one Libero per game is allowed. A Libero can change from game to game. The Libero's basic restrictions are she only plays back row, she may not serve, she may not block or attempt to block, she may not attack the ball above net height, and she may not set up a front row attack using an overhead pass from inside the 10-foot line. When the Libero is replaced, she must remain on the bench for one rally before reentering the game. If a Libero is entering a game for a front row player rotating to the back row to serve, she must wait until the server has failed to serve. (Many proponents are trying to change the rule to allow the Libero to serve with one normal rotation.) The Libero does not have to check in with the scorer but can only enter the game behind the attack line and only on a dead ball. There is an official Libero tracker at the desk who records her replacements. Many teams use the Libero for front row players who do not have consistent serve receive or defensive skills. The most common use of the Libero position is for the team's middle hitters. The middle hitters are not required to play defense while they are in their service rotation. Coaches usually choose to play the Libero at the 5 or 6 position. The Libero position has opened the door for better ball control but still allows the team to use other defensive specialists to improve play and maintain back row attacks.

The coach should decide which defense to use according to her team's strengths, the position of the team's setter, and the opponent's tendencies and strengths. As a team becomes more sophisticated and plays against higher level attacks, players may be called upon to use different defenses according to the complexity of the attack and the attacker's tendencies. Many scholastic teams play just one defense and make adjustments when needed while others train two or three defenses according to their need. What is really important is for a team to feel comfortable on the court with their defensive responsibilities and to have the coordination of play to counterattack on their opponents.

CHAPTER 13 PREPARING YOUR TEAM

We've all heard the expression, "Preparation is the key to success." This certainly holds true for volleyball, or any other competitive sport for that matter. I truly feel that I owe much of my success to the several facets of preparation that I established over the years. All of these elements relate to the actual game by providing a framework on which my players relied and which was the root of their success on the court.

SCOUTING

Scouting is a great tool to use for planning practices and creating strategies to outwit opponents. If a coach gives his team some insight on an opponent, his players will feel more confident, especially if they have this information before the practices to prepare for that specific match.

Unfortunately, many high school leagues play their matches on the same dates as others do, which makes it virtually impossible for a coach to scout an opponent in person. A coach can send an assistant to scout, but then he will have less help during a given match. Sometimes, when scheduling permits, a coaching staff divides the duties or attends another team's match together. Most college coaches

are not allowed to scout opponents, so they have to rely on swapping tapes. Junior clubs and high school teams frequently tape their own matches so they can have the video to assess for the next time they compete against that same opponent.

When I coached at the high school level, I used to assign my kids to scout, especially during tournaments where we had to check on more than one team. My setters always did a thorough job, especially in evaluating other setters. Other players frequently came back with information concerning an opponent's offense, who was their best hitter, or whom to aim at when serving. Of course, these sketchy facts included who had an awful hairstyle or who had an "attitude," and they always included a comment on that team's "tacky" uniforms! I knew my kids understood the game well enough to scout, but they just needed a template to use when observing an opponent's play.

There are many charts made for scouting; however, I needed to develop one that a high school player could use when time was limited. I kept it concise and easy to use (see figure 13.1).

As you can see, the chart includes offensive and defensive system, lineup order with provision for any player tendencies,

Scholastic Player Scouting Report on _____

Date _____ Vs _____ At _____

Player name _____

Serve receivers: #s _____ _____ _____ _____ _____ _____

Strong passers: #_____ #_____   Subs _____ for _____

Weak passers: #_____ #_____   _____ for _____

3 person_____ 4 person_____ 5 person_____   _____ for _____

Starting serve receive rotation _____(1)_____(2)_____(3)_____

_____(4)_____(5)_____(6)_____ Who served first? _____

Offense: 4-2_____   5-1_____   6-2_____

Block: Number of blockers in middle _____ What position helps? _____

Number of blockers on LS _____   Number of blockers on RS _____

Strong blockers: # _____ _____ _____ Weak blockers: # _____ _____ _____

Setter(s): # _____ _____ _____

Setter strengths _____ Comments _____

_____

Setter weaknesses _____ Comments _____

_____

Defense: Perimeter _____ Rotation _____ Other_____

OHs: #_____ _____ _____   Strong diggers: #_____ _____ _____

Strengths _____   Weak diggers: #_____ _____ _____

Weaknesses _____ Comments: _____

Serving tendencies: #_____-_____ #_____-_____ #_____-_____

#_____-_____ #_____-_____ #_____-_____ #_____-_____

Specifics we can do offensively to win: _____

_____

Specifics we can do defensively to win: _____

_____

Comments:_____

_____

Figure 13.1 Scouting form for players to use.

serve receive system, setter numbers and tendencies, hitters' tendencies, strong passers, weak passers, and space for comments. Comments are usually similar to the following: "#6 can't dig tips," "poor coverage on a 4 ball," "#7 is a blocking wall but can't close it," and "outside hitter #10 is all crosscourt, but outside hitter #9 can hit line." All of these are great comments that add to scouting information. Sometimes, coaches can deliver these messages to their players only in a pregame talk or while the other team is warming up. There are other scouting charts to use when a coach has the luxury of attending a match or to be used to accompany a tape. These are more detailed than the format followed by players scouting other players.

It is best for a coaching staff to develop their own chart to outline exactly what they want to record while scouting an opponent. For example, there is no reason to chart another team's hitting if that team doesn't attack! The information that is recorded is intended to raise a team's level of awareness and to prepare them to outplay that particular opponent.

Some examples of scouting report categories include tendencies in serving, blocking, and hitting, and which players are the strong and weak passers. The type of offense and defense used is also helpful information. Who is the setter and does she have any quirks or does she telegraph her sets? Does the setter cheat during transition? Can the team dig tips? Is their quick attack predictable? What are their play-option tendencies on serve receive, counterattack, free ball, and out-of-system play? What are the team's general strengths and weaknesses (e.g., poor transition, high posture on defense)? What are the characteristics of specific players that should be noted (e.g., the middle blocker doesn't close the block on the outside)? All of this information is key in preparing a team to play a specific opponent.

Normally, the higher a team's level is, the easier the scouting is because of predictability. Good teams know how to capitalize on their strengths, so they become consistent in tapping their own resources. Their atti-

tude is "try to stop us." Highly skilled teams usually have several plays to run off each serve receive, counterattack, and free ball situation.

The key to scouting is identifying the opponent's tendencies, strengths, and weaknesses. You can chart this information statistically or just record general tendencies. This information can be used to form lineups and matchups and to identify expectations by rotation, player tendencies, and methods to counteract opponents. The higher the level of play, the more a team is scrutinized. NCAA member schools are required to keep statistics on attack, assist, serve, dig, block, and general ball handling errors. Each school submits these statistics to its conference. Of course, most colleges have trained statisticians who use computerized programs to generate statistics. The AVCA provides a match summary form, also called a box score, that is used by most universities. This provides a consistent method for recording information. Statistics are meaningless if recorded differently and then compared as the same.

High schools and clubs generally keep statistics on attack and serve. Passing, assists, and blocking are frequently noted, too. Players, managers, and coaches tend to keep the stats so all must be trained to be consistent. Of course, the other key elements to record are the opponent's weaknesses, such as poor hitter coverage. The official score sheet can also be a wealth of information. The sheet provides the starting lineup, substitutes, points per rotation, and serving efficiency. A coach can see if another coach alters her lineup to change a matchup or remains steadfast to her starting rotation.

Any team is only as good as its weakest player, so when a team can identify and "pick on" that weakest link, they can force their opponent into out-of-systems plays or errors.

A coach needs to be careful not to spook his team or overload them with too much information if they are not skilled enough to use it. An example is a modified coach who has instructed his team that "number 32 can't pass her way out of a paper bag, so our team must serve and return every ball to number 32 to win." This is the same modified team that cheers when any serve goes over the net, between the antennas, and within the court boundaries!

In scholastic play, most scouting is minimal because teams within a league usually play on the same dates. For these coaches, "word of mouth" scouting, knowledge of returning players, and tendencies from past seasons are all elements that a coach can use to plan a prematch practice. If a scholastic coach films a match and then has another match against that same opponent, review of the film can help the coach plan more specifically for the match.

Discover Their Secret Weapon

Once we played a team from Pennsylvania that had a superstar on the team. The other five players were competent but not nearly as dynamic as Jen. Jen played outside hitter and the left back (5) position. Their team's game plan was to let Jen pass the first ball to the setter, and the setter would set up Jen whether she was in the front or back row. Jen had the focus and mobility to pass three quarters of the court and attack as well in the back row as she could in the front row. This was a two-person team. Everyone knew the key was to try to either block or dig Jen.

By knowing this team's tendency, we realized that what worked best was to not let Jen handle the first contact. In turn, the setter couldn't get a good set off to Jen, so she could not hit effectively. Even though it was tough to stop Jen from passing the first ball, we were effective in sticking to our game plan and gave this team their first defeat of the year.

It is important to know an opponent's strengths and weaknesses, but a coach needs to utilize her own team's strengths to defeat another team. By exploiting an opponent's weaknesses with her own team's strengths, a coach has a solid game plan. Additionally,

a coach needs to include in practice all the what-ifs that could occur during a match so her team doesn't feel panicked when she makes changes. If the strategy is team-specific and the team is well drilled, players will feel confident and physically prepared to play their best.

LINEUP

Devising a starting lineup is more than putting your most effective server first and your best hitter in the 4 position. Many considerations must be taken into account when developing a lineup.

Traditional 5-1 lineups resemble figures 13.2 and 13.3. The best middle hitter (MH-1) and the best outside hitter (OH-1) sandwich the setter. This helps the team's attack when its setter is in the front row. Accordingly, when the setter is in the back row, the front row attack includes three hitters. The starting rotation will depend on whether the setter has good blocking and net skills. Figures 13.2 and 13.3 show different rotation orders. Figure 13.2 diagrams the OH-1 following the setter, and figure 13.3 shows the MH-1 following the setter. A coach should try each option to discover which passing sequence most effectively uses the best hitters. Many two-person receiving teams use the option shown in figure 13.2.

A typical 6-2 lineup usually alternates a team's stronger players with its less effective players. This rotation order (figure 13.4) would balance the lineup and be less likely to suffer a poor rotation. Some coaches feel that the strongest setter should set the stronger hitters.

On the other hand, some coaches believe the stronger setter should set the more inconsistent hitters. It is important for the coach who uses the 6-2 to develop a lineup with at least two effective hitters in the front row at any given time.

A team's starting rotation should be determined by its strength and weakness. A team should start with a consistent or strong server, an effective hitter positioned in the

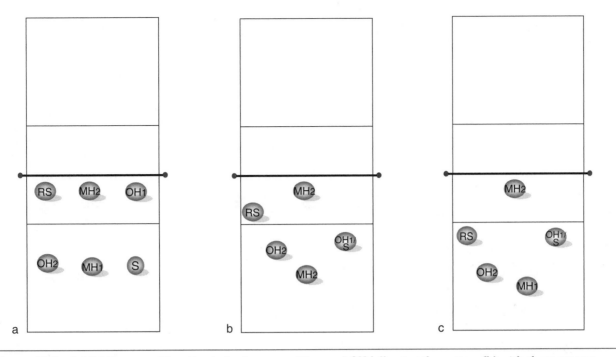

Figure 13.2 *(a)* 5-1 lineup, with setter in back row position and OH following the setter; *(b)* with three-person serve receive, and *(c)* with four-person serve receive.

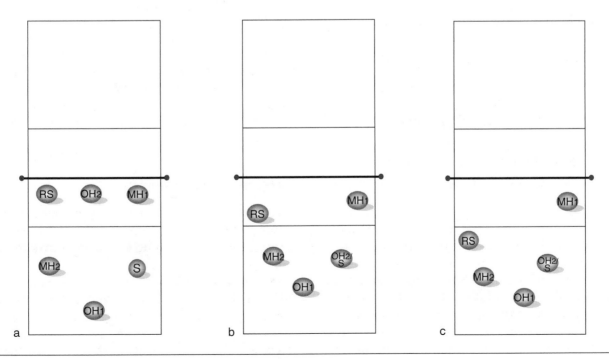

Figure 13.3 *(a)* 5-1 lineup, with setter in back row position and MH following the setter; *(b)* with three-person serve receive, and *(c)* with four-person serve receive.

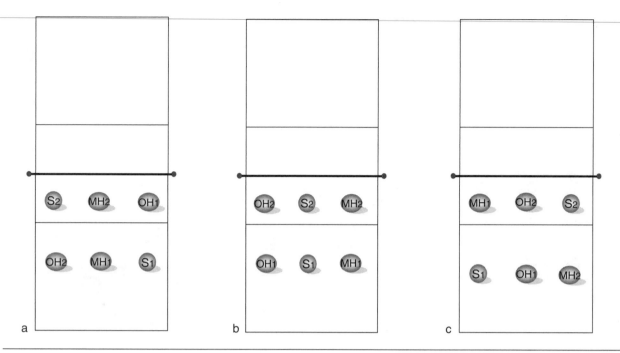

Figure 13.4 6-2 lineup.

front row, and two strong passers to receive the opponent's initially stronger serves.

The rotation order must be balanced so any weak rotation is minimized.

Other important considerations include the following:

- Lineup adjustments based on scouting reports or past competitions
- Teammates who play poorly next to each other
- Team chemistry
- Effective starters versus effective substitutes
- "Eye of the tiger" players under stress
- Players with good communication skills

A team is only as good as its worse rotation. Usually, a team's fifth or sixth rotation is its weakest. A team should practice this rotation more than its stronger rotations to minimize mistakes and nonaggressive play. Mistakes during one weak rotation can lead to a string of unearned points for the opponent, creating an emotional roller coaster ride that can throw a team off its game plan. With rally scoring in effect, it is difficult to come back from point deficits.

PREMATCH PREPARATION

The coach needs to take steps to prepare himself and his team before each match. Being well prepared for a game prevents last-minute chaos and feelings of uncertainty. It's important to have a good warm-up planned and to make sure your captain knows her responsibilities.

Team Warm-Up

Prematch warm-up serves several functions. Most important, it readies the body for game play. Secondly, it should help psych up a team for competition.

Physically, a player needs to warm up until she has broken a sweat. Suggested activities are court movements that replicate game play. Most high school teams have pregame rituals to psych the other team out. Many times they include running around the court, slapping hands, diving on the floor, and old-fashioned cheering! The initial warm-up could include side steps, crossover steps, blocking and attack patterns, skipping, sprinting, and jogging! Many teams stretch after their initial movement to ensure full range of motion in their joints. Most pregame movement drills are repetitious, creating an attitude of "let's get it over quickly!" Some teams pull out the flexible ladders to perform their agility step work. Some teams perform fun tag games to achieve quick movements with less pain and more fun! A coach should prevent his own team from staring at the other team who may be executing a "cooler" warm-up! During warm-up, players must focus on their own readiness, the team's readiness, and on their pregame rituals. Obviously, there is no score awarded at the end of warm-ups, but some warm-ups tend to be intimidating or better orchestrated, which can achieve better mental preparedness.

To stop our team from staring at other teams who were obviously having more fun during warm-up last season, we added a simple relay race at the end of our court movement drills. The players clapped and cheered for each of their groups, so we finally had other teams staring at us having fun during our warm-up!

Warm-up is also the time for a team to become familiar with the court. This includes testing the tautness of the net, identifying court lines and floor surface, and adjusting to the gym's lighting and overhead obstructions.

It is finally time to add some volleyballs! Most high school and club warm-up time is limited. A lot of our fans complain that the volleyball warm-up is longer than most played matches! But each team is usually allowed 10 to 20 minutes of shared court time and 3 to 12 minutes of whole court time. A team needs to simulate as many gamelike ball contacts as possible and use their time wisely. Important tune-up skills include passing and digging balls at gamelike angles, attacking, serving, setting, transition, and defensive run-through skills. Drills that can be performed on half a court should be used during the shared warm-up period. Serve

© Human Kinetics

Prematch warm-up can include simple ball movement drills, among other activities.

receive, hitting from a pass or from transition, and Libero/defensive specialist movement should be done during the whole court period. Many teams also use this time to play triples, quads, or review each serve receive pattern. Our high school league never allowed whole court warm-up, so we were notorious for starting with a 0-6 deficit until we warmed up serve receiving during the first game! Colleges follow more prematch protocol.

It is important not to "over warm up," too. Regardless of the time allotted, a coach should have his team practice the pregame warm-up and should time-manage it so it is efficient and prepares the team in all aspects. Warm-up drills can be centered on or initiated by the coach or by a player. A coach should focus on each player's readiness to play. He also wants to make some encouraging exchanges to remind individual players of specific strategies that are part of the game plan. Warm-up is not the time to make major changes in a player's technique. Warm-ups are for positively supporting the players so they feel mentally ready to compete. The coach initiates most drills so that he can help create what he needs and can motivate his players by testing their limitations but keeping each successful. Warm-ups sometimes help a coach read who is really ready to start in a game if he has any doubts about one or two positions.

Captain Responsibilities

The duties of a captain before a match should enhance the protocol of the event. The captain should take charge of whatever responsibilities the coach has assigned. These could include supervising court setup/takedown and team warm-up, greeting the opposing team and the officials, and always includes being team spokesperson at the official's coin toss. Some coaches organize the court setup by delegating specific duties to each player. The same is true for away matches. The underclassmen usually carry the brunt of the worse duties! Some schools or tournaments have booster clubs, event staff, or facility personnel to set up and take down the site. This is an ideal situation because it is a great way to use your team's parents who are so eager to help!

Captain responsibilities include being mature and clear thinking during the match, which aids the coaching staff in keeping the team focused both on and off the court. The floor captain is the only person who can directly, within the rules, speak to the official. The floor captain needs to have good knowledge of the rules, be tactful, stay focused on the game plan, and be well spoken. The captain should be the team representative to thank the officials after each match, too.

Other Pregame Procedures

The team captains and sometimes the coaches meet with the officials before a match to review ground rules. This is a pleasant exchange and good sporting behavior should be evident.

After the coin toss, the captain is the one who chooses either the side, the serve, or to receive. She may select a specific side if there is a physical problem that could make a difference. Examples are lighting or sun reflection problems, a crowded outside hitting area that would make transitional plays difficult, sitting near the opponent's noisy crowd, or playing below low overhead obstructions. Obviously, each team will have to play on each side eventually, but winning game one is the key in establishing the confidence level of the team. A captain may choose to serve first if her team has a tough server starting in the right back (1) position. A team that has an aggressive attack may choose to receive serve first so it gains a point and rotates into a strong pattern. A coach needs to examine the alternatives to correctly advise his captain before the toss.

After the toss, each team usually spends its formal warm-up time attacking on their side. After the warm-up, both teams should help with the ball shagging. This will give players ample time to return to the bench and get valuable last minute instructions from the coach.

THE HOME MATCH VERSUS THE AWAY MATCH

A team should have as much information as possible about the opponent's playing site before the contest. We used to play an opponent whose gym had a low ceiling and bright lights, and the end wall was three feet from the end line. The crowd noise was deafening. Days before a match, we would practice with our boom box blaring; we would play rebounding balls off our ceiling and shorten the pursuit area in our home gym to adequately prepare for this upcoming away match. We would also practice a quick huddle to make up for the lack of communication in that noisy gym!

Playing away is usually tougher than playing at home. The crowd is a factor. Boys taunting players can also be a problem for a girls' team. Girls distracting guys can be a factor in a boys' game, too! The only way to quiet an opposing crowd is by playing superior and winning! It is fun to hush a crowd! However, a coach must prepare a team to play under more pressure and negativity at away games. Players need to focus on the game and be thick-skinned. If a team understands that the crowd is trying to goad them, they can "win" by ignoring external pressures.

Usually players will know what they are up against from the warm-ups. When we used to play at Horseheads High School, there were several contests going on before the game. One was "Who is going to run out from the locker room last?" Another contest was "Who is going to win warm-ups by acting more excited and hitting more straight down spikes with the most power?" Intimidation and other emotional forces can be created.

Teams have to accept the other team's warm-up music. We have played at schools that turned off the music when it was our time on the court. My favorite opponent was the one who played opera music during our court warm-up time! Actually, I think it is important to psych up one's own team but at the same time not tick off the other team. That would be like throwing meat to a hungry tiger! The visiting team should also be respectful of a team's home side when entering the gym. If the home team has their equipment already assembled on one side, the visitors should politely "set up shop" on the other side. If one side of the court is extremely advantageous for play, this can be changed during the coin flip if the captain wins the toss.

A coach should also know who is providing the warm-up equipment and what the match protocol procedures are before taking the trip to another site. Once a team arrives, the coach or manager should find out what pregame rituals will occur. This could include introductions, the national anthem, and other hoopla home teams use to psych their team. Players should be polite and always be good sports before, during, and after a match . . . but they definitely need to play aggressively

to spoil a hometown victory! For safety reasons, a coach should closely supervise the team after the match until they get on the bus, especially if the visiting team wins a big road victory in front of a huge, sometimes hostile, crowd.

Home matches need to be well orchestrated and rich in tradition. A team needs to create the impression of being well organized and respectful of the rituals of the game. This includes things such as who sets up the court, chairs, scorer's table, bleachers, and sound system; who is the scorer/announcer; and any other match management concerns. It also includes who will meet the visiting team, where they will dress, how the warm-up will be conducted, how the teams will run out, whether there will be a formal march and introduction ceremony, and who possesses the team rosters and the names of the officials for introductions. An organized check off sheet is helpful so there is no last minute panic (see figure 13.5). Often it is easier to take the bus ride to an away match than to host a home event!

BENCH ORGANIZATION AND CONDUCT

The team bench must be organized efficiently. This is important during a time-out when time is limited. A coach should insist on the same procedures for every time-out and practice them before the first match. Here are some considerations:

- Will the starters come to the bench and sit or stand?
- Where will the towels and water bottles or cups be located?
- Will the team face the crowd during a time-out?
- Which coach does the talking during the time-out?
- Will the setter be spoken with separately at any time?

Home Match Checklist

Court
- ❏ Competition net
- ❏ Two antennae for net
- ❏ Standards
- ❏ Padding for standards
- ❏ Referee stand and padding
- ❏ Two ball carts
- ❏ Labeled practice balls in each cart for both teams
- ❏ Towels hung at each end of the net for wipe-ups
- ❏ Dust mop

Scorers' table
- ❏ Chairs
- ❏ Lineup sheets
- ❏ Duplicate score sheets, including game five special sheet
- ❏ Libero tracking sheet
- ❏ Pens and pencils in two colors
- ❏ Rosters from both teams
- ❏ Rule book
- ❏ Linesman flags
- ❏ Three game balls
- ❏ Ball inflator/deflator/needle
- ❏ Net height measuring device
- ❏ Flip score or electronic scoring/timing device
- ❏ Stopwatch
- ❏ Microphone for announcer
- ❏ National anthem CD
- ❏ Tape or CD set up for warm-up, time-out, and between game music
- ❏ Script for announcer including any special recognition and upcoming events
- ❏ Whistle
- ❏ Water for officials and scorers
- ❏ Area and supplies for statisticians unless seated at benches

Team bench area
- ❏ Chairs or benches to seat teams and staff
- ❏ Water cooler with cups or water bottles at end of each bench area
- ❏ Wipe towels
- ❏ Area for trainer and training needs (first aid kit, ice, and so on)

Personnel
- ❏ Event's host or hostess to attend to opponent's and officials' needs
- ❏ Two officials
- ❏ Two trained linespeople
- ❏ Six people to shag during warm-ups and utilize during three-ball system
- ❏ Scorer
- ❏ Libero tracker
- ❏ Announcer and music coordinator
- ❏ Electronic timer and scoreboard operator or flip scorer
- ❏ Chaperones for crowd control and security
- ❏ Video crew
- ❏ Two people to sell tickets, if applicable
- ❏ Statisticians

Video equipment
- ❏ Camera
- ❏ Tripod
- ❏ Labeled tape
- ❏ Extension cord to outlet
- ❏ Safe and secure area for video setups

Ticket sales (if applicable)
- ❏ Poster listing ticket prices
- ❏ Money box
- ❏ Cash to make change
- ❏ Tickets or hand stamp
- ❏ Table and two chairs
- ❏ Rosters for spectators, if possible

Figure 13.5 Home match checklist.

- How will the coach handle dealing with individuals during a time-out?
- Will the nonstarters listen during a time-out or will they ball handle at the end of the court?
- Are the players on the bench encouraged to perform organized cheers or just cheer in support?

The conduct of the nonstarters or substitutes during game play needs to be addressed. Some coaches use the bench players to do statistics. Some coaches have their subs stand at the end of the bench, but others have them sit. When a player comes out of a game, does she automatically go join the other subs or does she sit down next to the coach?

The coach also has some decisions to make about himself and his staff. Where will he sit on the bench? Will he stand at the end of the bench? Will he address each player as she comes out of the game? Will he talk to his team during the game to give instructions? Will he keep notes or stats? Will one of the coaches signal the server to indicate the area on the opponent's court to serve? These are just some of the questions a coaching staff should consider as part of its bench policy.

LEVEL OF COMPETITION

Preparing a team for an opponent's level of competition has to be handled correctly. A coach needs to mentally prepare her team without scaring them and without making them feel overconfident.

Pressure and confidence are two important elements to be instilled during each practice. If a team has trained to play their best in pressure situations, they are usually mentally prepared to take on the best competition. Of course, a team rarely plays as well as it practices, but a coach should emphasize that a team gets only as good as the competition it plays. Everyone knows the saying "On any given day . . . " The only way to beat a superior team is to play at the top of your game by minimizing unforced errors and to pick on the weaknesses of the opponent, hoping they are having an average day on the court. My frequent saying is "We practice this game to play against the best, yet both teams put their spandex on the same way!"

At Sweet Home, teams met us on the court with one of two outlooks. One was to come in with the attitude, "Hurry up and beat us, but don't hurt us too badly." The other was, "We have nothing to lose, so let's play our best." When playing teams that are not confident in their skills, it is difficult to maintain focus, so a coach can try to work on new offenses, can set different goals, and can change the lineup. On the other hand, the matches against teams that gave us a run for our money were the most memorable. We loved playing those teams, and both they and we increased our level of play, but even more important, we learned how to play under pressure.

One of the most difficult matches to prepare for is a play-off match. Usually the two teams have met during the season or have at least scouted each other. If a team has previously beaten their opponent, the coach may be dealing with an overconfidence problem. If the team lost in a previous meeting, she may have to deal with a lack of confidence. If the play-off is single elimination, the coach must be ready for her team to have an abrupt ending to its season, to advance further, or to ultimately be the State Champs! It is amazing to think that there are only a few happy teams at the end of a season. Those are the teams who finished the season with a victory, either as the State Champ or tournament winners! Nonetheless, coaches need to instill pride in accomplishment throughout the season so an abrupt ending is put in perspective.

Many people ask what was my favorite season during my years at Sweet Home. I can honestly say it was the year we were NYS Champion, NYS Scholar Athlete Team, and received the NYS Sportsmanship Award. It was like winning the trifecta.

The larger goal in team preparation is to provide composure for the coach and a stress-free environment for the team. By being free of stress, players can compete with wild abandon, and the coach can sit on the bench, able to focus on the needs at hand and not fret over what might have been.

CHAPTER 14 HANDLING MATCH SITUATIONS

Before a match, both teams' starting players line up along the net, shake hands, and say, "Gluck." It is supposed to be "Good luck" but really sounds like a chicken coop. The coaches will usually shake hands and exchange good wishes. Why teams would wish each other good luck is beyond my imagination. Every coach wants luck on her own side! At the collegiate level, these exchanges between coaches are rarely expressions of good luck to the opponents! A polite example would be to say, "Have a nice match," while really thinking, *We'd better beat you in three straight!* The starters and coach rejoin the team in a last huddle, the coach says a motivating statement, and the team resounds in a cheer for unity.

MAINTAINING FOCUS

One year I had a complete returning team. We had gone undefeated the year before in a Cinderella season. Obviously, I expected the next year to be a breeze. The team was loaded with Division I players who could have been coached by Santa Claus. Instead, I was faced with a team of individuals. We won matches based on reputation and comeback plays. I couldn't figure out why this team was struggling. I thought we lacked the chemistry we had the year before.

Two of my former players were playing in the MAC. I had the opportunity to watch them play against each other. About half of my team accompanied me on the trip to watch the match. Both teams seemed to have similar skills, but one team had a better overall record. As the match progressed, I noticed that players on team A were berating themselves quite demonstratively after an error. They would shake their heads and have scowls on their faces. Teammates were constantly trying to reassure them that everything was okay. Team B handled mistakes as if they were part of the game. After a mistake, they would quickly huddle in a display of support, and the setter would call the next play. The entire process was quick and displayed good sporting behavior and "teaminess." It was then that it struck me. My own team was playing like team A. They were a bunch of talented individuals who were too much into themselves. We lacked chemistry because of our own selfish element.

I pointed this out to my players who were with me, and they all agreed with my diagnosis. We were excited to report our findings to the other players. We felt enlightened and ready to share our vision with the entire team. On the trip home, we concluded that we lacked focus. Everyone makes mistakes; it is part of the game. We needed to learn how to shake off our individual mistakes and focus on the next play. When this negative force was lifted from our team, we had a wonderful conclusion to our season. More important, we learned how to accept and handle mistakes. We learned the importance of focus.

STARTERS VERSUS SUBSTITUTES

Preseason is always a glorious time on the volleyball court. Teams are excited and motivated for the start of the season. Coaches have the highest expectations. Players are showing off their best sides to win a starting position. Then the first scrimmage takes place. The coach tells the team that this will be the first true test. The coach says, "This scrimmage will show us what we need to work on" and "I am starting the best six from our practices so far" or "I don't know who the starters will be, but I have to put six players out to begin . . . it means nothing." After the scrimmage, the telltale process has begun. Players start fitting into a positional priority scheme. The coach keeps reiterating, "This lineup is not set in stone; any of you can win a starting position." Many times this is true; players do progress and the lineup changes. But it is the emotional mind-set of being a starter or a substitute that causes havoc on many teams.

Starters develop arrogance, and substitutes become the statisticians and cheerleaders. It is the lords and the serfs order of hierarchy in the manor. When a substitute is called upon to play, it is for one of several reasons. It could be to go out on the court and fix a bad situation. It could be because the team is so far ahead in score that the coach feels safe to let her play. It could be because the coach feels the team is so far behind in score that he may as well play his subs.

If a sub is called on to try to fix a problem, she usually feels like she has to show the coach how good she is and how she should be starting. Most nonstarters do not have the correct mind-set of being a substitute . . . because everyone wants to be a starter.

Appreciating the Band-Aids

During the 1987 Empire State Scholastic Games, I had a very versatile team. One of my own high school players, Amie, made the team and was chosen because she could effectively play left, middle, or right side. But Amie couldn't crack the lineup. She was the third-ranked player in all three positions. Amie ended up playing in *every* game of the tournament for whoever was flubbing up! She would go into the game and do a great job. Amie had made an extraordinary difference in our play during the five-game gold medal match against the great Hudson Valley team. Amie played three different positions in the five games and was a hero in the last game. A Syracuse newspaper journalist interviewed Amie after the match. I was standing behind Amie, but she didn't know it. The reporter asked Amie if she felt she had proved to me that she should have been a starter. I cringed! But Amie said, "Oh, anyone can be a starter. My coach has more faith in me. She trusts that I can go in and fix what's wrong. I'm like the Band-Aid." After that day, I made sure I shared this story with my Band-Aids, and they knew how important each one was to the team.

Of course, this story is effective for those substitutes who go in and make a difference. Most teams do not have the luxury of being five or six deep on the bench! Communication is important between the coach and substitutes. The coach must make sure there is not any dissension within the ranks and must remind players of their roles and needed areas of improvement.

During game play, if a team is ahead in score, a coach will usually sub a player in to give her more court time. Usually the coach will choose a player who is a senior or a player who is the 7th or 8th player on the team. The 11th and 12th players are the tough ones to squeeze into action. A suggestion made to me years ago, which has been very effective, is to sub that last player in with the starters. It will give her a chance to play with the consistent players. Usually, the lowest skilled players only get to play with other nonstarters in blow away games or doomed games.

Another option that needs to be considered is to put most of the subs on the court at once. Sometimes this shows a coach which subs are leaders, but usually it is a scary situation! Some coaches will leave a couple of stable starting players in the lineup. It is a poor situation when your starters sit on the bench and don't know how to handle being a nonplayer. Usually, they do not focus on the court and become silly and display poor sporting behavior. Coaches need to make sure bench players stay supportive but composed, whether they are starters or subs.

Substituting players also depends on the level of play. Usually, a grassroots, modified, or junior varsity program has an *everybody plays* philosophy. This philosophy will help ease some problems, but if it is not equal time and every player doesn't have an equal opportunity to start in the first game, there will always be moaning and groaning. As long as a coach maintains good communication, the players will know and understand their roles.

CONDUCT DURING THE GAME

Conduct during the game can refer to the duties of coaches, players, and nonplayers. It can also refer to verbal and body language. The head coach should model conduct during play to support his program's philosophy.

Most coaches agree that players and coaches should be in complete control of their emotions and display good sporting behavior. Anyone who has ever been to a volleyball match knows that this is an ideal and far from reality!

The floor captain is the only player on the court allowed to address an official. The floor captain must have good verbal skills, be respectful with adults, be tactful and calm, and have a very good knowledge of the game. The coach is not supposed to be able to address the referees, but there is always kibitzing going on, either verbally or with signals. First of all, it is important to designate only one coach for this type of naughty communication. Also, it should only be used to comment on or show dissatisfaction for outrageous calls. Nothing is worse than a whiny coach who argues every call. This type of coach displays poor sporting behavior, is a poor representative of the institution, and is a poor role model for the team. A coach who cries over every call loses credibility, and the referees will put him on their blacklist!

The bench players must know where they are supposed to stay during a match. Some coaches like them to stand at the end of the bench, and some like them to sit on the bench. One theory is that the players need to stay active, so standing at the end keeps them more ready to play. If the players sit down, they will become sedentary and stiff.

The other theory is that the players need to take a break, and sitting is more conducive to allowing a player to take a rest. Actually,

Establishing a policy on bench conduct and where the players, coach, and assistants will sit is important to do before the match.

many coaches use a combination of the two theories. Players who enter and reenter the game continually are given the opportunity to sit. Players who don't normally play and need to stay ready to go in usually stand. Again, some coaches allow substitutes who are keeping stats to sit because it is easier to write. Any of these methods is good, as long as the coach stays consistent.

Coaching the bench players is valuable since the input given could help a substitute when she enters the game. Even though the subs should be paying attention on the bench and envisioning themselves going into the game, a little advance notice always helps the substitute. Subs have to be ready to go in and be the momentum breaker, too. This can occur when a coach's time-outs are used up, a coach doesn't want to use a time-out, or after the opponents have scored a string of points. Sometimes the sub goes in for someone who is doing nothing wrong. Communication is always important with both players, so the wounded outgoing player isn't in a quandary sitting at the end of the bench! If a coach pulls a player from the game because she is making too many errors, the coach should instruct her as she comes out of the game on how to avoid the mistakes she just made and should give her a few encouraging words. Sometimes this is difficult because it is obvious why the player is coming out of the game and she needs to recoup composure.

The head coach will usually dictate to his assistants where they should sit or stand. Many coaches like to stand because they actively coach during a match. This easily gives them the opportunity to interact with the subs, the court players, the staff, and the officials. Many coaches like to sit because they feel it is important to display a calm demeanor during the match. If they choose to stand and make a point, it appears more effective. Most coaches feel that it is the kids' time to play, so the coach should sit down and enjoy the match! Coaching is not just instructing the technique and tactics; it is also about teaching the players how to handle any game situation as it develops. A coach needs to be in control of his emotions. Players need to look at the

bench and see a stable leader; however, that doesn't mean the coach can't be emotional. Players love to see the excitement and support from their coach during exciting play, but the coach has to be a calming influence during the emotional downswings in a game. If the coach has extreme mood swings, the team can be expected to reflect those same highs and lows in play. If a coach can maintain the appearance of being in control of his emotions during a "disaster," it should help the team to be in better control during chaos. If a coach displays extreme highs and lows, that roller coaster of emotions has a disastrous effect on his players. A team usually takes on the persona of the coach's outward expression. Emotion can certainly be a positive driving force, but acting on emotion alone will not lead to success.

The head coach usually takes on the role of being the main speaker during the game. If a team has two or three coaches giving instructions and badgering the players on the court, it confuses the team and takes the focus off the play. It also shows that the coaches do not trust the players to adapt to game situations. In addition, a coach should usually limit the amount of information given to a team during a time-out . . . that is what practice is all about. The players should have developed into self-thinkers and problem solvers through practice situations. Many young teams do need some suggestions during game play, but it should be limited. A coach does not want his team constantly looking over to the bench for advice or instruction. He should try to limit complicated instruction to practices and simply give advice during time-outs. The use of key phrases during play can be effective but should be kept limited. Many coaches feel that every mistake must be addressed at the end of play. Volleyball is a game of mistakes. Some mistakes are avoidable, so practice should be about "bettering the ball." However, many coaches feel that when a player makes a mistake, it is a reflection of what a poor technical coach they are . . . Get over it and let the kids play! One other exception to this is the coach who calls the plays for the setter. In addition, it is common for a coach and setter to have a special communication system. Many times, coaches will signal when to switch defenses or give other tactical signals.

A coach may choose to switch defenses because the opponent has changed their offensive tactics or because a change in rotation doesn't lend itself to defend an attack successfully. An example of the former is when an opponent starts sending tips over the block; in response, a coach may change his defense from perimeter to rotation. An example of the latter is when an opponent who hits crosscourt rotates to the front row; in response, a coach may change from rotation to perimeter defense. Other common changes include changing front row players to beef up an attack route or changing blocking assignments. A team that practices these changes will be versatile and confident under duress.

A common strategy in game play is a coach signaling where the server should direct the serve. The controversy is whether a coach should call the signal or allow the player to make the decision. It will depend on whether the coach has taught his players the strategy of serving, if the player can serve to all the areas, and if the player has different kinds of serves. Coaches know the best area to serve to because of scouting information and their understanding of the tactics of deterring a team from siding out easily.

The most common signals coaches use are the 1-2-3-4-5-fist signals. The coach uses a clipboard to hide his hand from the opponent (making sure his server can see it). The numbers correspond with the serving areas on the opponent's court with the fist signal indicating the 6 area. The coach puts up the number of fingers according to the serving area. The other signal frequently used is one where the coach only lifts the index and pinkie fingers. This signal means serve in between the antennas please!

TIME-OUTS

Time-outs are taken for many reasons during a game. Usually it is the team that is losing that takes the time-out. Sometimes a coach takes a time-out to break the action in the game. This happens after a string of lost points, during a tough server, late in the game, or when a coach gets a gut feeling that the tide is turning. Sometimes a coach who has a comfortable lead will also take a time-out when the opponents have gained a string of points. Time-outs need to be structured so that time is used efficiently.

The coach should instruct the team on the correct time-out procedures. Players' water bottles and towels should be kept in the same accessible place. The coach can have the players sit or stand but should try to maintain an environment of focus on the coach. This will probably mean that the players are not facing the spectators. We don't need Grandma waving from the bleachers, or a dad giving his child instruction, or that "special" friend in the stands taking a player's attention off the coach.

During a Christmas reunion party I was hosting for my past players, a revelation took place. Many of the players were now playing

Make the most of time-outs by mixing in motivational comments along with the instruction.

in college, and they were discussing their likes and dislikes about their college programs. Stories were flying through the room. Roberta, the player who was at the most prestigious volleyball program, was stealing the show. She had always gotten the attention, and now the kids wanted to hear how she liked playing at such a high level of play. Roberta said that her coach was a great practice coach but "sucked" as a game coach. I jumped in and asked her why she felt that way. Roberta said that during time-outs, he would just say "insipid" statements. She went on to say that during a time-out a team needs to know how to fix things or needs answers. All her coach would say was things like, "Pass the ball" or "Move your feet."

I started reflecting on how often I said those things in time-outs, too. During a time-out when we were ahead, I used to laugh and joke and keep the spirits high. I think I sometimes took focus off play, and we went back overconfident and less focused.

So, from then on, I made sure I was ready for the time-out. If we were ahead, I made sure to compliment what was working, give advice on what might happen next, and tell them something to do better. I did not overload them. I made sure to end with a defensive cheer.

If we were behind, I tried not to emphasize the mistakes unless I could say something concrete to improve play. Instead, I refocused the team by giving suggestions on what to do next and what the opponents might do next. I made sure I didn't overload the team and confuse them. I gave a positive, supportive finishing statement. I usually spoke to the setter on the side and offered several suggestions in case the first one I gave the team failed. The setter had an alternative and remained calm on the court. I made sure to finish with a supportive, "teamy" cheer.

As the game progresses, a coach can jot down statements he wants to make at the next time-out on his clipboard. I developed an organized template to help me record information I'd need during a time-out. It includes rotations, time-out notes, court outlines, and a place to write down essentials to help me plan the next practice from game mistakes (see figure 14.1). My assistant also formed a template that helped her record pertinent information (see figure 14.2). These forms kept our time-outs efficient, and I didn't have to rely on my memory. The coach should know the rotation of the teams before the time-out so he can offer suggested areas to attack, remind the team what the opponents might do next, and remind the team whether the opponent's setter is front or back row.

During the game, a 60-second time-out is the only time a coach can give valuable input to the team without disrupting play. If a coach stays organized, it can be a valuable minute that affects the outcome of play. Nothing is better than an opponent who misses a serve after a time-out!

BETWEEN GAMES

Between games is a time similar to a time-out, but there are two problems. One problem is the coach must turn in his lineup, and the other problem is the team has to change benches. If the team is organized, changing benches can be efficient. Also, after a team has just lost, many coaches will make an adjustment in the lineup to improve it.

Between games, a coach may make adjustments to the lineup to improve matchups. This means starting his team in a certain rotation order to best match up with the other team's order—in other words, who will be blocking and hitting against each other. Considerations are similar to those made before the first game, but if the matchups were different than expected or ineffective, the coach will make a change. The biggest problem is a coach doesn't know the changes the other coach may make. A crystal ball would be a good coaching tool to possess! Sometimes a coach can have better odds by knowing the opposing coach's tendencies from past experience. A coach may choose to put his best hitter attacking against a different blocker because of tendencies he saw throughout the previous game. He may change a digger

Subs

Time-out notes

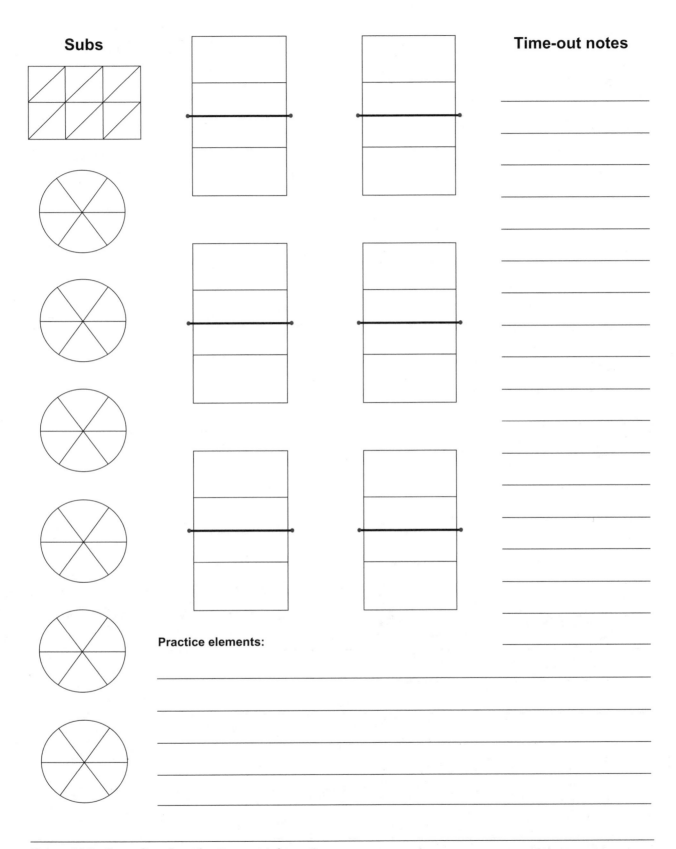

Practice elements:

Figure 14.1 Recording sheet for time-out information.

195

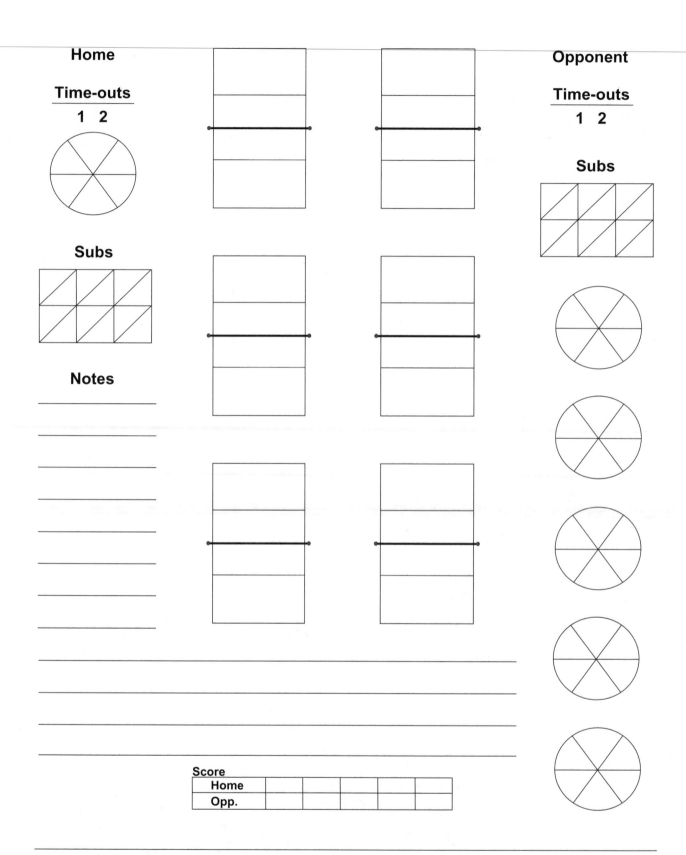

Figure 14.2 Assistant coach's recording sheet.

to a different position to make her more apt to dig the opponent's best hitter and cover that hitter's tendencies. These are all examples of why a coach may change a lineup. If a coach maintains the same lineup over and over again, and it does not produce a win, players can lose faith in the process.

Once a team has settled on the other side of the court, the next minute is similar to a time-out. The coach will show the team the starting lineup. If they lost the prior game, the coach will point out why this lineup should help. This will help the players refocus on the next game and help them see that the coach is solving problems. Sometimes it might be a change in personnel, and other times it may be just rotating the lineup to face different matchups. The coach will then proceed to remind the team of what the opponents did that this team needs to stop and what this team can do to be more effective. The "don'ts" have to be limited, and the "we're going tos" have to be flowing. All coaches have some key phrases to use to finish, such as "That's why we play the best of five" or "You're just trying to get our money's worth." A supportive cheer before a team leaves the huddle is a must.

MAINTAINING MOMENTUM

Everyone wants to know the formula for momentum. Volleyball is such a roller coaster ride. When a team is ahead, it's like sitting in the front seat and anticipating the thrill. When a team is behind, it is like sitting in the back seat and gasping for air. Maintaining momentum is the key to success. It can be as easy as *A, B, C.*

A stands for aggressiveness. If a team stays aggressive in everything they do, it will keep the other team scrambling. Aggressiveness is not just hitting. It can be diving for a key dig, serving to a weak zone, covering a hitter, pursuing a shanked pass, placing a free ball in a strategic area on the opponent's court, setting a tight pass, or penetrating the net when blocking. Aggressiveness usually

means confidence. Confidence is an attitude. Attitude is usually developed from a player's environment and experiences. This aggressive attitude has to be a constant in practice so teams don't learn to play safe.

B stands for believing. Believing is commitment and loyalty. Believing in winning means never giving up and never regretting how you play. True believing will produce adrenaline and desire!

C is for communication. When things go wrong in a game, communication usually ceases. If a team is always talking, a team is anticipating. Communication maintains focus, helps the struggling player, and supports aggressiveness.

This is a formula. The key to it is to be able to coach it in practice, exhibit it in games, live it in life, and keep humming the *A, B, C* jingle.

RALLY SCORE

Rally score is the newest change in the game. It used to be a team would be aggressive during rallies when they were serving and more conservative when the opponents had the serve. When rally score was first introduced, it started changing the aggressive mind-set of play. Players made conservative plays because errors caused the opponents to gain a point no matter who was serving. Now that people are comfortable with this method, aggressiveness is back. A team must have aggressive play in a game in order to play with excellence and to win. Playing safe by serving easy or by hitting it "to just keep it in" allows the other team to side out and gain a point. So, the best philosophy is to be aggressive, force your opponent to err, and stick to the game plan.

During the coin toss before a match, most teams choose to receive serve. The rotation order lends itself to siding out first, gaining the first point, and rotating into the team's best rotation. This gives a team the ability to set the tempo and attack first. Of course, many feel that the first attack is the serve, and the serving team gets to use their first line of defense, which is an effective block. A coach's philosophy has to be based on the abilities of his team.

The rally score method scores games to 25 or 30 points. This allows teams to accept aggressive errors and still recover lost points. If the last game is limited to 15 points, teams have to score early and maintain composure. These are the games where safe play is prevalent and the players develop feathers. These are games where officials tend to swallow the whistle to allow the teams to decide their own fate. A team is more successful if they stick to their game plan.

CHAPTER 15 EVALUATING PLAYERS

Evaluating players is not limited to tryouts. In fact, evaluation is a coach's constant role. A coach needs to appraise players throughout the season, both during practices and in game situations. These three areas of evaluation are distinct, so there are specific strategies for each category.

PRESEASON TRYOUTS

It used to be that a coach's judgment was trusted when it came to picking a team. Now a coach has to be more accountable and protect his integrity. A tryout cannot be subjective anymore. A tryout must be objective. A coach has to be able to show specific player ratings in case he is challenged. He needs to show in black and white that the player was unable to demonstrate the skill or didn't have the athleticism needed to be a contributing player on the team. The coach can no longer say, "She's not quick enough or she can't pass." A coach must have a rating process for all participants. Each rating must reflect specific goals to achieve the grade. See table 15.1 for an example of a rating scale for passing.

This is a general passing guideline. The grassroots player could not be judged on this scale. The coach can adjust the grading "cue" sentences according to his highest expectations for players at his team's level of play. This seems like a tedious process, but it really involves integrating your key words into sentences. Once it is developed, a coach can review and improve it to make it easier to administer. From experience, I have learned to be critical in appraisal. It is very easy to assign a rating of 3 to many participants. This will leave the coach with too many participants with the same grade. Don't be afraid to assign 1s to very poor participants and 2s to mediocre players.

Along with having a rating system, a comment column can be very helpful when a coach reviews his scores. Comments like "quick feet" or "slow to the ball" can become very helpful when choosing that 12th player. A comment like "verbalizes well" or "is supportive of teammates" can be helpful when assessing focus and attitude.

Actually, my favorite rating system is Y, M, and N. That is my judgment when watching a player try out or play. Y is yes, M is maybe, and N is no. It is simple but I bet most veteran coaches could effectively choose a team with this method!

Table 15.1 Rating Scale for Passing

Score (1-5; 5 is highest)	Description	Comments
5	Participant faces the ball in a medium posture and is focused on the flight of the ball. Participant maintains her posture and moves her feet efficiently to the ball and stops in a wide, balanced base position before the ball arrives. Participant places the heels of her hands together outstretched from her body and creates a platform angle that is aimed at the target. Participant focuses on the ball contacting the forearms and the ball effectively finishing to the target.	
4	Participant usually faces the ball in a medium posture and focuses on the flight of the ball. Participant usually maintains her posture throughout her movement to the ball. She usually stops her feet before the ball arrives. Participant usually places the heels of her hands together outstretched from her body and creates a platform angle that is aimed near the target area.	
3	Participant sometimes faces the ball, and so on.	
2	Participant seldom faces the ball, and so on.	
1	Participant never faces the ball, and so on.	

Challenges in Assessing Tryouts

There are two major challenges with tryouts. One is learning to focus on the *maybes*. The maybes are the last few players you will choose for your team. This is where balancing the grade and position within the coach's philosophy has to be clear. Here are some considerations a coach will weigh when choosing his last three to six players:

- A coach believes in taking young players to develop the future, but it is easier to take veteran players who know the system. Young players may be drill stoppers in practice.

- A coach believes in keeping seniors who have been part of the program but have never developed to expectations; however, these seniors could become disgruntled when younger players receive more game time.

- A coach believes in taking a chance on some taller players, but these players may be drill stoppers in practice.

- A coach believes in taking athletes to finish his roster to keep his scrimmages competitive, but these athletes may be unfocused when learning drills and just there to play.

A coach should also consider taking the players with the best attitudes, since these last few players will probably ride a lot of pine. This is your "Rudy" player. It's hard to argue against a player with a great attitude unless she is a drill stopper in practice.

A coach needs to compare all the maybes against each other in a gamelike situation. This is where the cream rises to the top! If a coach is fortunate to have two courts, he can place the maybes on one court and mix the yeses and nos playing together on the other court. If he only has use of one court, he should watch the maybes play first and the other group second. This will give him more time to assess the maybes. The coach might even choose to watch a few of the maybes again in the second group.

The other major challenge with tryouts is to learn to focus on the nonball side of a court during competitive drills. Many skills are not performed well because a player has poor trajectory reading. Flight recognition and arriving at the ball before the ball arrives at the spot can be learned, but they are usually developed earlier in childhood. Kids who play catch with a ball outside in the summer, versus playing Barbie Dolls or playing on the Internet, learn this skill through play and early sport interaction.

Evaluating Younger Players

A coach must decide what is important when choosing what volleyball or athletic skills to assess. Obviously, the evaluation process at the grassroots level would differ greatly from the process used at the varsity level.

When evaluating the grassroots player, a coach has to look back on his philosophy and decide what he feels is most important in his farm system. It is always best to have a no cut policy with young players since your only basis is athleticism. If too many children attend the first day, perhaps they can be divided into two groups, and the coach can alternate days to accommodate all the children. If this is not possible and the coach must eliminate players from the program, it is best if he can steer the children that are not chosen to another level of volleyball. An example would be to participate in an intramural or YMCA program.

A coach who must run a tryout for these young players must base his evaluation on his philosophy. When I coached at the middle school level, I had the fortunate situation where I could teach and watch players in physical education class and in intramurals. When choosing players for my sixth grade team, I evaluated each player during two drills. One drill was throwing a baseball across the gym. The throwing motion is similar to the serving and spiking motion. The next drill was watching the kids play quads from a coach (usually an eighth grader) initiated toss. From this drill, I could evaluate two distinct qualities. One was agility and aggressiveness to the ball. The other was to watch the side that was NOT playing the ball to see who had feet focus. By this I mean who was moving with each touch of the ball . . . not just standing with her knees locked and nodding her head up and down like a bobble head doll. Again, this showed agility and focus. All of these skills are natural or developed from a cross-trained sport. Either way, the kid who moved to the ball and moved with the ball defensively was the player I wanted. My philosophy is aggressiveness, agility, leadership, and focus.

Another consideration that may seem ridiculous is to check out the size of the parents. A boy usually grows taller than his dad and a girl taller than her mom. Does the kid have big feet? What about the size of the siblings? It is tough with grassroots programs because a coach wants to end up with a blend of athletes and taller players.

Tall Tales

I was using my family comparisons with a great young athlete named Colleen. Both of her parents and her sister were over six feet tall, and her brother was over six-foot-six. In sixth grade, Colleen could pass nails, hit aggressively, and had very quick feet. Colleen was about five-foot-six. I decided that Colleen should become a setter. I knew with her genetic potential she would be a national team prospect in 10 years! Well, Colleen did develop into a Division I setter but never grew past five-foot-seven!

Another story concerns a gawky, six-foot-plus middle school boy named Chris. He appeared to have no coordination, but our middle school coach put him on the team. After the tryout, there was a lot of chuckling about Chris making the squad. In the end, Chris grew to be six-foot-ten, was a star on the Penn State team, and made the national B team!

The same coach cut a young man named Rich in middle school. Rich was determined and asked the coach if he could be the manager. The coach said yes, and Rich ended up participating in many practices. The next year, Rich made junior varsity and proceeded to become a varsity star in high school. Of course, this success story ends with this man becoming a starter at Penn State! The lesson in this is to allow those eager kids who get cut to become a future Rich by letting them be the manager!

These stories should help coaches realize that mistakes will be made, but they should trust their instincts.

A coach will always make mistakes in tryouts. On a team of 14 players, the 10th through the 14th player will usually change throughout the season. The unfortunate part is number 15 might have developed into number 8. Potential is a tricky assessment. It is impossible to justly assess potential because only experience proves it. Many players with the most potential don't have the desire to achieve it. Does a coach want a self-made volleyball player who has the desire or a natural athlete who can freelance and be successful?

When selecting a team, it is easiest to post the names of the players who have been chosen on the bulletin board and then run and hide! A true teacher will take the time and share the rating with those who did not make it. This is very difficult but will help maintain integrity. It will also squelch some of the complaining that will take place and the blame shifting that will occur. It will usually deter parental interference. Parents tend to live vicariously through their child athlete. They tend to get involved when their child gets cut if they suspect favoritism, subjective selection, or after a child has been successful in a prior experience.

One example of a prior successful experience is a summer camp evaluation. Some camps evaluate each camper on a written form. Camps want to attract kids back the next summer and tend to be generous when assessing a child's skill level. The other problem with a written evaluation is it usually doesn't state whom the camper is being compared with or the rating process. So, if a child receives glowing remarks following summer camp and proceeds to get cut from the junior varsity team, somebody needs to be responsible for breaking her heart.

Time may not permit individual assessment meetings with those players not chosen on a team. If this is the case, the coach should meet with the children as a group and state his case. These 10 minutes are the longest in history! The coach should extend the option to meet with him to discuss the evaluation (few players will accept this invitation). The coach should thank each participant and give each the option of playing at an alternate level.

Once a team has been chosen, the coach can also use the written evaluation process to identify the level his team is at. This will help him plan his preseason and season practices. He can also share his rating with his players to help them understand where each needs to improve.

Look Beneath the Surface

Back in the '80s, I was coaching the NYS Western Scholastic volleyball team. We only had a few tryouts based on skill and court play. There was only a month of biweekly practices before the state event. So, most of the practices were devoted to developing playing systems and team chemistry. The coach was allowed to choose 12 players and 2 alternates. An alternate could become a team player if a teammate was injured or quit. One young lady, Lisa, from a very small school district, was quite an image at the net but did not possess the finer qualities to make it through the tryout. She was selected as an alternate. After a month of practice,

Lisa would have been the number one starting middle blocker on the team. The kids affectionately called her "The Beast." Lisa possessed all the virtues that the selection committee would not know about. She was a quick learner, a student of the game, and a great, aggressive athlete. Through her tryout, she only demonstrated what she knew and was somewhat intimidated by the more savvy players. Lisa ended up being a force during her senior year and gained a Division I scholarship. She went on to coach Division I. Since that tryout, I have learned to look out for any possible Lisas that might be in the gym!

Another consideration when choosing a team is to balance the team with enough veteran players to compete and enough younger players to ensure the future of the program. Not all programs have this luxury and have to recruit from their middle schools, physical education classes, or intramurals. Many junior clubs recruit during the high school season, too. If a program has the luxury of choosing players from many participants, a coach's philosophy will come into effect during tryouts. Many coaches want to put the best six players on the court . . . no matter what grade those players are in. Some coaches believe that there is a hierarchy in the program, and the seniors have earned the starting position. This coach usually feels that the younger player should pay her dues within the pipeline of the farm system.

To be a successful team, the coach must also choose the proper balance of players based on specific positions. On a team of 12 to 14 players, each position should be at least three deep for outsides, middles, right sides, and setters. With the addition of the Libero position, one or two players are needed to fill that invaluable role. Many coaches train their backup setter, utility, or extra outside player to play Libero. Some coaches feel that training one or two players to play only Libero strengthens ball control and team chemistry. Traditionally, lefties usually train as setters or right-side hitters. Some coaches train lefties

as outsides or middles to wreak more havoc with the opposing defense. Another valuable position is the defensive specialist. There is still a role, in addition to the Libero, for at least one defensive specialist. This player can go in and play defense along with the Libero to strengthen back row play. The defensive specialist is also allowed to attack out of the back row. It is a great way to add another option and some zip to the offense. A blend of players needs to be chosen to complement a lineup. As for grassroots programs, a blend of agile athleticism with potentially taller players is smart.

PRACTICE ASSESSMENT

Coaches insist that starters are selected based on their performance in practice. The keen eye of the coach is enough judgment for him to decide who should be in the starting lineup. But sometimes a player or parent (who wears rose-colored glasses) will question the coach's decision on the starting lineup. This is why a coach should remember that practice stats don't lie! The statistics recorded during matches can also be recorded in practice. But, the coach will need a few loyal managers to fulfill this role. If a coach has a manager, he can assign her some simple stats to keep in practice. If the coach does not have a manager, players not involved in the drill can record stats or each player can keep track of her own stats. An example of a simple stat is during a serve receive or passing drill. Depending upon the level of the team, the coach will assign a grade of 3, 2, 1, or 0 for each pass.

At a varsity level, a 3 pass would be a pass right on target. It is a pass the setter could set any tempo or any position along the net. A 2 pass would be a pass the setter can handle but must set as a second or third tempo set along the net or back row. A 1 pass is a pass that forces the setter to call "help" or results in a free ball to the opposition. A 0 pass is a ball that is shanked or hits the floor. A coach and player will quickly see who the best passers are by their average. It is also a good way to find out who a team's primary passers are, who should be placed defensively to pass more balls, or who the best defensive specialists are on the team. Similar point systems can be developed for any skill. Few teams have the personnel to keep stats for every skill or drill, but these scores are helpful in evaluating players.

Another way to use stats in drills is to use the scale for a scoring method. An example of this is a serve receive or passing drill. Using the same scoring method as in the previous example, a player or group of players are finished with the drill when they accumulate a set number of points in the drill. Here are some examples of how a drill could be scored if three players are passing in the drill:

- The group goal could be 77 points, and the drill would be over when it is reached. They can rotate every 15 points to allow them to pass from each position.

- Three additional players could be on the other side of the net or a second court performing the same drill. The two groups compete against each other to see who can achieve 77 first.

- Each passer could be required to score 3 in a row. When a team can score a 3-3-3, they can rotate to the next position. Again, a team on the other side or a team on an adjacent court is a more competitive method to score the drill.

- An individual method could be to score the drill by requiring each player to pass 27 points before exiting the drill. This type of scoring makes passers aggressive to get to the ball and no one wants to be the last one on the court!

The coach needs to remember that the more competitive the drill becomes, the more the players will rush through the drill. If the coach's objective is to develop and train good habits, then competing against another court may not be a good idea until the players have more consistent passing skills.

Drills like the previous example are easy to develop, and changing the scoring method makes them easy to reuse.

Another easy method of recording stats is to use the +, 0, – method. In a serving drill, a + would be a point that is a direct result of the serve. This is an ace serve. A 0 would be a serve that is handled by the opposition and the ball remains in play. A – would be a serve that is not in play and results in a point and side-out. This method can be developed for each skill. The coach can assign a point value if he chooses to develop an average.

Another stat that can be used in practice is to record each player's percentage when performing a specific skill (all the players perform a specific number of repetitions at one time). An example is if each player had to set attack 10 tossed balls. If the hitter attacked 7 of 10 tossed balls, she hit 70 percent or .700. Of course, a variable a coach would have to take into account is the consistency of the toss. The other problem with this stat is players may tend to hit safe or be less aggressive to keep up their percentage.

Another similar stat is for the coach to run a drill where the hitter has to hit 10 balls in the opposing court. The counter could keep track of how many tosses or sets it takes for the hitter to accomplish the goal.

GAME EVALUATION

According to league or conference rules, some teams must keep specific game stats and submit them to the governing body. The NCAA requires teams to keep the following statistics:

Number of games played in the match

Attack kills—point is awarded to the attacking team as a direct result of the attacking motion

Attack errors—results in a point for the opponent

TA—total attack attempts in the game

Kill percentage—the number of kills per attempts (similar to a batting average)

Set assists that lead to a kill

Serve aces—point is awarded to the serving team as a direct result of the serve

Serve errors—opponent is awarded a point as a direct result of the serve

Serve receive—a service error that is a direct point for the opponent

Defense—a dig performed from an attacked ball

Solo block—a block performed by one player that results in a point

Assist block—a block performed with one or two other players that results in a point

Block error—an error that results in a point for the other team

General handling errors—a ball handling error called by an official that awards a point

All of these statistics are compiled, and averages are posted for the individual and team by game and match.

These are just some of the statistics used by college teams. More sophisticated methods are used to more closely identify the skill used. An example is the attack. Some statistics keep track of the type of attack (e.g., tip, roll, wipe, off the block, caused by a blocking error, caused by a center line violation, back row attacker crossing the three-meter line) and areas the ball was attacked into the opponent's court. A coach can get as intricate as he wishes and has the personnel to facilitate. If bench players are used to keep statistics, they must be trained to be consistent. Statistics are only as good as the person who holds the pencil! Parents are generally not consistent at statistics, especially if their child seems to be at the top of every component!

Scholastic and club teams usually account for service, assist, and attack statistics. Some keep passing, digging, and blocking statistics if they have the need for them. Most coaches tend to keep statistics to help them identify skill weaknesses rather than successes. Skill weaknesses will help identify what the next practice should contain. On the bench, I have always recorded on my clipboard a shortened version of what caused the point. This shows me our success and our failure. I have two columns, one for the goods and one for the bads. If Molly, who is number 4 and plays OH (position 4), has an attack kill, I would chart it as 4K-4X, which would mean the 4 player hit a four ball (high outside) crosscourt for a kill. If the same player shanks a serve receive, I would write 4s/r E. Obviously, I found myself not having time to write after a string of poor plays. I developed an easy graph for my manager that I wish I had made for myself. Figure 15.1 shows the NCAA's box score for recording stats.

Another good chart to develop is a passing area frequency chart. It is a simple chart that identifies where the serve receive or pass arrives on the court. Some coaches use dots and some use the number of the passer who passed the ball on the court diagram. Either way, it shows the passing tendency of the player or team. This is a simple chart that can be kept by a sideline player or manager.

A high school or club coach can keep statistics by using a numbering system, a +, 0, − system, or any method that proves easiest to administer and results in what the coach wants to identify and use. Statistics should help identify a player's and team's successes and failures. How a coach uses this information is just as important as careful compilation. As stated, I have always kept the negatives of my team during game play. My first year at the University of Buffalo, for the first time in my coaching career, I was called negative. I arranged for a team meeting. Upon further questioning, the players thought I was charting our negatives so I could display them on a bar graph. After I explained to them that it helped me plan the next week of practices, all was forgiven. This is when I turned the negative graphing over to my manager and focused more on better communication. Players need to understand the use of statistics and how it implicates game play. Players should get used to tactful constructive criticism but also be praised for their individual efforts, which result in team success.

Some youth teams keep statistics to show success and improvement. Generally, the most important statistics are serving and passing. A simple + and − is easy to administer. Once the team can pass to target or

OFFICIAL NCAA® VOLLEYBALL BOX SCORE

Site: _____ Date: _____ Attendance: _____

TEAM			ATTACK				SET	SERVE		PASS	DEF	BLOCK			GEN.
NO.	PLAYER	GP	K	E	TA	PCT.	A	SA	SE	RE	DIG	BS	BA	BE	BHE
TEAM TOTALS:															

TEAM ATTACKS PER GAME:
TOTAL TEAM BLOCKS:

	K	E	TA	PCT.		GAME SCORES:	1	2	3	4	5	TEAM RECORDS:
GAME 1												
2												
3												
4												
5												

TEAM			ATTACK				SET	SERVE		PASS	DEF	BLOCK			GEN.
NO.	PLAYER	GP	K	E	TA	PCT.	A	SA	SE	RE	DIG	BS	BA	BE	BHE
TEAM TOTALS:															

TEAM ATTACKS PER GAME:
TOTAL TEAM BLOCKS:

	K	E	TA	PCT.
GAME 1				
2				
3				
4				
5				

KEY

A = Assists	BHE = Ball-Handling Errors
K = Kills	TA = Total Attempts
E = Errors	RE = Receiving Errors
D = Digs	BS = Block Solos
PCT. = %	BA = Block Assists
	BE = Block Errors

SA = Service Aces
SE = Service Errors
GP = Games Played
TEAM BLOCKS = BS + 1/2 BA
HITTING PCT. = (K - E) ÷TA

Length of Match: _____ 1st Referee: _____ 2nd Referee: _____

NCAA 15830-6/01

Figure 15.1 Box score for recording stats.

Reprinted, by permission, from The National Collegiate Athletic Association.

an attack is generated, the 0 statistic can be added. It is important with youth teams to show improvement and success no matter what the score.

When I first coached our middle school team, we used two scoring methods: the game score and the *real score*. The game score was the actual score at the end of the match. The real score was the point I awarded after an attempted bump, set, and spike. Most of the teams in our league returned the ball on the first contact. We usually tried to pass, hit, and attack every ball, which was easy to attempt since we were receiving all free balls. Because we had practiced passing and setting every practice, most of our errors were in our attack. But we were playing the game the way it was supposed to be played. Sometimes, it is difficult to lose a game when you are playing the game correctly but the other team is winning. Our best statistic was the number of pass, set, hit attempts we recorded in a game.

Some coaches keep their own statistics by viewing video of game play. This is a great method if a coach has the time to perform this duty. Video can be used to show a player or the team different aspects of their performance. The video can be used to have the player chart her own statistics, too.

Statistics are valid only if the rater is consistent. Statistics can be used throughout a game to chart successes and errors. This can help the coach decide on lineup changes. Statistics must be used to help a team's success and improve play. Individual statistics must be used to improve team play and not to bolster the player's ego so she loses the team concept.

Players are acutely aware that they are being evaluated during tryouts. A coach must remind his players that they are also being evaluated throughout the season. The coach must give players feedback from this evaluation when appropriate. Stats provide objective evidence of player performance and can prove useful in discussions with players. A coach needs to prevent the response, "Why didn't you ever tell me what I was doing wrong?"

CHAPTER 16
EVALUATING YOUR PROGRAM

The drive home from the state championship should be spent relaxing and reminiscing. I always found myself developing next year's lineup. That is when I knew I was assessing (or obsessing?) our players and thinking of the future needs for being successful. I would try to plan what coaching clinic to attend, what age to coach in the upcoming club season, and what camps were the best for me to coach at and for my players to attend. There were also thoughts of other volleyball experiences my players could aspire to, including different all-star, state games, and junior elite experiences through USA Volleyball. It was important for my players to grow in the sport and for me to remain a student of the game. At the end of my off-season experiences, I would always revel in the new things I had learned, and I would think, *If I only knew that last year, we would have been so much better!* As long as I could annually say that, I knew coaching was for me.

Assessing the program has to start with preseason and the players' and coach's recommendations from the last postseason evaluation. It includes goal setting, player responsibilities, and performance plans for the assistant and head coaches. It also has to include recruiting new players, scheduling, fund-raising, and any new ideas to spark the upcoming season.

SETTING GOALS AND RESPONSIBILITIES

Goals must be established before the season so the players know what they are shooting for in the season. If the program does not have goals, it is difficult to set individual player goals. Goals must be realistic but challenging. Examples of team goals could include the following:

- To finish a certain place in the conference, league, regional, or state
- To focus on the next point after an error
- To motivate and challenge teammates constructively
- To play every point as if the team is behind
- To practice aggressively and hone in on basics
- To hit .250 as a team
- To achieve 15 kills per game as a team
- To serve more aces than errors as a team
- To serve 2 aces per game as a team
- To keep reception errors below 1.5 per game

- To achieve 15 digs per game as a team
- To keep fun in volleyball but never regret how you play
- To enjoy your teammates on and off the court and respect and appreciate each other's differences
- To communicate well with teammates and the staff; treat each other as a family
- To play on the road as well as you play at home matches
- To be a positive and respectful representative of the school or club
- To always play aggressively

Some junior varsity or modified goals could be the following:

- To attempt a pass, set, hit from every free ball
- To serve more than 75 percent as a team
- To praise my passer after an attack
- To communicate on every first contact
- To be respectful of officials and be a good sport
- To be helpful and thankful to my coaches, teammates, and bus driver
- To be tolerant of my teammates' mistakes and focus on the next play
- To cheer and celebrate good play

These goals should be developed from player and staff input. This could mean preseason meetings, individual meetings, mailings, e-mail solicitation, and previous postseason evaluation. The players' input must be included or they will not believe in what they need to achieve to have a successful season. Kids come up with the darnedest things! Varsity and collegiate players appreciate the opportunity to give input and feel the staff respects them if they're included in the process.

Player responsibilities should be clearly stated so they know what is expected of them in practice, in a match, or off the court. The responsibilities include conduct, practice expectations, home and away match procedures, travel procedures, and team policies.

Conduct includes good sporting behavior, respectfulness, and pride. Practice expectations include drill organizational procedures (e.g., player responsibilities and practice skills needed to run a successful drill). Responsibilities should be assigned for all aspects of a home or away match to take the burden off the staff and develop a valuable character trait. Team policies must be written, and they must be reviewed by the players and their parents. The signed team policy is a contract, and if a rule is broken, it will help to avoid the excuse of "I didn't know."

Performance plans for the coaching staff are also important to have in place. These are similar to a job description.

Wearing Many Hats

The first collegiate coaching job I accepted was a revelation. Every day I found I was supposed to do something I didn't know was my task. Van arrangements, academic advisor, compliance, scheduling, motel reservation specialist, restaurant choosing, financier, budget, counseling, equipment and apparel purchasing, and fund-raising are just a few of the items that should be on a job description. I usually found out it was my responsibility after I hadn't done it! It was a small school so there was little support staff. I had come from a large high school where there was support and "spoon-feeding!" My husband kept saying to me, "That's what you get when you accept a job without a description."

A performance plan spells out the major responsibilities of each staff member. The plan is written by the immediate supervisor and sometimes with input from the coach. The head coach writes the plan for her assistants. It is best if both parties discuss the tasks. With good communication, duties can be delegated that the coach excels in or has interest in developing. If a coach does not have the luxury of a staff (which in scholastic settings would include assistants, junior varsity, freshman, and modified coaches), the coach may assign some duties to captains, players, or responsible parents. The performance plan can be detailed, but a coach wants to have some freedom to develop and promote individual assignments. From time to time, the athletic director should meet with the head coach, and the head coach should meet with her assistants, to make sure all assignments are being performed.

A performance appraisal is a written assessment at the end of the season on how well the plan was carried out by the coach. It is an easy and reliable method of assessment. The immediate supervisor and the coach sign the appraisal. It is placed in the coach's folder and can also be used as an employment reference.

IDENTIFYING FUTURE NEEDS

Building for the future must be a plan. A coach can use player, staff, and program assessment to help identify future needs. Examples of needs include player and position, equipment and apparel, facility, staffing, fund-raising, and any need that will help develop and support a better program in the years ahead. Some needs that are identified must be developed during the off-season. If a coach waits until preseason, it might be too late to effectively organize and administer the task. An example is a team who wants to play in a tournament out of state during the next season. Permission from the governing bodies, legal issues, missing classes, travel, food, overnight arrangements, and outside educational opportunities are just a few of the considerations that need to be explored, identified, and arranged. A coach doesn't want to hear, "We should have planned earlier" after a botched mess has occurred!

Other important needs are players and personnel. Before recruiting or tryouts, a coach must identify what positions are needed to balance a team. Replacing players who have moved to the next level or graduated is important. If a new staff member has to be hired or recruited, the coach must identify the qualities needed to support and complement her skills and personality.

Input from players helps coaches identify strengths and weaknesses in the program.

MIDSEASON AND POSTSEASON PLAYER MEETINGS

Many coaches say they do not have time to meet with players in the middle of the season. Schedule, travel, midterms, and practice time are the frequent excuses. Early communication will put out small fires that could flare up into major blazes. There are also other methods of meeting with players. One idea is to meet with one player before and another player after each practice. Another is to meet with groups or the entire team. Some players will be inhibited to disclose problems in front of their peers, but at least this opens the door. With open dialogue, it may encourage a player to talk to the coach privately about an issue. A coach should "keep her ears open," without being too obtrusive, for any disputes in the making. With luck, she can mediate and squelch a growing problem that may hinder team chemistry. Canceling one day of practice to heal wounds or ward off problems will probably accomplish more than the practice. During the meeting, interchange of ideas, accomplishments, goals, and review of statistics can be refreshing. It also allows everyone the opportunity to review, adjust, and focus on the goals set from preseason.

Postseason meetings are a true reflection of the entire season. Individual meetings and written evaluations will help the staff review what should be eliminated or improved for the next season.

Consider individual meeting topics such as review of academics, grade estimates, injury and rehab status, athlete's assessment of her season performance, assessment of the team's season, coach's assessment of the athlete, personal and team goals for the off-season, brainstorming for the next season, individual and team goals for next season, and things to continue to do next season. It is helpful if a coach creates a form and lists the questions to remain consistent in all meetings. This doesn't mean that the answers will be consistent! The players should have the questions before the meeting so each can reflect and have meaningful answers. The coach should paraphrase the answers from each individual. This paraphrasing will help the coach accumulate valid data to help plan for the next season.

Many coaches replace the individual meeting or enhance it with a written evaluation. As much as a coach wants to have an open dialogue with her players, some kids find it easier to be more upright on paper. The only problem with a written statement is it can be misconstrued and it is a material fact. A coach can avoid perplexing questions by keeping the questions individual and team oriented and less confrontational.

Without being redundant, a coach should give the team the opportunity to evaluate the program. This can be done in discussions during individual meetings but is best done on paper. Some schools have a policy to conduct the evaluation so the player has anonymity and does not fear retaliation from the coach. It is best to format the answers with a yes/no or 1 to 5 rating system. Space to comment should be included, but essays should be discouraged! These questions pertain to the program and staff and their reaction to the player and team.

SENIOR INPUT

Seniors have one mission. It is to have fun and have a great personal and program finish to their career at the high school, club, or collegiate level. The senior knows the philosophy of the program, has lived through the ups and downs of each season, and wants to leave a legacy. The coach should tap their leadership qualities. Many seniors leave programs disgruntled and bitter. A main goal of the coaching staff is to make sure the senior is a model student-athlete and ambassador of the program when she graduates. Giving special attention to the seniors is important before and during the season. Giving them input and respecting their opinions can be a valuable tool for building better team chemistry.

At Sweet Home, whenever one of my seniors went on a recruiting trip, I told her to ask questions of the seniors. These were the players who tended to give honest answers because they had nothing to lose and had lived through the program for many years. I found that most collegiate coaches placed recruits with freshmen or sophomores who may be more enthusiastic and less critical. A recruit should stay with players who are closer in age or will be her teammates but should not be excluded from meeting the seniors.

Evaluation is difficult because it is like walking around nude. In other words, it's hard to leave yourself vulnerable to criticism. Coaches need to accept criticism as constructive advice to help a program improve. When a coach self-evaluates her program, she tends to have tunnel vision and rationalizes whatever she sees. However, when players, staff, and administration all have their say, an evaluation is more thorough and eye-opening and presents the coach with a more accurate picture. Evaluation from others gives the coach the rest of the story. I can handle another's evaluation of me, but unless I act on that evaluation, it's worthless.

INDEX

Note: The italicized *f* following page numbers refers to figures.

ABOUT THE AUTHOR

Michael Groll/The Buffalo News

Sally Kus is the head volleyball coach at the University of Buffalo. Before taking over the reigns at UB in December of 2001, Kus enjoyed four successful seasons at Daemen College (New York), where she was named NAIA Conference Coach of the Year twice.

A veteran coach at the collegiate, high school, and club levels, Kus is best known for her remarkable 23-year coaching tenure at Sweet Home High School in Amherst, New York, where she compiled a record of 794-29 with teams that *Volleyball Magazine* called

"the best prep program ever in the history of the sport." Kus coached her teams to a National Federation of State High Schools record of 292 consecutive wins (1978-1987), six consecutive state titles (1990-1995), and a number one national ranking by *USA Today* (1991). Kus was named the National Women's Sports Foundation Coach of the Year in 1983 and National Federation Volleyball Coach of the Year in 1987, and she was inducted into the National Volleyball Hall of Fame in 1996.

Kus is a 1970 graduate of the University of Akron and a graduate of the University of Buffalo, having earned a master's degree in health and physical education in 1974. She coached the girls' scholastic team at the Empire State Games from 1978 to 1991, where her teams won 10 gold and 3 silver medals. She is the founder and coordinator of the nationally renowned Cheetah Junior Olympic Development Program and is a USA Volleyball National Coaching Accreditation Program clinician (CADRE).

When not coaching, teaching, or speaking at clinics about volleyball, Kus enjoys traveling, water sports, and shopping. She and her husband, Larry, live near Buffalo, New York.

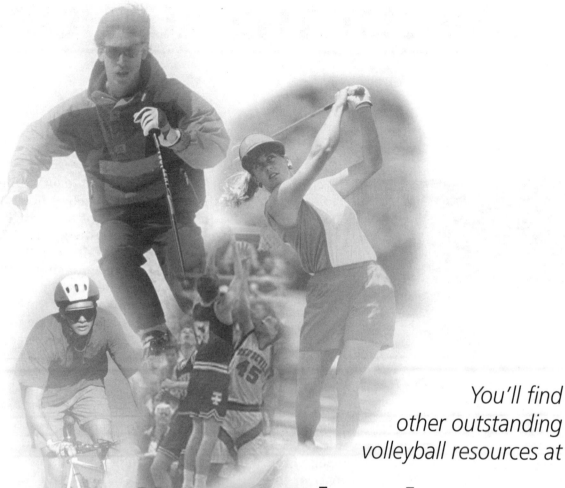